Islamism and Globalisation in Jordan

This book explores the activities of the Muslim Brotherhood in Jordan. It examines how the Brotherhood, working to establish an alternative social, political and moral order through a network of Islamic institutions, transformed Jordanian society. It also reveals that the Brotherhood's involvement in the economic realm, in Islamic financial activities, led it to engage with the neoliberal approach to the economy, with the result that the Islamic social institutions created by the Brotherhood, such as charities, lost their importance in favour of profit-oriented activities owned by leading Islamist individuals. The book thereby demonstrates the 'hybridisation' of Islamism, and argues that Islamism is not an abstract set of beliefs, but rather a collection of historically constructed practices. The book also illustrates how globalisation is profoundly influencing culture and society in the Arab world, though modified by the adoption of an Islamic framework.

Daniel Atzori (Daniele Atzori) is a Senior Energy Analyst at FC Business Intelligence and completed his doctorate at the University of Durham, UK. He has previously been the editorial team coordinator of the magazine *Papers of Dialogue*, published by the AGI (Agenzia Italia) news agency, and a columnist for *Oil*, a publication that focuses on energy.

Durham Modern Middle East and Islamic World Series

Series Editor: Anoushiravan Ehteshami, University of Durham

1. **Economic Development in Saudi Arabia**
   Rodney Wilson, with Abdullah Al-Salamah, Monica Malik and Ahmed Al-Rajhi

2. **Islam Encountering Globalisation**
   Edited by Ali Mohammadi

3. **China's Relations with Arabia and the Gulf, 1949–1999**
   Mohamed Bin Huwaidin

4. **Good Governance in the Middle East Oil Monarchies**
   Edited by Tom Pierre Najem and Martin Hetherington

5. **The Middle East's Relations with Asia and Russia**
   Edited by Hannah Carter and Anoushiravan Ehteshami

6. **Israeli Politics and the Middle East Peace Process, 1988–2002**
   Hassan A. Barari

7. **The Communist Movement in the Arab World**
   Tareq Y. Ismael

8. **Oman – The Islamic Democratic Tradition**
   Hussein Ghubash

9. **The Secret Israeli–Palestinian Negotiations in Oslo**
   Their success and why the process ultimately failed
   Sven Behrendt

10. **Globalization and Geopolitics in the Middle East**
    Old games, new rules
    Anoushiravan Ehteshami

11. **Iran–Europe Relations**
    Challenges and opportunities
    Seyyed Hossein Mousavian

12. **Islands and International Politics in the Persian Gulf**
    The Abu Musa and Tunbs in strategic perspective
    Kourosh Ahmadi

13. **Monetary Union in the Gulf**
    Prospects for a single currency in the Arabian Peninsula
    Emilie Rutledge

14. **Contested Sudan**
    The political economy of war and reconstruction
    Ibrahim Elnur

15. **Palestinian Politics and the Middle East Peace Process**
    Consensus and competition in the Palestinian negotiation team
    Ghassan Khatib

16. **Islam in the Eyes of the West**
    Images and realities in an age of terror
    Edited by Tareq Y. Ismael and Andrew Rippin

17. **Islamic Extremism in Kuwait**
    From the Muslim Brotherhood to Al-Qaeda and other Islamic political groups
    Falah Abdullah al-Mdaires

18. **Iraq, Democracy and the Future of the Muslim World**
    Edited by Ali Paya and John Esposito

19. **Islamic Entrepreneurship**
    Rasem N. Kayed and M. Kabir Hassan

20. **Iran and the International System**
    Edited by Anoushiravan Ehteshami and Reza Molavi

21. **The International Politics of the Red Sea**
    Anoushiravan Ehteshami and Emma C. Murphy

22. **Palestinian Christians in Israel**
    State attitudes towards non-Muslims in a Jewish State
    Una McGahern

23. **Iran–Turkey Relations, 1979–2011**
    Conceptualising the dynamics of politics, religion and security in middle-power States
    Suleyman Elik

24. **The Sudanese Communist Party**
    Ideology and party politics
    Tareq Y. Ismael

25. **The Muslim Brotherhood in Contemporary Egypt**
    Democracy defined or confined?
    Mariz Tadros

26. **Social and Gender Inequality in Oman**
    The power of religious and political tradition
    Khalid M. Al-Azri

27. **American Democracy Promotion in the Changing Middle East**
    From Bush to Obama
    Edited by Shahram Akbarzadeh, James Piscatori, Benjamin MacQueen and Amin Saikal

28. **China–Saudi Arabia Relations, 1990–2012**
    Marriage of convenience or strategic alliance?
    Naser M. Al-Tamimi

29. **Adjudicating Family Law in Muslim Courts**
    Cases from the contemporary Muslim world
    Edited by Elisa Giunchi

30. **Muslim Family Law in Western Courts**
    Edited by Elisa Giunchi

31. **Anti-Veiling Campaigns in the Muslim World**
    Gender, modernism and the politics of dress
    Edited by Stephanie Cronin

32. **Russia–Iran Relations Since the End of the Cold War**
    Eric D. Moore

33. **Islam and Pakistan's Political Culture**
    Farhan Mujahid Chak

34. **Iraq in the Twenty-First Century**
    Regime change and the making of a failed state
    Tareq Y. Ismael and Jacqueline S. Ismael

35. **Islamism and Cultural Expression in the Arab World**
    Abir Hamdar and Lindsey Moore

36. **The Emerging Middle East – East Asia Nexus**
    Edited by Anoushiravan Ehteshami and Yukiko Miyagi

37. **Islamism and Globalisation in Jordan**
    Daniel Atzori

Islamism and Globalisation in Jordan

The Muslim brotherhood's quest for hegemony

Daniel Atzori

LONDON AND NEW YORK

First published 2015
by Routledge
2 Park Square, Milton Park, Abingdon, Oxon OX14 4RN

and by Routledge
711 Third Avenue, New York, NY 10017

Routledge is an imprint of the Taylor & Francis Group, an informa business

© 2015 Daniel Atzori

The right of Daniel Atzori to be identified as author of this work has been asserted by him in accordance with sections 77 and 78 of the Copyright, Designs and Patents Act 1988.

All rights reserved. No part of this book may be reprinted or reproduced or utilised in any form or by any electronic, mechanical, or other means, now known or hereafter invented, including photocopying and recording, or in any information storage or retrieval system, without permission in writing from the publishers.

Trademark notice: Product or corporate names may be trademarks or registered trademarks, and are used only for identification and explanation without intent to infringe.

British Library Cataloguing in Publication Data
A catalogue record for this book is available from the British Library

Library of Congress Cataloging in Publication Data
Atzori, Daniel.
Islamism and globalisation in Jordan / Daniel Atzori.
    pages cm. -- (Durham modern middle east and islamic world series ; v. 37)
    Includes bibliographical references and index.
    1. Islam--Jordan--History. 2. Islam and state--Jordan. 3. Islamic fundamentalism--Jordan. 4. Globalization--Jordan. I. Title.
    BP63.J6A89 2015
    322'.1095695--dc23
                2014046918

ISBN: 978-1-138-82096-8 (hbk)
ISBN: 978-1-315-74359-2 (ebk)

Typeset in Times New Roman
by Taylor & Francis Books

To the memory of my grandfather, Ignazio Cannella (1921–2009)

Contents

	Acknowledgement	x
	Introduction	1
1	Political economy perspectives on Islamism	11
2	Understanding Islamism: theoretical and conceptual framework	37
3	Articulations of Islamism in Jordan	54
4	Trajectories of political identity development in Jordan	82
5	The social construction of contemporary Islamic identities: the case of Jordan	118
	Conclusion	146
	Bibliography	152
	Index	159

Acknowledgement

Writing a PhD dissertation, and then transforming it into a book, is a long and laborious process. Throughout these years, I have benefited from the help and support of several teachers, colleagues, friends and family members. Firstly, I would like to express my gratitude to my supervisor, Dr Mehmet Asutay, whose expertise and wisdom added considerably to my research experience. The intellectual engagement I had with him has been crucial for the development of my research. I also wish to thank my second supervisor, Professor Rodney Wilson, for patiently helping me through the process of conducting a PhD. In these years, Professor Giulio Sapelli, friend and mentor, has always been a constant source of inspiration and encouragement. I also had the privilege to have, as my external examiners during my Viva, Professor James Piscatori and Professor Salwa Ismail, two scholars I greatly admire. Their profound observations have been invaluable in triggering in me new questions and new interests.

Moroever, I also would like say how grateful I am to my employers, Roberto Iadicicco, Editor-in-Chief of AGI (Agenzia Italia), Daniela Viglione, former AGI's Chief Executive Officer, and Gianni Di Giovanni, current AGI's Chief Executive Officer, for allowing me to conduct my research, for their support and for believing in my potential.

Furthermore, I thank all the interviewees and respondents who participated in this research, as well as all of those extraordinary people that, in Jordan, supported me in my fieldwork. In particular, the help of Professor Zu'bi al-Zu'bi, currently Dean of the Faculty of Business of the University of Jordan, was invaluable in facilitating my research. Professor Amir al-Sabaileh of the University of Jordan considerably helped me to deepen my understanding of Jordanian society. Several other researchers and students helped me a lot. Also in Durham, where I spent years of study and personal growth, there are innumerable people to whom I would like to express my gratitude. I apologise for not thanking them individually here.

Finally, I want to wholeheartedly thank my parents, Francesco Atzori and Maria Rosaria Cannella, for their support throughout these years. Their contribution has been simply invaluable. I would also like to add my appreciation to my wife, Jenny Carlino, for her understanding and – most of all – for her love.

I dedicate this book to my grandfather, Ignazio Cannella, who passed away while I was about to start my fieldwork in Jordan, and whose moral example has been, and still is, a constant source of inspiration for me.

Daniel Atzori
London, March 2015

Introduction

In the 1990s, influential studies such as Roy's *The Failure of Political Islam* (1994) announced the exhaustion of Islamism. However, the aftermath of the Arab uprisings of 2011 has shown that Islamism managed to transform itself, to the point that our very understanding of the existence of a single phenomenon such as 'political Islam' may be questioned. This text argues that Islamism is a multi-layered phenomenon and its analysis cannot merely focus on its political aspects, but that its social, economic and cultural dimensions need to be explored as well. To put it simply, Islamism is not a static phenomenon, but a dynamic and multi-faceted reality.

So what is, exactly, Islamism? The literature on this issue is vast and heterogeneous, and concepts such as Islamism and Islamisation have been defined in profoundly different ways. Before proposing the working definition of Islamism adopted in this study, it is crucial to note that Islamism is here considered a 'modern' phenomenon, therefore challenging the approaches which see it as the manifestation of an alleged Islamic nature. Parenthetically, as it can be seen throughout this work, the very rise of Islamism brings into question the current definition of 'modernity'. To put it simply, this study considers Islamism as a modern socio-political movement of the twentieth and twenty-first centuries, and not as the mere development of a religious movement which started in the seventh century. Overall, it is of the utmost importance to underline that in this book the terms 'modern' and 'modernity' are never used with any sort of positive, sympathetic or favourable connotations, especially with regard to Islamism and Islamist movements. They have been merely adopted as neutral terms, useful to differentiate Islamism from 'traditional' Islamic beliefs and practices.

Reconstructing the history of Islamic politics from the community of the Prophet Muhammad to the present often leads to assuming an immutable continuity in the political and religious history of Islam. The flaw of the grand narratives based on this approach consists in their tendency to confer agency to Islam itself, neglecting the specific historical, political and economic contexts, with the effect of transforming the history of Muslim societies into a *Bildungsroman*. Accepting these attempts of constructing an organic and coherent narrative exposes the researcher to the risk of ignoring the specific features of contemporary Islamist politics, as well as their similarities with non-Islamic contemporary ideologies and social movements.

Marranci (2009: 54) suggests that much of the current essentialist discourse stems from Gellner's influential book *Muslim Society* (1981). Indeed, according to Gellner (1981), 'fundamentalism' is, to a certain degree, intrinsic to Islam as such. Gellner (1981) depicts an essentially homogenous Islamic civilisation, which extends both in space and time, always presenting recognisable features. One of those is an intrinsic tendency to fundamentalism. Foucault's (1969: 37) critique of history, his 'archaeology of knowledge', is an invitation to be suspicious of interpretations, which assume homogeneity and continuity; according to him, these continuities and coherences imposed on history are merely due to processes of social construction.

Grand narratives that postulate a coherent development of Islamic politics are here criticised insofar as they consider Islam as an agent (Ismail, 2006: 9). In general, essentialist approaches tend to see Islamic societies not as socially constructed historical products, but as the different phases of a unique and coherent Islamic project that starts from the Prophet Muhammad onward. Islamic history is presented as a sort of literary novel, where Islam plays the role of the major character. Anderson (1983) highlighted, in his *Imagined Communities* (1983), the connection between the social construction of nationalism and romantic literature. This 'romantic' approach to Islamic civilisation is often shared by both so-called Orientalists and Islamists. Following this approach, the rise of Islamism has therefore been entirely explained by the fact Islam is intrinsically prone to periodical waves of fundamentalism. Muslims are not seen as individuals free to choose their destiny, but as if they were acted upon by an impersonal, monolithic and extra-historical force called Islam, which evolves according to predetermined laws.

An essentialist approach to Islamism is exemplified by Dekmejian's (1985) contribution. In fact, Dekmejian states (1985: 8):

> The present phase of Islamic resurgence can be viewed as conforming to the cyclical appearance of revivalist movements in times of crisis reaching back to the Prophet's area. ... The practice of present-day Islamists to view Islamist history in terms of cycles of decline and resurgence possesses considerable historical validity.

It is precisely the alleged validity of this paradigm that the present research attempts to deconstruct, since contemporary Islamic identities are here seen as socially constructed products, outcomes of processes of articulations conducted by historically situated social actors. Dekmejian interprets Islamic history in terms of a coherent narrative. Responding to analogous tendency in social sciences, Michel Foucault and Edward Said, identifying a crucial nexus between knowledge and power, illustrate to what extent apparently neutral attempts to define the 'other' may mask the will of domination. Dekmejian (1985: 19–22) claims to adopt a 'dialectical perspective' in the analysis of Islamic history, identifying eleven dialectical relationships. However, his use of the term 'dialectics' appears peculiar: the dialectic poles (for example, Islamic modernism *versus* Islamic conservatism, establishment Islam *versus* fundamentalist Islam, ruling elites *versus* Islamist militants, economic elites *versus* Islamic radicals, ethnic nationalism *versus* Islamic unity) are seen by this author as purely static metaphysical essences.

Contemporary forms of Islamism, hence, are not analysed as contingent historical products, but as predetermined, mechanical patterns. According to this framework, Dekmejian ventures to draw a psychological profile of Islamists, affirming that 'the fundamentalist is, above all, an acutely alienated individual' and claiming that 'his alienation' is a 'direct consequence of the Arab-Islamic crisis environment' (Dekmejian, 1985: 32–35). Islamism, thus, is interpreted as a social pathology, which is a consequence of the nature of Islam. Such a conclusion shows how the apparent scientific discourse of essentialism could mask the desire to control the 'other' through the imposition of arbitrary notions of rationality and irrationality, health and pathology.

Cognizant of the shortcomings of essentialist approaches, this research argues that contemporary Islamic movements need to be analysed as historically situated, rejecting the supposed continuity and coherence of Islamic history, which implies that 'contemporary Islamist movements represent basic responses and express modes of action which have been patterned in earlier historical periods' (Ismail, 2006: 6). Analyses of Islamic movements that rely on comparative history avoid the risks inherent in the essentialist and deterministic approaches, such as singling out the history of Islam in the name of an alleged 'Islamic exceptionalism'.

What is Islamism, then? Terms such as 'Islamism' or 'Islamic fundamentalism' are usually employed to indicate 'modern political movements and ideas, mostly oppositional, which seek to establish, in one sense or another, an Islamic state' (Zubaida, 2009: 38). Similarly, in the *Columbia World Dictionary of Islamism*, Islamism is defined as 'a political and religious ideology that aims to establish an Islamic state under the Shari'a law and to reunify the Muslim *ummah* (*i.e.* the Islamic community)' (Sfeir, 2007: 170).

The limitation of these definitions, it is maintained in this study, consists in their over-emphasis on the political goals of Islamism at the expense of its socio-economic and cultural dimensions. In order to avoid confusion, the label 'political Islam' is therefore discarded and the term 'Islamism' is adopted instead. Hence, this study suggests overturning what Milton-Edwards calls a 'state-centric' designation of Islamism (2004: 20), out of the persuasion that in order to understand Islamism the political, economic, social and cultural dimensions need to be all put under scrutiny. Also Mandaville (2007: 6) has suggested widening our understanding of 'politics' when studying 'political Islam', in order to also comprehend movements whose primary emphasis is not on the conquest of the state apparatus, but which focus on the construction of an Islamic society 'through the collectivization of individually pious Muslims'. Göle (1997: 47) has proposed a valuable definition of Islamism inasmuch as she emphasises the counter-hegemonic character of the Islamist project: '"Islamism" indicates the re-appropriation of Muslim identity and values as a basis for an alternative social and political agenda'. She also crucially underlines the importance of differentiating between the term 'Muslim', which indicates a 'religious identity', and 'Islamist', which denotes 'political consciousness and social action' (Göle, 1997: 47). This distinction between Muslim and Islamist is adopted in this research, as is Ismail's (2006: 2) proposed definition of Islamism:

> The term 'Islamism' is used to encompass both Islamist politics as well as re-Islamisation, the process whereby various domains of social life are invested with signs and symbols associated with Islamic cultural traditions. ... Islamism, as I conceive it, is not just the expression of a political project; it also covers the invocation of frames with an Islamic referent in social and cultural spheres.

Such a definition, by broadening the focus to include socio-economic and cultural facets of Islamism, allows a more sophisticated and holistic analysis of the phenomenon. Islamism and re-Islamisation are not seen as two distinct facts. On the contrary, they are seen as the attribution of meanings to social life through the production and reproduction of frames pertaining to the symbolic universes of Islam. Islam is thus seen here, alongside other religious traditions, as a nexus of 'historically produced systems of meanings' (Ismail, 2006: 6). The history of modern Islamic movements such as the Muslim Brotherhood is therefore the history of the articulation of historically and socially constructed meanings by modern socio-political movements, in dynamic and ever-changing settings. The Muslim Brotherhood is, in this context, one of the most important collective social agents participating in the social construction of an anthropological paradigm here defined as *homo islamicus*. Such a term is here used to describe the 'ideal type' of Islamic economics, that is to say an individual that, in contrast with the *homo economicus* theorised by neoclassical economics, pursues the welfare of the Islamic community instead of his or her own self-interest (Asutay, 2007b: 167).

The term re-Islamisation may be contentious, since it implies that contemporary Arab societies are today more 'Islamic' than they used to be. This raises questions on what 'Islamic' means. In fact, the claim can be questioned by affirming that the fact that Islamic frames are used more often in the public sphere may certainly indicate a higher penetration of Islamism as an ideology, but not necessarily of Islam as a religion. However, for lack of a better expression, the term re-Islamisation is used in this text as indicating the growing utilisation of Islamic frames and symbols, which have occurred in Arab societies at least since the defeat in 1967 of Nasser's Pan-Arab secular project.

For Bayat, the process of Islamisation 'ceased to be primarily a political project and became simply an "Islamic phenomenon", a struggle against secular values in order to elevate personal piety, morality, Islamic identity and ethos' (Bayat, 2007: 145). Thus, Islamism is conceptualised as a 'modern' phenomenon, where the notion of 'modernity' 'refers to a whole range of phenomena that accompany the spread of capitalism and the inclusion of ever-more regions of the world in its revolutionary processes' (Zubaida, 2011: 2). In this respect, Göle analysed the concept of Islamic modernities in reference to the Turkish case, arguing that 'Islamism can be thought of as a critical introduction of Muslim agency into the modern arenas of social life' (Göle, 2000: 93), since Islamism is seen as a challenge to both the traditional readings of Islam and the universalistic claims of Western modernity.

The present research, hence, considers Islamism as part of these processes of reframing of modernity, intertwined with the rise and development of capitalism. In particular, by drawing attention to political economy, this research explores the role played by the dialectic between Islamism and socio-economic changes in the formation of contemporary Muslim identities in the Hashemite Kingdom of Jordan. Jordan has been chosen as a case study because of its alleged 'exceptionalism' (Moaddel, 2002): while in other Arab countries, such as Egypt, Tunisia and Syria, Islamism was seen by the establishment as a threat to their regimes, in Jordan Islamism, as represented by the Muslim Brotherhood, played an important role in the construction of the nation. The Hashemite Kingdom of Jordan, then Transjordan, was established as a nation-state in 1921, while the Muslim Brotherhood of Jordan was founded in 1945. The Islamist movement developed a 'symbiotic relationship with the regime from 1945 through to the early 1990s' (Boulby, 1999: 1) and it became the largest and best organised social movement of the Kingdom. The freedom and the opportunity spaces allowed by the Hashemites to the Muslim Brotherhood, since its foundation in 1945, let the Islamists develop a pervasive network of political, economic and social institutions, which played an important part in Jordanian history as well as in shaping contemporary Islamic identities in Jordan. Its social, political and economic activities became deeply interwoven with the fabric of Jordanian society, having played a remarkable role in moulding the consciousness of ordinary citizens. The Muslim Brotherhood were, at times, supportive of the hegemonic official narrative and at times counter-hegemonic. In any case, the Islamist movement has always been a central character in the history of the country. Its influence, over the years, on two decisive ministries such as education and religious affairs, as well as the establishment of a vast network of Islamic social institutions, granted the movement sway over the *fora* of production of the Jordanian subject. Islamist discourses permeated Jordanian society and have been crucial in defining what 'authentic' Islam really is for ordinary Jordanians.

The Hashemite Kingdom of Jordan was chosen as a case study in this research for two reasons. Firstly, following the economic reforms started in the 1990s, its society underwent a process of growing integration into the global economy, which caused dramatic changes in Jordanian society. The second reason is that Jordanian society has known, since the 1970s, an intense process of re-Islamisation, which has been mainly articulated by the Muslim Brotherhood of Jordan. Jordan has therefore been chosen as a case study to analyse the interactions between these two concomitant processes of globalisation and Islamisation in shaping contemporary Islamic identities in Jordan.

The fieldwork of this research was carried out in the second half of 2010, immediately before the uprisings which became known as the Arab Spring. Thus, this study provides an exceptional historical document of an extremely important phase of Jordanian, and Arab, history. At the time this research was conducted, the Muslim Brotherhood, as well as its political wing, the Islamic Action Front Party, were not only legal and free to operate, but were considered a mainstream movement. Thus, it was easy for me to get in touch with the leaders and founders of the movement. However, since in the last years the political landscape of the Arab world has changed dramatically, I decided to anonymise all my interviewees and respondents, in order to preserve their privacy.

Overall, it is a contention of this study that, since the Brotherhood articulates discourses which are, at the same time, 'Islamic' and 'modern', the study of such articulations can shed light on processes of social construction of identities, examined in their dialectical relationships with political economy. It can also contribute to explain the emergence of new social classes, whose aspirations and frustrations the Brotherhood managed to partially interpret also by contributing to the social construction of models of 'Islamic capitalism', which can be conceptualised as hybrid forms of modernity through the theoretical framework of the 'multiple modernities' concept (Eisenstadt, 2009).

Overall, from a theoretical point of view, this study challenges essentialist readings, which postulate an alleged meta-historical nature of Islam, which would predetermine not only the behaviours of Muslim individuals, but also the developments of Muslim societies. At the same time, this study aims to critically respond to the approaches which assume deterministic relationships between economy and culture, adopting instead an analytical perspective which conceptualises the relationships between socio-economic changes and ideology reproduction in dialectical terms through social constructivism. These considerations, instead of providing answers, raise new fundamental questions for the interpretation and analysis of Islamism.

The correlation between the economy and culture has been one of the main theoretical acquisitions of Marx's thinking, but the principal flaw of orthodox Marxism has been to postulate a deterministic, and unidirectional, relationship between the former and the latter. In this respect, the contribution of Gramsci's concept of hegemony *qua* articulation, of social constructivism and of social movement theory is seen as decisive in formulating approaches that emphasise processes of articulation, without overlooking the economic dimensions. Also Max Weber was aware of the fact that religion can be used to legitimise positions of social privilege, as well as to put forward critiques of the establishment (Weber, 1978: 490–491). However, Weberian interpretations often tend to conceptualise religions in an essentialist fashion, neglecting the fact that also cultural and religious frames, as Goffman (1974) argued, are historical products, thus subject to transformation and change. This articulation of frames is also deeply entangled with relations of power, as Foucault has shown.

Here, these phenomena are studied in their dialectical relationships out of the persuasion that '"culture" is a process intertwined with the dynamics of economy and power, and not a fixed essence working itself out through history' (Zubaida, 2011: 6). Hence, the analysis of processes of articulation of 'modern' and 'Islamic' identities, as well as the interdependences between these two, is carried out in the historically situated contexts of contemporary Jordanian society, by focusing on the articulation of these interdependent processes in the domain of political economy. This emphasis on political economy stems from a theoretically informed persuasion of the relevance of this sphere with regard to processes of social construction of identities. In other words, establishing a dialectical relationship between social being and consciousness implies that both the emergence of 'modernity' and of 'Islamism' can be read in the context of simultaneous transformations of the capitalistic mode of production. Such an approach allows to explore to what extent capitalism itself is 'Islamised' through the adoption of the symbolic language of Islamism (Atia, 2012).

In this regard, an important arena where Islamic identity construction is articulated is the emergence of Islamic moral economy and Islamic finance; inasmuch as, since the 1960s, Islamic banking became a successful paradigm, being the very first 'Islamic' institution to be realised in 'modern' times. As argued, Islamism is a larger concept than what directly refers to the 'politics' of Islamism. Thus, it is important to locate the extent to which Islamic moral economy, banking and finance have been, on the one hand, the product of the perceived Islamisation through processes of construction of Islamic identity, and, on the other hand, to what extent Islamic moral economy, banking and finance, in turn shaped Muslim identities in everyday life. It is hence among the aims of this study to search these dialectical relationships in the case of Jordan, where an Islamist social movement, the Muslim Brotherhood, has played a major social, political and economic role since its foundation in 1945. This is expected to help to understand how 'modern' institutions, in this case banking and finance, have shaped or have been shaped by Islamists discourse, thus providing insights into the articulation of particular relationships between social being and consciousness. This research focuses on the Muslim Brotherhood, whose role is seen as pivotal in the development of contemporary Islamism in Jordan; however, it has already been affirmed here that Islamism is a complex and multifaceted phenomenon that cannot be reduced to a single movement. Different and competing trends of Islamism, such as Salafism, have a significant role in the Jordanian society; while they do not constitute the focus of the present research, their importance needs not to be ignored. Similarly, the Muslim Brotherhood should not be seen as a monolithic social actor, since different trends and the competing definitions and discourses of Islamism, in terms of contemplation and action, coexist even within the Brotherhood itself.

Thus, the present research identifies a relationship between the development of contemporary Islamism and the emergence of new educated middle classes. On a global level, the development of a new Muslim middle class has been studied by Nasr (2009). More specifically, Clark (2004) analysed the extent to which a new social formation, mainly constituted by educated professionals and entrepreneurs, has become the incubator of Islamism in countries such as Egypt, Jordan and Yemen, also thanks to the aggregating role of Islamic social institutions networks. This middle class is called 'new' to distinguish it from traditional Arab social groups such as landowners and merchants or embryonic forms of bourgeoisie. The new middle class, as it will be argued in Chapter 1, developed in relation with profound transformations of the political economy of the Arab world, such as the decline of Arab socialism and the emergence of new social groups. The notion of 'middle class Islamism', hence, is adopted in this study to identify the novelty constituted by the appearance of a cluster of social groups that identify neither with the traditional middle class (landowners and merchants) nor with the 'modern' secular bourgeoisie; Islam plays an essential role in their attempt at seeing and understanding social reality and acting upon it.

In summary, three aspects are, therefore, crucial to the present research: (i) the theoretical relationships between Islamism and modernity; (ii) the relationships between articulations of Islamism and modernity, on the one hand, and their links with political economy on the other hand, through the exploration of how Islamic discourses shape individual economic and financial behaviour in everyday life; and (iii) the empirical observation of these processes in contemporary Jordanian society.

The research questions are analysed in specific historic contexts; for example, the emergence of Islamism is understood in the context of the crisis of the Arab state and of its model of development. The hypothesis is that, since Nasser's defeat in 1967, Islamism has been articulated as an alternative, as a counter-hegemonic project, thus interpreting the aspirations and the grievances of social strata, which felt, in varying degrees, that they had not benefited from the current model of economic development. The research questions are then investigated in the context of the relationships between the development of Islamism and the current phase of capitalist development, that of globalisation, in order to explore the impact of globalisation on the social construction of Islamic identities.

This issue raises two related questions: if Islamism constructed a *homo islamicus* paradigm, and globalisation exported a *homo economicus* paradigm, are these two paradigms clashing or undergoing a process of hybridisation? The final, related research question, is the following issue: are we witnessing the emergence of Islamic modernities that are challenging the mono-civilisational claims of Western modernity? As this research indicates, the frames produced and reproduced by Islamism now constitute one of the predominant forms through which Muslim individuals both conceptualise and transform social reality. Consequently, traditional Islamic frames have been reinterpreted and transformed. The process through which these Islamist frames have become one of the prevailing languages to interpret reality in several Muslim societies such as Jordan is here conceptualised in terms of a hegemonic struggle. Following this line of reasoning, the research on which this book is based focused on ethnographically informed empirical investigations in order to analyse processes of social construction of Islamic discourses. This stems from the conviction that the social construction of Islamic frames can be observed not only in the political domain, narrowly defined, but also in the social and financial attitudes, as well as in the patterns of consumption, of the social actors. This research is, hence, primarily a qualitative research aiming to explore the research questions through the analysis of the perceptions of various social actors in the Hashemite Kingdom of Jordan. For this, primary data in the form of questionnaire and interviews were collected to provide the necessary empirical evidence to respond to the identified research questions. As regards the research method, triangulation was adopted as an efficient method comprising of qualitative and quantitative data collection and analysis methods. The fieldwork in the Hashemite Kingdom of Jordan was conducted in the form of interviews, focus groups and a questionnaire survey. The interviews were conducted mainly with Islamist politicians and activists, journalists and researchers with the goal of shedding light on the recent transformations of Jordanian society in the light of the aforementioned concomitant processes of globalisation and Islamisation. The focus groups and the survey questionnaire, which have been carried out with students of the University of Jordan, investigated their social, financial and religious attitudes, exploring to what extent the paradigms of global capitalism and Islamism cross-fertilised in their lives. A crucial research question to answer was, therefore, whether the paradigms of *homo economicus* and *homo islamicus* are clashing in the lives of Jordanian students or whether they are undergoing processes of hybridisation. On the whole, as it has already been stressed, this study argues for a broadening of the concept of Islamism, out of the theoretically informed persuasion that contemporary Islamism represents not only a chapter of the political history of Muslim societies, but a moment in the social construction of Islamic modernities. To put it simply, Islamism can be conceptualised as a cluster of symbolic frames produced and reproduced by social actors to interpret social reality, as a language in which social actors, and social groups, articulate their aspirations and grievances.

Since this research argues that Islamism is a multi-layered phenomenon, it needs to be analysed adopting an interdisciplinary approach. Different disciplines, such as sociology, political economy, political science, economics, history, anthropology, philosophy, psychology and statistics can shed light on different aspects of a complex phenomenon such as that of contemporary Islamic identities. This is particularly relevant to the analysis of the discourses related to the research questions. In this regard, Islamism is defined, in this research, by employing terms such as 'worldview', 'ideology' and 'language'. It should be noted that different expressions are used to describe different facets of Islamism. Here, 'worldview' (*Weltanschauung*) refers to a set of opinions and beliefs, since Islamism shapes the collective cognition of reality. The term 'ideology' adds to the above a critical awareness of the dialectical relationship between these ideas and the social group which expresses them. Islamism is also seen here as a 'language', that is to say a 'discursive tradition' (Asad, 1986) that is constantly reinterpreted by social actors in developing their vernacular in relating to the realities of everyday life.

Synopsis of the research

This research is composed of five chapters. Chapter 1 argues that Islamism should be comprehended in relation with political economy transformations, and especially in relation to the crisis of the Arab state and the emergence of globalisation. Chapter 2 locates the study of Islamism in social theory, elaborating the theoretical framework this study is based upon. Such a framework conceptualises to what extent the opportunity structures provided by economic transformations contribute to shape both the ideology and the strategies of Islamic movements. On the whole, this part provides the theoretical tools to understand how Islamic movements have been involved in the social construction of multiple Islamic modernities. The first chapters lay the foundations on which Chapter 3 builds. Indeed, the theoretical issues previously discussed allow to analyse the historical process of re-Islamisation of Jordanian society in the last decades in relation to broader political and economic transformations, and in particular to the impact of globalisation. On the whole, these chapters examine, from different perspectives, the relationship between social actors and Islamic consciousness, locating these processes in the historical context of contemporary Jordanian society. Chapter 4 analyses the findings of the interviews and of the focus groups conducted during the fieldwork of this research. Elite interviews focused on selected people such as Islamist leaders and political analysts with the goal of understanding a multi-layered phenomenon such as Islamism in the historical, social and economic context of Jordanian society. Focus groups endeavoured to shed light on the processes of social construction of Islamic identity among students of the University of Jordan. Chapter 5 provides a critical discussion of the findings of this study against the background of the theoretical framework proposed in the first four chapters. Broadly, it aims at the critical discussion of the concept of 'Islamic modernities' to provide a theoretical understanding of the processes of hybridisation between the paradigms of *homo economicus* and *homo islamicus* analysed by this research. The conclusion offers a review of the main arguments of this text.

1 Political economy perspectives on Islamism

Introduction

The objective of this chapter is to locate the emergence of Islamism in the context of political economy, highlighting the dialectic relationships between Islamist ideologies and socio-economic transformations. Marxist thinkers have often tended to conceptualise the relationships between economy and culture in a deterministic fashion. In his *Preface* to *A Contribution to the Critique of Political Economy*, Marx (1971: 20) famously affirmed: 'neither legal relations nor political forms could be comprehended whether by themselves or on the basis of a so-called general development of the human mind, but that on the contrary they originate in the material conditions of life'. In fact, this passage has led several Marxist thinkers to postulate deterministic relations between economic structure and ideological superstructure. Thus, culture has been seen as a mere by-product of the interplay between forces of production and relations of productions, and ideologies as the masks of underlying economic interests. However, thinkers such as Gramsci and the early Lukács have deconstructed these forms of economic reductionism and developed readings that emphasise the creative role of social actors in the historical process, as well as highlighting the importance of studying ideologies as autonomous from the economic structure. This approach recognises the autonomy of ideological factors, affirming at the same time their interdependence with economic and social practices and possibly providing the footprint for a theoretically informed conceptualisation of the relationships between economy and ideology.

This research, while rejecting the assumption of the existence of a fixed and unchangeable 'nature' of Islam, which predetermines Muslims and Muslim society, explores the formation of contemporary Islamic identities in living connection with socioeconomic developments. So-called Orientalist approaches to the study of Islamic movements tend to postulate an immutable nature of Islamism, which was deducted by assumptions about the nature of Islam. Such an attitude is commonly referred to as 'essentialism' and, following Sami Zubaida's (2009: 122) definition, is 'based on the idea that "Islamic" societies share essential elements which mark their history and determine or limit the possibilities of their social and political developments in the present'. In the last decades, following Edward Said's (1979) seminal work, the essentialism of the Orientalist schools has been deconstructed. In particular, Binder (1988: 85) has conducted a critique of Orientalism, recognising in it 'an attempt to articulate an interpretation of Islam', and therefore rejecting its claim of producing objective and impartial descriptions of an alleged nature and essence of Muslim societies. By exposing the crucial nexus between knowledge and power, Said (1979) illustrated the extent to which the study of Arab and Islamic societies was tainted by ideologies that merely masked the colonialist project of the West. A thorough critique of essentialism has also been conducted by al-Azmeh (2009), who illustrates the degree to which anti-historical conceptions of Islam are shared by both Orientalists and 'Islamic fundamentalists'. Thorough critiques of essentialist approaches have been conducted by studying Islamic activism using the analytical tools provided by social movement theory (Wiktorowicz, 2004).

The main contribution of this theoretical lineage consists in the rejection of the notion according to which Islamism presents exceptional features, which impede it from being examined with the same analytical tools used to study other social and political movements. A new generation of scholars has suggested reading the struggle between secular and Islamist discourses, taking into consideration their broad economic, social and cultural aspects. In other words, the conflict between the two competing narratives of Islamism and secularism has been seen both as an ideological conflict and as a clash between two social formations. This approach stems from the conviction that an analysis of power, both hegemonic and counter-hegemonic, should examine also its economic, political and cultural dimensions (Ayubi, 1995: 38). The underlying logic of this argument consists in the critique of both idealistic approaches, which emphasise the role of ideas at the expense of social and economic factors, and economic approaches, which assume that ideology, religion and culture are mere reflections of the contradictions of material life. With reference to the Turkish experience, Öniş (1997: 745) affirms that Islamism should be understood as 'a manifestation or a reflection of the far-reaching transformations that are occurring at the global level both in the economic and the cultural sphere'. In particular, contemporary Islamism needs to be read, according to Öniş (1997), against the background of globalisation. Coherent with this understanding, Islamism has to be understood in specific historical, social and economic contexts, that have contributed to shaping its ideology and strategies (Ismail, 2006: 26) and that have been in turn shaped by Islamism. Yet it is this two-sided relationship or bi-causation, which can be termed dialectical, that is crucial here.

This chapter, hence, discusses the political economy of Islamism. The first part of this chapter explores the emergence of Islamism in relation to the social and ideological crisis of the Arab state, while the second section analyses the rise of a new middle class that has identified in Islamist ideologies the language through which it expresses its frustrations and aspirations. In the conclusion, civil society is identified as the main battleground between the hegemonic narrative and practice of the state and the counter-hegemonic narrative and practice of Islamism. Such a conclusion will be the starting point to properly address, in the subsequent chapter, the theoretical framework that informs this study.

The crisis of the Arab state and the rise of Islamism

The relationship between the Arab state and Islamism

In order to conceptualise the process of Islamisation from decolonisation to the present era, some key features of the post-colonial Arab state need to be addressed, since in our understanding the development of this state has had a remarkable influence in shaping both the ideology and the strategies of Islamic movements. Thus, the examination of the political and economic context in which Islamic movements have been operating is central to critically analyse their developments. Several scholars have highlighted the significance of the relationship between the state and Islamist movements, often identifying the latter as a challenge to the former. As Tripp (1996: 51–52) affirms: 'The goals and methods of the organizations associated with the reassertion of Islamic values in political life are to a large degree shaped by the structures of imagination and power appropriate to the state'.

Tibi (2005: 2), also, maintains that 'the contemporary politicisation of Islam is a response to the on-going crisis of the modern secular nation-state in the world of Islam'. Supporting this, Moaddel (2005: 207) establishes a fundamental link between the state and its ideology, affirming that: 'Crucial in the development of the Islamic opposition were the rise of the secularist state and the rationalist outlooks of the intellectual leaders connected to it'.

As the present discussion argues, not only Islamism is a response to the crisis of the modern Arab nation state, but also Islamism has historically represented a threat for the legitimacy of its secular credentials. Ayubi (1995: 442) affirms in his seminal *Over-Stating the Arab State* that 'it is the "*cultural*" private sector – so to speak – that currently represents the main challenge to the state, in the form of the Islamist organisations' and in his *Political Islam* (1991: 161) he identified the *raison d'être* of Islamism in its opposition to the state. In addition, Zubaida (2009: 121) maintains the very concept of state is 'at issue and on the defensive in the face of the Islamic challenge'.

Following this line of reasoning, the developments of the modern secular Arab state and its legitimacy crisis in the 1970s can be conceptualised as a decisive factor in shaping contemporary Islamist movements and contemporary Islamic identities. A central argument is that the transition from state capitalism to forms of market economy with strong rentier features (Ismail, 2006) opened up new opportunity spaces for Islamism. At the same time, the crisis of the discourse of Arab nationalism paved the way for the rise and development of the so-called Islamic alternative. Thus, a relationship can be recognised between the twilight of allegedly 'socialist' forms of state capitalism in the economic structure and the loss of hegemony of Arab socialism in the ideological superstructure. Similarly, the emergence of a market economy and the expansion of Islamism appear to be connected, as well as the emergence of Islamic business and the rise of the political facets of the Islamist project.

An important point of the present research is that the link between these processes should not be considered in a deterministic fashion, postulating automatic transformations of the superstructure after changes in the economic structure, but as dialectically intertwined (Ismail, 2006: 22). These theoretical assumptions explain why, in this study, the analysis of the development of the Islamic private sector acquires relevance. Indeed, the rise of the Islamic private sector transformed Islamist ideology by providing opportunity spaces to social movements to expand horizontally and vertically, while at the same time Islamist ideology shaped the Islamic private sector. In other words, Islam provided new social formations with a language in which to express their frustrations, aspirations and their critique of the *status quo*, represented by the Arab and other nation states in the Muslim world. In turn, social and economic processes taking place within the expanding opportunity spaces have influenced the production, articulation and transformation of Islamist discourse. Hence, it is important to highlight the dialectic between the secular elite in power and the Islamist opposition that challenges the legitimacy claims of the regimes. The production of these two discourses rests on the social construction of the self and on the social construction of the 'other'.

Ideological and social dimensions of the struggle between secularism and Islamism

Ayubi (1995) attributes the weakness of the idea of nation state in the Arab world to the fact that it has been perceived as a recent and culturally alien product. He stresses that Arabs tended to imagine themselves as *ummah*, seen as a 'religio-political community', and have reluctantly accepted the territorial conception on which the notion of the Arab state is based (Ayubi, 1995: 135). In response to this, Islamist movements have claimed to be the true representatives of authentic Muslim identity, as they are likely to identify in the secular Arab state their enemy, conceptualised as the Pharaoh (al-Ghazali, 1994), who allegedly subdued Muslims in the name of alien values. This framework even reappears in the discourse of al-Qaeda, which distinguishes between the 'far enemy', a term which refers to the West and in particular to the United States of America and Israel, and the 'near enemy', represented by the Muslim states that are seen as instruments of Western domination (Springer, Regens and Edger, 2009: 59–73).

The ideology of the Arab state, as exemplified by the Nasserite model, has been criticised by the Islamist discourse, because of its secular, nationalistic and socialist features, seen as extraneous to Muslim identity. The paradox is that, by operating in the post-colonial Arab nation states, Islamist movements have thoroughly internalised in their theory and practice the concept of the nation state, contributing to its indigenisation, as will be seen in the course of this study. The model of the Arab state followed a pattern originally set by Atatürk, founder of the Republic of Turkey, which identified in the state the prime mover of a vast transformation of economy and society that would have led to the emancipation of the country from the heritage of colonialism and 'backwardness' (Richards and Waterbury, 2008: 182). Turkish society would become 'modern', embracing the Western model of modernity and progress. This experiment set an example for Muslim and Arab countries after the achievement of independence, since most of their state institutions were established according to Western models based on secular values (Esposito, 1999: 75). Pan-Arab ideology was animated by a similar desire to embrace Western ideas, such as the idea of the nation state, in order to free Arabs from foreign domination. However, it can be argued that the emancipation from the colonial 'other' was carried out through an adoption of its values and its epistemology. As Milton-Edwards (2005: 32) states: 'being modern and Muslim was viewed as an oxymoron and the secular project left no room for Islam'. As is discussed later, contemporary Islamist discourses claim instead to promote a selective and critical approach to modernity. What needs to be seen is whether this critical approach to modernity has also managed to elaborate a critique of Western epistemologies. As Ayubi (1995: 146) notes, Pan-Arab ideology has been successful during confrontation with the 'other', firstly the Ottoman state, then Western colonialism. However, following Nasser's defeat by Israel in 1967, this ideology suffered an identity crisis, thus paving the way for the emergence of the 'Islamist alternative' (Sidahmed and Ehteshami, 1996: 6). This defeat is indeed the watershed between an era dominated by Arab nationalism and the so-called 'awakening' of Islam (Piscatori, 1986: 26). Islamists accused the Pan-Arab project of being responsible not only for not having thoroughly solved the problem of the political and economic dependence of the Arabs from the West, but also of having introduced a more subtle form of enslavement, a cultural enslavement. Thus, Islamism articulated what Choueiri (2010: 157) defines as 'a qualitative contradiction between Western civilization and the religion of Islam'.

Islamists, thus, tended to refuse the ideals of Arab nationalism in favour of the concept of a renaissance of the Islamic *ummah*. They recognised the centrality of the ideological domain, a realm in which Western values exerted their cultural hegemony over Arab societies. This is one of the factors which explains why, since their very beginning, Islamist movements such as the Muslim Brotherhood have focused on grass-root institutions, aiming at a bottom-up method of promoting cultural and religious change, thus constructing a 'moral community that should be developed from below' (Harmsen, 2008: 59). However, it would be reductive to analyse the struggle between nationalism and secularism as exclusively pertaining to ideological realms: integral to the struggle between the nationalist and the Islamist narratives was also its socio-economic character. From a social point of view, the emergence of Islamic revivalism has to be understood against the development of Western educated secular elites, which proposed a model of transformation of Arab societies consistent with Western values and emancipated from what was seen as the burden of Islamic law. The link between ideology and social class has cogently been highlighted by Khoury (1983: 218), who highlighted the extent to which the new elite 'maintained no strong attachment to the weakened religious institutions'.

This heterogeneous class, unified by its secular attitude, had led the struggle for independence and, after the liberation from colonialism, established its rule on Arab societies. Once in power, this elite became what Khoury (1983: 202–221) defines as a 'state bourgeoisie'. These social strata, deeply influenced by Western education, produced a model of state that closely followed Western examples, seen as the embodiment of a Weberian rational legal authority. In order for such a model to be successful, it was essential to lead a struggle against 'traditional' Islam, identified as the cause of the perceived underdevelopment of Arab societies compared with Western ones. In its struggle for emancipation, thus, the post-colonial elite fought against Islamic traditions, often seen as a burden to development. Hence, the post-colonial state was simultaneously the product and the producer of a new, Western-educated state bourgeoisie. According to Khoury (1983: 216), nationalism was a mere expression of bourgeois class interests. Nationalism and socialism were therefore, in Khoury's (1983) understanding, the ideologies through which this Arab bourgeoisie justified and legitimised its power. The secularised elites managed to lead the masses and at the same time to negotiate with the colonial powers, given the crisis of legitimacy of the traditional religious establishment (Khoury, 1983: 219).

This bourgeoisie was distant, especially from a cultural point of view, from the Arab masses. Its Western education and its proclivity towards secularism and nationalism isolated it from the people whose everyday life was shaped by Islamic frames. The secular elite initially enjoyed consensus for its prominent role in the decolonisation struggle and for its promises to build a more just society. However, the gap between the ruling elite and the masses became evident when the governments demonstrated their incapacity to fulfil their promises, especially in terms of creation and redistribution of wealth. The ruling elites promoted policies inspired by *etatism* and populism in line with Atatürk's model (Richards and Waterbury, 2008: 180–185), which not only meant the hegemony of the state over economy, but also necessitated a strong state being hegemonic in every aspect of the public sphere. The promotion of an import substitution model and the growth of a massive public sector were accompanied by suspicions towards the private sector, hindering the development of a class of entrepreneurs, autonomous from the power of the state. However, as Ayubi (1991: 171) states:

> One of the characteristics of late, uneven and dependent capitalist 'development' is that the rates of growth in urbanisation, education and

bureaucratisation are never matched by similar rates of growth in industrialisation. ... A relatively small consumerist class is created in the cities, whose counterpart is usually a noticeably large sub-proletariat involved in the services and a fairly large lumpenproletariat scavenging for the leftovers of the consumerist segment.

This social frustration springing from this 'distorted transformation towards capitalism' (Ayubi, 1991: 171) has contributed to the shaping of the current developments in Islamism. State-led growth was not merely a characteristic of Arab 'socialist' regimes: also pro-Western countries, such as Jordan and Saudi Arabia, encouraged a massive growth of the public sector. On the whole, the interventionist state paradigm, based on state capitalism, caused profound imbalances in the socio-economic development of the Arab world. Besides, a clear link can be established between patronage-based authoritarian systems and the repression of civil society, because the growth of the public sector was often accompanied by the remarkable expansion of the repressive apparatuses (Khoury, 1983: 220). Since the legitimacy claims of the regimes were resting on fragile bases, the expansion of the patronage networks throughout civil society was a way to 'buy' legitimacy (Henry and Springborg, 2001: 11).

The emergence of the Islamic alternative

As Piscatori (1986: 37) affirms, 'although revivalist sentiments run broad and deep and are unquestionably genuine, their catalyst is the variety of discontents associated with the development process'. The crisis of secular Arab nationalism and its failure in delivering its social and economic promises is generally seen as the single major factor that paved the way for the growing appeal of Islamic revivalism. In other words, the Arab state dialectically contributed to shape its nemesis. In particular, Khoury (1983) and Ayubi (1991) located the main roots of the emergence of Islamism in political economy. According to Khoury, Islamic revivalism has to be chiefly understood as a reaction to the modernisation project carried out by Arab secular elites. As Khoury (1983: 215) states:

> for the classes sponsoring revivalism, Islam must be seen as the vehicle for political and economic demands, rather than as being itself the 'impulse' behind these demands. Given the positions of these classes in the social hierarchy and their continued attachment to the traditional sectors, Islam is their most convenient, readily available ideological instrument.

Islamism provided the traditional classes excluded from power with the language in which to express their hostility to what Khoury (1983: 232) calls the 'modern secular state'. Khoury's contribution is important inasmuch as it denies the agency to an alleged meta-historical Islam, but it is problematic since his analysis fails to acknowledge the agency of Islamists *qua* social actors, by considering Islamism merely as an instrument (Khoury, 1983: 233). His interpretation, therefore, seems tainted by an economistic tendency to debase ideology, and religion, as a mere *instrumentum regni*. However, the perceived failure of Arab socialism, as a socio-political project, undoubtedly contributed to the appeal of the alternative solution represented by Islamism, which claimed that Islam provides an organic answer to all the political and socio-economic problems of contemporary Muslim societies. According to Ayubi, socio-economic frustration has been crucial in the development of Islamist movements, from the 1970s onwards (1991: 176). Harsh methods of government and the withering of Islam from the public sphere resulted in the emergence of Islamism as an opposition force, also given the fact that mosques became almost the only incubators of socio-political change, since opposition parties were seldom allowed to operate freely. Moreover, the rank and file of Islamism were often educated in schools and universities that followed the Western model and had thus incorporated Western values and epistemologies in their symbolic universe. Islamism has been greatly influenced by these factors.

According to Khoury (1983: 222–225), the process of 'state exhaustion' is particularly evident in the failed effort of the state bourgeoisie to modernise society on its own terms. In this context, Islamism managed to express the frustration of the urban lower-middle classes, the social class that provided the leadership to the Islamist movement (Khoury, 1983: 226–229). This social stratum partially enjoyed the benefits of the new system, in particular in terms of access to higher education. However, during their studies, they matured their expectations of social mobility, which had not been fulfilled (Khoury, 1983: 227). Ayubi (1991: 158), also, stresses the importance of examining the social basis of Islamism, establishing a link between the latter and a frustrated intelligentsia. Ayubi (1991: 158–159) affirms: 'political Islam … is a movement of the students and of the "new middle class" of officials (including army officers), professionals and technocrats'. While, according to Ayubi, the presence of merchants and artisans among Islamists has been significant in Iran, in no Arab country has their presence been remarkable, although they have been involved in Islamic movements in countries such as Syria and Egypt (Ayubi, 1991: 159). Another crucial difference with Iran is that, while here the clergy has been active in the Islamist movement, the majority of traditional Sunni legal scholars, the *ulama*, have not been sympathetic towards Islamism. Moreover, Islamism also had, in the Arab world, a limited appeal on urban factory workers and peasants (Ayubi, 1991: 159). The social engineering promoted by Nasser led to the emergence of new social strata, in particular of a middle class which 'in some sense owes its existence to Arab socialism' (Noland and Pack, 2007: 201); however, Arab socialism failed to fulfil its promises, thus transforming this social group in a huge reservoir of discontent. This process has been analysed, with regard to the Egyptian case, in particular by Wickham (2002: 36), who identifies in the frustration and resentment of what she defines the '*lumpen intelligentsia*' a crucial element in contributing to the appeal of the Islamic alternative, pivotal in the articulation of the Islamist counter-hegemonic challenge among the excluded from the benefits of crony capitalism. Wickham's thesis echoes Ayubi's (1991: 162) persuasion that 'a major source of frustration is over the unfulfilled promise of education' and 'the unfulfilled promise of urbanisation'. These two phenomena happened in the context of a wider 'distorted transformation towards capitalism' (Ayubi, 1991: 171), which led to the breakdown of pre-existing forms of community (Zubaida, 2009: 67). The dramatic expansion of urban population in the entire Arab world, with the migration of thousands of people from rural areas to the cities, triggered a feeling of displacement and contributed to the crisis of traditional religious authorities (Piscatori, 1986: 27).

Another crucial factor in the emergence of Islamism, as has been mentioned before, was the unexpected outcome of the project of mass education. Nasser launched an ambitious programme intended to expand higher education, with the goal of promoting class equality in the country, substituting the principle of privilege with that of merit (Wickham, 2002: 25). The huge expansion of university education was accompanied by a policy labelled 'graduate appointment', which guaranteed all the graduates a job in the public sector (Wickham, 2002: 27). This policy, coherent with the socialist leanings of the regime, was also aimed at creating consensus. However, in the long term, this became economically and politically unsustainable, since state intervention was no longer possible due to fiscal reasons. The situation, already critical in the 1970s, became increasingly untenable in the following decade. A growing number of graduate youth could not obtain the jobs in the public sector that had been promised to them, and had to accept jobs that were deemed inadequate for a degree-holder or were forced into a situation of unemployment. This added to the frustration of these classes, recently migrated to urban areas (Ayubi, 1991: 162). Thus, discontent and resentment spread throughout Egyptian society, and the Islamists, many of whom were the expression of those strata, managed to represent those grievances (Utvik, 2006: 10).

Overall, therefore, Islamist movements have been particularly effective in exploiting the failure of the Arab state. In particular, the Muslim Brotherhood managed to expand its control on Egyptian society. If the educated and unemployed youth provided the movement with the rank and file, the strategy of the Muslim Brotherhood was also based on its creation of a so-called 'parallel Islamic sector' (Wickham, 2002: 97). A significant part of this sector was devoted to welfare activities that, according to Tripp (1996: 62), were 'designed more directly and instrumentally to reinforce the electoral strategies of organized groupings such as the Muslim Brotherhood'. On a theoretical level, the frustrated *lumpen intelligentsia* developed a critique of the *status quo* based on Islamic frames and symbols. In other words, Islamism offered a language to elaborate a critical evaluation of the status of contemporary Arab societies. This led to a 'politicisation of religion' that, according to Moaddel (2005: 207), has been made possible by the official policy of secularisation endorsed by Arab states such as Egypt. In so doing, Islamic discourse was recreated and renovated, making possible the construction of Islamism as a modern political ideology. The articulation of discontent in Islamic terms is, therefore, part of the development of Islamism as an oppositional, counter-hegemonic discourse that permeates society. *Micro-ijtihad*, which conceptualise everyday life according to Islamic frames, as interpreted by the social agents, is to be read in the context of these transformations, which in turn they contribute to shaping. The term *micro-ijtihad* is here used to imply that the rational interpretive effort (*ijtihad*), once considered as a prerogative of Muslim legal experts, is growingly exerted at an individual level for everyday life choices (Yilmaz, 2003). In other words, individual Muslims facing realities, for which there is no previous religious consensus, refer to their rational understanding in an attempt to construct 'Islamic' interpretation and meaning.

In the following decades, Islamists articulated their critique of Western civilization through the prism of Islamic frames and symbols: Islam has been portrayed as the key to discover 'true' democracy, 'true' socialism, 'true' free market, 'true' science, 'true' emancipation of women. Often, Western values are not rejected, but presented as Islamic, and reinterpreted according to alleged Islamic categories, often relying on a Western epistemology. In this context, the Islamist critique of the Western state has been crucial in elaborating the doctrine of the 'Islamic state'; that is to say, the Western concept of 'state' has been internalised and indigenised. Thus, in the process, Islamic modernisation has been unconsciously and unwillingly theorised in a subaltern manner, since Western epistemology has been extensively employed to understand social reality. The responses of the Arab states towards Islamist movements have been crucial in shaping the Islamist narrative itself. Hence, Qutbism, the ideology that developed following Sayyid Qutb's theorisations, also needs to be understood against the background of the repression of Nasser's regime. Ayubi (1995: 26) recognised that Arab states reacted in different ways to the Islamist challenge:

> Whereas the more conservative systems have managed to internalise certain elements of an Islamic ideology into the ideological apparatus of the state (by co-opting, rather than simply controlling, the Islamic clerics), the more 'radical' modernising systems have seen their marginalised groups adopting political Islam as a counter-hegemonic ideology in recent years.

The 'divide and rule' strategy adopted by regimes against Islamist movements is particularly evident in the Jordanian case, where co-option and repression have been selectively used by the regime against Islamic groups. In supporting the argument that a regime's policies contribute to shaping Islamism, Esposito (1997: 9) affirmed with reference to Egypt: 'Egypt reveals the diversity of political Islam even within a single country and also demonstrates the extent to which Islamist responses and tactics ... are often a reaction to government policies.'

Regarding the Jordanian case, Wiktorowicz's (2001) analysis has shown how the regime has been able to deal with both the 'moderate' Muslim Brotherhood and the 'radical' Salafism through the adoption of different strategies. What his research implies is that the regime has not only dealt with Islamism but, through its strategy, has helped to shape the trajectories of the movement. Moderate and radical outcomes are not written *a priori*, but are also produced by the initiatives of the regime. Consequently, Wiktorowicz's (2001) research is particularly interesting in showing to what extent the regime has managed to control and regulate Islamism, and concomitantly to what extent this attitude has affected the developments of Islamic movements. According to Wiktorowicz (2001), the regime has created a complex system of incentives and disincentives, enforced through administrative apparatuses, which have ended up persuading Islamist groups to adopt certain forms of social action, while dismissing others. This system allowed 'moderate' Islamists such as the Muslim Brotherhood to create their network of formal Islamic social institutions, while it compelled the Salafis to develop informal underground networks (Wiktorowicz, 2001: 14–15), resulting in the development of various strategies of survival by these groups. However, the peculiarity of the Jordanian case relies on the fact that the regime conceived a sophisticated system of bureaucratic processes and practices through which to control social action, instead of relying on sheer coercion, such as in the case of the Muslim Brotherhood of Syria in 1982.

The example of Jordan also highlights the importance of controlling the loci of production and reproduction of religious discourse, such as the mosques, in order to avoid the Islamists claiming a monopoly over religious discourse (Wiktorowicz, 2001: 150). The significance of Wiktorowicz's findings is important in recognising the centrality of the role of the state in providing opportunities and constraints to Islamic movements, in turn deeply influencing their strategies and social practices. In other words, the Jordanian case shows to what extent the state has played a significant role in the processes of social construction of the different trends of Islamism. Thus, the role of the state in contributing to shaping the Islamic 'other' emerges in its dialectical complexity. Understanding, however, the links between the actions of the state and the developments of Islamic movements should not lead to considering their mutual relationship in a purely deterministic fashion. In this respect, Schwedler (2006) deconstructs the so-called 'inclusion-moderation hypothesis', the argument according to which inclusion of Islamist movements in the political process automatically and necessarily leads to their moderation. For this, Schwedler (2006) compared the Islamic Action Front Party (IAFP) in Jordan with the Islah Party in Yemen, maintaining that the inclusion-moderation hypothesis presents several flaws. The Jordanian experience shows that political liberalisations contributed to the moderation of the IAFP in Jordan, while similar openings in Yemen did not have the same effect on the Islah party (Schwedler, 2006: 194). According to Schwedler (2006: 195–196), one of the decisive factors that explains the different stances of the Islamist parties in the two countries concerns 'changes in the boundaries of what the party can justify on ideological grounds and still recognize as Islamic practices'. Schwedler (2006: 197) invites us to focus on 'shifting boundaries of justifiable action' as 'one mechanism that can explain moderation', identifying ethnographic study as the most helpful methodology to carry out this endeavour. According to Schwedler's (2006) findings, the inclusion-moderation hypothesis risks assuming that shifts in the state's policies lead to mechanical adjustments in the strategies and ideologies of Islamist movements, thus implicitly denying Islamic movements' agency. Also Browers (2009: 179) has criticised the determinism of the inclusion-moderation hypothesis, advocating the adoption of a more dynamic model by affirming that 'structures and agents, material conditions, and ideological contexts exist within a dialectical relationship'. To sum up, national and international political economy profoundly influences the emergence, strategy and ideologies of Islamist movements. However, such an emphasis on the economic structure should not lead to a denial of the autonomy of ideology: an ideological sphere that is influenced by the political and economic structure, but which presents its own originality and autonomy, since social actors are primarily individuals, who constantly interpret and transform social reality. In other words, if political economy presents opportunities and constraints, individuals creatively react to social 'facts'.

It is precisely in the context of the cross-fertilisation between different narratives that it is possible to go beyond the dichotomy between secular state and Islamist opposition, in order to convincingly analyse contemporary Arab societies. On the one hand, Arab regimes increasingly relied on Islamic discourse to justify their claims to power. On the other hand, Islamic movements identified in the Western model of state an alien product imposed on Muslim societies. What is more, Islamist movements constructed themselves as the alternative *par excellence* to such a paradigm. The Western model of nation state, adopted in the Arab world after decolonisation and based on ideas such as the separation between church and state, was considered by Islamist movements extraneous to Islamic civilisation, whose history was seen as a coherent narrative (Vatikiotis, 1987: 35–57). Thus, it is possible to analyse two competing yet overlapping discourses of Islamism, the official one, which was endorsed by the regime and by its apparatuses, and the oppositional one of the Islamists. The Jordanian case is particularly instructive in this respect, showing convergences between the discourse of nationalism and Islamism, and therefore revealing to what extent this dichotomy fails to capture the complexity of contemporary Arab societies. Indeed, the discourse of the Jordanian Muslim Brotherhood increasingly used to rely on a sort of Islamo-nationalist ideology, while also the official discourse of the state developed a melange of nationalistic and Islamist themes.

The case of Jordan is obviously peculiar, since the Hashemite dynasty's legitimacy claim is based, since its very beginning, on its descent from the Prophet Muhammad. In Jordan, thus, instead of a cultural struggle between secularism and Islamism, what can be witnessed is the complex relationship between competing Islamo-nationalist ideologies, whose discourses are constantly shifting and overlapping. Thus, the struggle between nationalism and Islamism that has characterised the cultural landscape of the Arab world, at least from the 1970s to the 1990s, seems to have been superseded by the emergence of different Islamo-nationalist ideologies (Roy, 1994: 194). The crisis of Pan-Arab ideology and the spread of the Islamist discourse throughout society have led various regimes, such as the Egyptian regime under Mubarak and the Jordanian one, to adopt a religious narrative as an integral part of their discourse. This shift, characterised by the endorsement of Islamist discourse and by the co-option of the 'periphery' of moderate Islamists by the 'centre' of the regime in order to avoid disruptive social change, will be addressed in the next chapter. The next section, hence, addresses the phenomenon of Islamism against the background of the development of an Islamist middle class and of an Islamist private sector.

The Islamist middle class and the Islamic private sector

In the analysis of the transformation of Islamism, it is argued that the partial unleashing of market forces, triggered by the adoption of neoliberal policies, has opened up opportunity spaces that Islamist groups have managed to exploit. Cognizant of the experience of the Turkish Islamists, contenders to the debate, such as Öniş (1997), Gülalp (2001) and Yavuz (2003) have convincingly argued that globalisation has been conducive to the development of Islamic movements. Their arguments can be helpful in analysing analogous phenomena that took place in the Arab world. However, before exposing their theses, it is useful to critically address the concept of globalisation.

A critical approach to globalisation

Neoliberal economic globalisation has dramatically altered the relationships between state and market forces worldwide, leading to question the very sovereignty of a nation state, in particular with regard to what concerns economic sovereignty. The awareness of this process has led critical globalisation scholars to question the validity of a discipline such as 'international studies', since this can be 'an impediment to understanding the discourses of globalization', 'for emergent interactions ... are now between the state-centric and multi-centric worlds' (Mittelman, 2005: 20). It can be argued that conceptualising globalisation merely in terms of the expansion of American, or Western, imperialism, risks being reductionist, since it underemphasises the profound interplay between global market forces and local societies. Categories such as 'imperialism' and 'colonialism' seem indeed inadequate to fully explain the profound transformations of world economics currently defined as 'globalisation'. Conceiving globalisation solely as an exploitative process imposed by the 'centre', represented by the Western world, to the 'periphery' of developing countries neglects the fact that globalisation is reproducing the same dynamics between 'centre' and 'periphery' within both developed and developing societies. The persistence of 'the core-periphery structure of the global political economy' (Arrighi, 2005: 33) should not therefore be understood in exclusively international terms, but as a complex interplay between state actors, market and social forces.

In order to understand globalisation, it is useful to differentiate between globalisation as a structural process and globalisation as a political ideology. The former has been defined as 'the expansion and intensification of large-scale interaction networks relative to more local interactions', while the latter as 'a specific political ideology that glorifies the efficiency of markets and privately held firms' (Chase-Dunn and Gills, 2005: 450). Critical globalisation studies argue that blurring the distinction between globalisation as a structural phenomenon and as a political ideology is a socio-political act, since it aims to conceal to what extent dominant knowledge is entrenched with power. Indeed, according to Robinson, 'the exercise of studying the world, or trying to know the world, is itself a social act, committed by agents with a definite relationship to the social order. Intellectual production is always a collective process, and knowledge, a social product' (Robinson, 2005: 13). Robinson therefore radically challenges the existence of what he defines as 'free-floating academics', instead grounding the role of the Gramscian 'organic intellectual' in historically situated relations of power (Robinson, 2005: 12–14). Acknowledging the extent to which the producer and reproducer of social knowledge is embedded in society becomes crucial to examine the phenomenon of globalisation and its effects on societies.

The process of globalisation and the development of Islamism

The concept of 'critical globalisation studies' is a useful premise to the actual analysis of the reactions and the resistances generated by the worldwide diffusion of global socio-economic practices and patterns of consumptions. The process of globalisation can indeed contribute to explaining the appeal of the Islamist alternative against the background of the new importance of identity politics in the globalised world. Öniş (1997: 763), for example, discusses the extent to which neoliberal policies, associated with globalisation, were 'instrumental' in the development of the Islamic Welfare Party in Turkey. In addition, Gülalp (2001: 435) affirms that globalisation has actually paved the way for the blossoming of Islamism in Turkey. Moreover, Öniş (1997: 763) considers the Welfare Party 'the political expression of rising Islamic capital', therefore identifying a relationship between the growth of an Islamist bourgeoisie and the development of an Islamist party against the historical background of globalisation. This relationship has also been convincingly highlighted, as far as the Turkish case is concerned, by Gülalp (2001) and Yavuz (2003). This thesis, as Gülalp (2001: 435) emphasises, radically challenges the hypothesis according to which 'modernisation' leads to secularisation. According to Öniş, globalisation has challenged the economic sovereignty of nation state, since the latter is not anymore able to control economic activity (Öniş, 1997: 746).

This process has led to the crisis of social-democratic parties in Western Europe, since these political movements can no longer provide a genuine alternative to neoliberal policies. The crisis of the nation state is therefore closely connected with the crisis of the left, unable to articulate a counter-hegemonic project. In Muslim majority countries, Islamism has often successfully managed to play this role. With regard to what concerns us, the profound transformations that took place in the global economy also had far reaching consequences in the cultural sphere, where a tendency towards homogenisation, especially evident in the patterns of consumption, co-exists with an emergence of identity politics, which has partially dislocated traditional axes such as left and right (Öniş, 1997: 747). The dichotomy between left and right is indeed displaced by the emergence, or re-emergence, of other polarising axes, such as secularism versus religiosity. Simply equating 'secularism' with 'left' and 'religiosity' with 'right' would be utterly inadequate, since religious language can be equally used to promote agendas purported as progressive or conservative or both. On the other hand, the Turkish case clearly shows to what extent the secularist narrative has been employed to justify positions of power, through the exclusion of the 'periphery' from the 'centre'. According to Gülalp, a crucial difference between Latin American Catholic liberation theology and Islamism of the Welfare Party consists in the fact that liberation theology mainly uses religious language to promote social change, while Welfare's Islamism deals with social issues in order to promote cultural change (Gülalp, 2001: 434). However, following Öniş and Yavuz, it can be argued that also the Welfare Party has been truly engaged in socio-economic change. Both these social movements claimed to empower the 'excluded', but while this category refers, in liberation theology, to the poor, in the case of Turkey it also included segments of the new bourgeoisie. Öniş (1997: 748) correctly points out that, given the crisis of the left, Islamism has therefore become in Turkey the language through which the excluded have been clamouring for social, economic and political change. However, as Öniş (1997: 763) indicates, the category of the excluded is in fact extremely broad, since it includes not only the 'losers' of globalisation, but also the 'winners', such as professionals and businesspersons who are not part of the ruling class. Islamism provides a language in which both the marginalized and the wealthy articulate their grievances, allowing them to give birth to a Gramscian social bloc.

The different meanings attributed to the category of the excluded explains why liberation theology used to promote radical and disruptive social change, while Welfare Party's Islamism appeared remarkably more moderate. The former was addressing the losers of globalisation and aimed at a drastic redistribution of wealth, while the latter expressed the grievances of a more articulated social bloc, whose wealthier strata were not interested in radical social change. However, this does not imply that Turkey's Welfare Party was not interested in social change, and that its goal was merely cultural: the social change the Welfare Party was envisaging was one conducive to the development of Islamic business. In this context, the emergence of the Welfare Party in Turkey is seen as 'a parallel phenomenon to and a reflection of the growing power of Islamic business in the Turkish economy and society in the context of the 1990s' (Öniş, 1997: 760). The Welfare Party was therefore the political representative of an 'Islamic bourgeoisie', which demanded not only 'elite status', but 'to obtain a greater share of public resources, both at the central and local levels, in competition with other segments of private business in Turkey' (Öniş, 1997: 760). It is in order to reach this goal that the Islamic bourgeoisie rallied the poor to combat secularist crony capitalism (Gülalp, 2001: 435), thus giving birth to a counter-hegemonic 'Islamic social bloc'. Yavuz (2003) argues that globalisation and economic liberalisation created the necessary opportunity space for Islamists to expand in economy, education and welfare related areas. In Turkey, the dialectics between globalisation and Islamism, hence, seem to have produced new forms of Islamism, represented by the Justice and Development Party (AKP), which are compatible with a free market economy and liberal democracy (Mandaville, 2007: 120–128). A similar process took place in Egypt, with the emergence of the Hizb al-Wasat from the Muslim Brotherhood (Mandaville, 2007: 117–119). The establishment of an interpretative link between the development of an Islamic bourgeoisie and the growing appeal of Islamism, which has been highlighted through an analysis of the Turkish case, is indeed the hypothesis that informs this study. This link is here seen as a dialectical relationship and it is located in a precise historical context, characterised by the decline of the Arab state and by the globalisation of social, economic and cultural practices.

The market as an opportunity space for Islamist movements

This section examines how Islamism has developed alternative strategies of existence using available opportunity spaces, such as economic practices. In fact, Islamism, seen as a nexus of groups and activities whose declared aim is the spreading of Islamic values, has identified in the market a locus in which to carry out a counter-hegemonic struggle against the hegemonic narrative of the establishment. Since the political domain has generally been precluded from the initiatives of Islamic movements, the market has been identified by those groups as a crucial opportunity space in which to carry out their strategies. As Ismail (2006: 28) argues, 'the appropriation of the public sphere' through its Islamisation is a crucial strategic goal for Islamist activism. The establishment of an Islamic private sector will be read into this context. Wickham (2002: 97) sees the 'parallel Islamic sector' as including:

(1) private mosques; (2) Islamic voluntary associations, including welfare societies, cultural organizations, health clinics, and schools; and (3) Islamic for-profit commercial and business enterprises, such as Islamic banks, investment companies, manufacturing firms, and publishing houses.

Thus, Islamism managed to express the frustrations and aspirations of new social formations, in particular of the new middle classes (Clark, 2004: 1–41), while the marketplace became a crucial battlefield in which to undertake a struggle over meaning. The economic restructuring policies allowed a new middle class that adopted, produced and transformed Islamist ideology to thrive. Thus, the frames provided by Islam have been useful in helping the new middle class to create 'insurgent consciousness' (McAdam, 1999), through mobilisation of dissent and expansion of networks of alliances. However, such an 'insurgency' did not take place as a political struggle, since the political domain was out of the reach of Islamism, but as a hegemonic struggle over society, in which the market, as well as the cultural sphere, has been a crucial battleground. Such a peaceful struggle expressed the development of a rift between the political society, and the state bourgeoisie linked to it, and a new bourgeoisie, emancipated from the state. The outcome of this struggle has been the birth of an embryonic Islamic civil society (Warde, 2004: 47). The Islamic middle class, emancipated from both the secularist middle class and the masses, developed its own specific identity, a melange of traditional Islamic practices and modern Islamist ideologies and middle class patterns of consumption. Yavuz (2003: 94) defines this class, in the Turkish case, as follows:

> they are religiously and socially conservative, economically liberal, and oriented towards private initiative; able to generate initial capital through family and religious networks and thus more prone to accumulate wealth; and very critical of state intervention in the economy. This causes them to support free market conditions, in contrast to the state, which supports the big secularist business oligarchs.

This new Islamist middle class constitutes the stronghold of Islamism, the social strata where Islamist movements mainly recruit their cadres. The example of Turkey is pivotal in order to understand the challenge to the *status quo* posed by Islamism in the context of a struggle for hegemony between two social groups. Indeed, in his ground-breaking research on Islamic political identity in Turkey, Yavuz (2003) identified in the marketplace the battlefield where a struggle for hegemony took place between secularism and Islamism. Following the economic restructuring promoted by Özal in the 1980s, the state partially withdrew from the economic realm, allowing other forces to occupy this space. Such an argument is, as will be seen in the following chapters, relevant to the analysis of the Jordanian experience. According to Yavuz (2003), the reforms promoted by Özal caused a remarkable waning of the control over Turkish society wielded by the secularist bourgeoisie, which enjoyed the patronage of the state. In this period, a new middle class, alien to Kemalist ideology, started to challenge the *status quo*. This new middle class was predominantly from the Anatolian mainland, conceptualised by Yavuz (2003) as a 'periphery' as opposed to the 'centre' represented by the urban Kemalist middle class linked to the state apparatus. Its worldview was imbued by Sufi Islam, and it was radically challenging the implicit assumption of Kemalism, which identifies religion with 'backwardness' and secularism with 'progress' (Yavuz, 2003: 268–269): this discourse was accused of being constructed in order to exclude the 'periphery' from the 'centre'. Indeed, this new thriving middle class could not easily fit in categories such as 'reactionary' and 'progressive': its moral viewpoint was conservative and traditional, while its attitude toward market and society was liberal, if not neoliberal. On the contrary, Yavuz (2003) argues, the secular bourgeoisie was deeply connected, and owed its status and wealth to the proximity to the state. These features of crony capitalism are even more evident in Arab societies.

The new middle class of Turkey, identifying new opportunity spaces in the neoliberal economic reforms, embraced a version of Islamism that expressed a radical critique of the secularist oligarchy. With regard to the Turkish case, Öniş (1997: 744) scrutinised the political economy causes behind 'the tensions between the authoritarian secularism of the Republican elite at the "centre" and the broad masses quite congenial to Islamic principles and values on the "periphery"'. Concepts such as 'centre' and 'periphery' allow the deconstruction of the idealistic and essentialist approaches, which assume that the struggle between secularism and Islamism needs to be merely understood as an ideological conflict, without taking into account the economic structure. Thus, according to Yavuz (2003), the struggle between secularism and Islamism in Turkey can be better comprehended in the light of a struggle between big oligarchs and small and medium enterprises, crony capitalism and free market supporters.

Clearly, this middle class trend of Islam, which enthusiastically embraced a free market, represents merely a small fraction of the entire spectrum of Turkish 'political' Islam. Indeed, social strata that did not benefit from the economic adjustment attacked the Islamist middle class, accusing it of betrayal of 'true' Islam. When segments of the Islamic 'periphery' began to share the same pattern of consumption of secularist 'centre', the segments of the Islamic 'periphery' who did not partake the benefits of free market started to criticise the others, accusing them of betrayal. Also in this case, the social struggle was conducted under the flags of Islam, while the underlying issues were mainly of economic and social nature. Therefore, according to Yavuz (2003), Islam provided a frame in which the new Islamist middle class managed to express its grievances but also its desire for political and economic emancipation from the 'iron cage' of Kemalist etatism.

Noland and Pack (2007: 205) notice that, in the Syrian case, 'the Syrian Moslem [sic] Brotherhood counts among its supporters local Sunni capitalists who are more favourably disposed to policy reform than the minority Alawites' and that also the Egyptian Muslim Brotherhood 'are bourgeois in their economic orientation and with greater democratic legitimacy might actually have an easier time implementing reforms than the incumbent authoritarian regimes'. For Islamic business to work efficiently to generate resources to channel the socio-economic activities of the Islamic groupings, they had to work in an environment in which they could have the freedom to further their own strategies of expanding religious activism. This made them the sometimes reluctant supporters of a liberal economic framework, due to the fact that it provided them with the opportunity spaces to emerge and thrive. Hence, political reform and economic de-regulation were required so that opportunity spaces for their existence could be created.

Locating the emergence of the 'Islamic private sector'

The discussion in the previous section argued that the economic realm is one of the main loci in which it is possible to recognise the political action of Islamism. This section argues, on the other hand, that also the development of Islamist consciousness can be conceptualised in the light of the emergence of a new social formation. The two processes, far from being mutually exclusive, appear dialectically related. Islam offered to politically and socially marginalised social strata the frames to express their critique to the *status quo*. New economic and social actors identified, in the language of Islamic symbols, frames in which to utter their social frustrations and aspirations. Thus, Islamism became the language in which social and economic forces articulated their challenges. Arab socialism, with its nationalist and secular feature, became the main object of critique. Islamism, seen as the ideology of the social forces excluded from the patronage networks of the governments, represented an organic and integral challenge to the Arab state, since it contested its political, social and economic foundations, as well as its ideological claims and its very legitimacy.

A question, which will be dealt with elsewhere in this study, is whether Islamism also proposes a truly alternative epistemology. In this contest, the economic realm acquires a crucial importance as the structural level of the struggle between different socio-political formations, whose boundaries are often blurred and shifting. The rise and expansion of Islamic business can be properly understood against the background of the political economy strategies of Islamism. In particular, the Muslim Brothers seem to have fostered the development of Islamic finance, as has been demonstrated at least in the cases of Jordan and Kuwait (Henry and Wilson, 2004). As will be seen, the Muslim Brotherhood of Jordan played a major role in lobbying for the establishment of an Islamic bank in the Hashemite kingdom (Malley, 2004). Some Arab states fostered the creation of Islamic banks, considered as bulwarks against the penetration and spread of secular ideologies such as Nasserism, communism and socialism. As stated above, the creation of a strong middle class was useful in order to defend the *status quo* against potential threats, and Islamic finance has been a significant factor in cementing this social bloc. In particular, Kahf (2004: 22) identifies in the establishment of the Faisal Islamic Bank of Egypt in 1976 the 'beginning of the new alliance between *shari'a* scholars and bankers', the foundation of which is interpreted as the outcome of the collaboration between the Egyptian President Anwar al-Sadat, the

Grand Mufti of Egypt and the Saudi Prince Muhammad al-Faisal, indefatigable advocate of Islamic banking (Warde, 2004: 40). This convergence of interests, which occurred under the aegis of the Muslim Brotherhood, was part of Sadat's broader project of development of an Islamic middle class. The *infitah* (open door) policy of the Egyptian President Sadat in the 1970s determined the crisis of the *etatist* development strategy of Arab socialism, which had characterised the experience of his predecessor Nasser, in favour of policies open to free market and individual enterprise. Such a process determined a reconfiguration of the Egyptian socio-economic structure. In particular, a new Islamist bourgeoisie developed, a new '*infitah* class' that managed to take full advantage of the transformations of Egyptian society and economy (Beinin, 2005: 120). According to data quoted by Beinin (2005), in 1980, eight out of the 18 families who towered above the Egyptian economy were closely linked to the Muslim Brotherhood, while 40% of the whole private sector was connected to the Muslim Brotherhood (Beinin, 2005). At the same time, the new Islamist bourgeoisie extended its control over the Muslim Brotherhood itself, which was, according to Warde (2004: 38), 'squarely in the anti-Soviet, pro-US camp' and played a significant role in mobilising this Islamist middle class against the legacy of Nasserism.

If it is undeniable that this middle class presented some features of crony capitalism, due to the patronage links with the state, nevertheless it presented original features, since its wealth was not merely acquired through patronage networks, but mainly benefited from private sector economic activities and international links. Moreover, this Islamic bourgeoisie, despite its support for the *status quo*, did not entirely share the hegemonic narrative of the state, nor the ultimate goals of the Arab regimes. In fact, its worldview was intensely shaped by the narrative of the moderate trend of Islamism represented by the Muslim Brotherhood, which attempted to provide political representation for this class. Throughout the 1970s, the 1980s and the 1990s, the Muslim Brotherhood supported the economic reforms which allowed this '*intifah* class' to thrive (Utvik, 2006: 150–152). The development trajectories of the Islamist middle class, whose previous wealth had been predominantly related to land owning, show that, through a paradigm shift in their attitudes, they commenced investing in the financial sector (Beinin, 2005: 120–123). The ideology of Islamism managed to guarantee the cohesion of this class, legitimising its newly acquired riches and justifying its desire for political participation through the frames of Islam. It is clear that the 'pact' between the regime and the new Islamist middle class gave birth to a contradiction: on the one hand, the regime identified in this class a pillar of socio-economic stability, since both of them were opposed to radical social change. On the other hand, this class gradually became a potential political threat, given that it aspired to play a larger role in the decision-making process. Indeed, despite the fact that the rise of this social class had been supported by several Arab regimes, the new Islamic bourgeoisie became at the same time largely autonomous from them, due to its transnational characteristics.

The marriage between capitalism and Islamism has been blessed by the *ulama*, who guaranteed the rising Islamic banking sector the support of 'new clienteles' (Kahf, 2004: 17), in particular small and medium entrepreneurs, a social class traditionally close to them. On the ground, small and medium entrepreneurs mobilised their savings and supported Islamic finance and Islamism, providing cadres to both.

Such a new power centre had a 'modernising' function, in promoting economic and political reform, and it had a crucial role in opening up new opportunity spaces for Islamist activism. According to Kahf (2004: 23), this role is particularly evident in Sudan, Turkey and Jordan. In Sudan, 'business owned and run by associates of the Islamist movement', close to Hassan al-Turabi, challenged the existing business establishment, and the Saudi Prince Muhammad al-Faisal played a crucial role in supporting the Islamist movement, also through the establishment of an Islamic bank (Kahf, 2004: 23). In this country, Islamic business, relying on the resources of the Islamic movement and on the capital of al-Faisal, decisively contributed to destabilising the traditional political and economic elite through the promotion of social change. In Kahf's (2004: 30) view, the rise of Islamic business in Sudan can be understood as a conscious effort to create an 'economic base' for the Islamist movement. A similar pattern can be observed in Turkey, where the Faisal Islamic Bank of Turkey obtained the support of the MÜSIAD, the powerful association of Islamist businesspersons and industrialists (Kahf, 2004: 23). The role of the MÜSIAD in promoting economic and political reform has been examined by Yavuz (2003), who argues that this association, representing the interests of the small and medium Anatolian enterprises, provided an economic basis to the Islamist movement and a religio-political foundation to an economic formation. According to Yavuz (2003: 97), indeed the MÜSIAD has also been the cradle of a Weberian 'entrepreneurial spirit', spreading capitalistic values such as the willingness to take risks and, most of all, providing an ethical framework and creating networks for the development of business interactions (ESI, 2005). Overall, the MÜSIAD has been pivotal in fostering new interpretations of Islam supportive of a free market economy. As Roy (2004: 40) acknowledges:

> The Islamist organisation Müsiad (Independent Industrialists' and Businessmen Association) in Turkey explicitly extols the 'work ethic' in Islam and is more Weberian in deed than many Western culturalists are in their writing. In this sense changing patterns of religiosity are in line with the entrenching of modern models of economic liberalism, entrepreneurial individualism and compassionate conservatism.

A striking example of the links between Islamist activism and Islamic business is represented by Kuwait. In Kuwait, the banking system was traditionally controlled by the merchant oligarchy, on which the al-Sabah ruling family was highly dependent (Smith, 2004: 170). In such a context, the establishment of the Kuwait Finance House (KFH), now one of the most important Islamic banks in the world, has been explained as the result of a pact between the Islamists and the ruling family, whose goal was the breaking up of the oligopolistic position of the merchants. Smith (2004: 169) maintains that:

> KFH is a concrete expression of the de facto alliance between the ruling family and the Islamic movement ... Islamic finance in Kuwait, then, embodies the growing Islamization of public life in Kuwait under the benign gaze of the Kuwaiti government.

Indeed, Islamists represented in Kuwait, as in several other Arab countries, an ally of the regime against the penetration of leftist ideologies, spread in Kuwait by Arab migrant workers, particularly Palestinians (Smith, 2004: 172). The al-Sabah ruling family, therefore, managed, through the alliance with the Islamists, to stem both the growing power of the merchants and the diffusion of political ideas considered subversive. Islamists obtained the support of recently urbanised Bedouins (Smith, 2004: 173), who represented a new middle class excluded by the patronage networks of the merchant oligarchy. According to Smith (2004: 179), 'The role of the Kuwait Finance House is that of an engine of the Islamist movements, through the alleged support of Islamist candidates and the support of Islamic charities throughout the Arab world.' Most of those charities are eagerly engaged in the spread of *da'wa*, promoting conformity to Islamic values and supporting several Muslim causes. Furthermore, Smith argues that the Kuwait Finance House may even support Islamist student movements, guaranteeing the activists jobs in the bank (Smith, 2004: 178–179). These cases highlight the interdependence between the rise of new socio-economic formations and the development of Islamism as a religious-political phenomenon.

Locating the emergence of Islamic economics and finance

The emergence of new social formations that expressed their grievances and aspirations through Islamic frames contributed to the blossoming of new research activities in the field of economics and finance throughout the Arab and Islamic world, part of a broader process of 'Islamisation of knowledge'. One of the most famous centres, the Islamic Research and Training Institute of the Islamic Development Bank, has been a herald of economic reforms in the Islamic world, educating Muslim students and scholars in Islamic economics and finance.

Indeed, this new discipline determined a vast and profound process of *ijtihad* in Islamic thought, persuading generations of Muslim students to participate in the social construction of a discipline which could conciliate the most recent acquisitions in economics and finance with Islamic tenets, promising at the same time material wealth and rewards in the hereafter. Such a cultural trend can be considered one of the most original contributions of Islamic thought in the second half of the twentieth century. Presented by several Muslim scholars as a mere rediscovery of the hidden socio-economic message of Islam, Islamic economics can be more persuasively considered as a re-invention of tradition. The development of Islamic economics may be partially seen as a reaction of Muslim intellectuals against the shortcomings of Arab socialism. As Warde (2004: 43) argues, 'ideologically both liberalism and economic Islam were driven by their common opposition to socialism and economic *dirigisme*' (Warde, 2004: 43). The *Kulturkampf* engaged by Islamic economists against Arab socialism must be read against the historical background of the Arab world and of its aftermath. To put it differently, the rise of Islamic economics discourse has to be contextualised in the ideological struggle between leftist ideologies, such as communism, socialism, Nasserism and Ba'athism, and an alternative model, compatible with capitalism.

It can be argued that Islamic economics, reifying the pillars of the capitalist economy, i.e. private property and a free market, provides stronger foundations to the capitalist system. Warde (2004: 47) argues that the first point shared by Islamism and neoliberalism is 'the Islamic commitment to private property, free enterprise and the sanctity of contracts, in contrast to state-led economic policies'. Moreover, Warde (2004: 47) continues to state that 'Islam became the tool of entrepreneurs seeking to get around restrictive regulation and an instrumental factor in privatisation and deregulation – and the best excuse to disengage the state from the economy'. According to Warde, not only neoliberals and Islamic bankers cooperated, but governments used this trend of Islam to promote financial restructuring, such as in Malaysia and Bahrain (Warde, 2004: 47). Secondly, another area of convergence between Islamic economics and neoliberalism was the support of private welfare and philanthropy, and the critique against state intervention, out of the convictions that 'the voluntary provision of charity reduces the need for public welfare organisations that are usually costlier to run' (Warde, 2004: 47). Also Noland and Pack (2007: 2000) argue that 'the widespread support for subjecting business to *shari'a* law ... could be interpreted as forming a coherent basis for adapting the demands of globalization to local values'. However, a rift developed between Islamic economics, which promoted a reform of the economic system based on the paradigm of the ethically conscious *homo islamicus*, and Islamic finance, which increasingly integrated into the international financial system and de facto adopted the *Weltanschauung* of the individualistic and profit driven *homo economicus* (Asutay, 2007b). Indeed, it may be argued that while Islamic economics aimed at creating an alternative system consistent with the 'substance' of Islam, Islamic banking and finance developed an approach consistent with the 'form' of Islam. In other words, Islamic banking and finance accepted the hegemony of capitalism, while articulating itself through the language of Islam. Hence, it may be argued that Islamic business, and in particular Islamic finance, has played the role of one of the driving forces of globalisation in the Islamic world, contributing to the integration of Islamic societies in global capitalism. Such a role is shown by the fact that Islamic business has identified, since its inception, a political-ideological rival and an obstacle for the expansion of its activities in the authoritarian and *dirigiste* Arab state. It should be noted that Islamic business supports free market ideology, legitimising capital accumulation in a liberal framework, encouraging the growth of the private sector and criticising state-led development policies. At the same time, a moderate trend of Islamism has managed to interpret the aspirations of a new middle class, whose rise occurred during the *infitah* policies implemented by the Arab regimes during the 1970s and the 1980s. Therefore, both moderate Islamic movements and the Islamic private sector seem to have been supportive of political and economic liberalisation policies. Undoubtedly, the rise of Islamic economics has to be read as a chapter in the wider history of the project of 'Islamisation of knowledge' as part of the construction of an 'authentic' Islamic identity. In terms of political economy, it needs to be understood against the background of the crisis of Arab socialism and the shift towards market economies.

In conclusion, Islamism became the ideology in which social strata managed to express their dissatisfaction with the shortcomings of Arab socialism. For example, Islamism became the language in which both the *infitah* bourgeoisie and the lumpen intelligentsia framed their critique against the Egyptian state. The *infitah* bourgeoisie, like the Anatolian middle class, emphasised the notion that Islam was fully compatible with the free market, and that Islam favoured trade and wealth creation since its very inception. Moreover, the concept of *shura* has been widely used by this social class to claim the right to be represented and participate in the decision making process. On the other hand, the lumpen intelligentsia found in Islamism the language in which to articulate its dissatisfaction for the failure of the Arab state to fulfil its promises of social equality. Thus, Islamic frames managed to cover a broad spectrum of position, from the medium and small entrepreneurs who were asking for more economic freedom to the deprived masses who were demanding social justice. Similarly, Islamic economics provided the language in which to express these grievances in economic terms. Islamic economics presented Islam as the solution to the economic and social problems of humankind; a third way which, after the alleged failure of capitalism and socialism, would have been able to guarantee both efficiency and equity. In the last decades, the counter hegemonic potential of such a solution has been extremely high, since it can cement both the winners of globalisation, when focusing on free market, and the losers, when stressing social justice. However, there is an intrinsic risk, which will be highlighted by the Jordanian case, of the occurrence of a rift between these two social formations, whose alliance is precarious and linked to political and economic developments.

Conclusion

The aim of this chapter is to show the process of Islamisation in its complex dialectical relationship with the economic structure. The analysis of Islamism has been primarily located in the realm of political economy, in the attempt to demonstrate that, in order to understand Islamism, it is essential to include both the economic and cultural domains. Thus, supporting Ismail's argument, Roy's (1994) notion of a failure of 'political Islam' is here challenged. Indeed, as Ismail points out, Roy's argument lies on the assumption that, in order to assess the success or failure of Islamic movements, attention should be concentrated on the political domain, narrowly intended. As Ismail (2006: 161) argues, 'this conclusion, however, rests on a problematic conception of politics; one that limits "the political" solely to activities that concern the state and government'. Ismail (2006: 25) also points out that 'a widening of the conception of politics to recognise the relations of power structuring everyday communities allows us to see the terms of Islamist insertion into the political field'. Her conclusions underline 'the centrality of the cultural domain for the Islamists' struggle for power' (2006: 77).

The present study aims to propose an integrated understanding of Islamism that takes into account the economic, political, social and cultural dimensions of its power. Hence, the theoretical framework that informs the present study to be exposed in the next chapter, suggests adopting a broader conception of politics that also includes the 'ideological sphere' of the society. Following this line of reasoning, a more nuanced and sophisticated theoretical understanding will lead to observing the strategies of the Muslim Brotherhood in the economic, cultural and social realms. These domains constitute 'political' areas in which its struggle over meanings took place, battlegrounds between the hegemonic narrative of the state and the counter-hegemonic narrative of Islamism.

The argument is that a dissociation of the analysis of the political, narrowly defined, from the social, economic and cultural domains, wrongly led to the conclusion that the cycle of Islamism was concluded. The aftermath of the so-called Arab Spring has clearly shown the flaws of these readings. On the other hand, a study that takes into account the dialectic through which Islamism shapes society and, in turn, is shaped by society, can lead to very different conclusions regarding the vitality of Islamism. In other words, the discursive tradition of Islam still provides signs, symbols and frames through which grievances, frustrations and aspirations are expressed. Moreover, the discursive tradition of Islam reveals itself as a primary object of interpretation and contestation, given the fact that both the hegemonic narratives of the Arab regimes and the counter-hegemonic narratives of different social strata tend to elaborate and to articulate distinct Islamic discourses. Hence, it is vital to highlight the links between these Islamist narratives and political economy.

Relying on Ismail's (2006: 23) argument, the relationships between the Arab state and Islamist movements have been seen as influenced by the decline of state capitalism and the transition to 'rentier market economies'. These transformations have also been read in relation to the crisis of the once hegemonic Pan-Arab narrative and to the 'expansion of the arena of informal politics' (Ismail, 2006: 23). As discussed, the contribution of Nazih Ayubi has been central to our argument: according to Ayubi (1995), the Arab state has been 'over-stated'; in other words its strength was merely apparent. The Arab state may have looked strong because of its coercive apparatus but, as soon as civil society was included in our analysis, it was clear that the consensus enjoyed by Islamist movements threatened the very legitimacy claims upon which the Arab state was built (Ayubi, 1995: 457–458). The emergence of the Islamist challenge has been made possible by the fact that the Arab states 'have annexed parts of society and the economy "from the outside" without penetrating society at large' (Ayubi, 1995: 447). On the other hand, the penetration of the society has been the main endeavour of the Islamist movement.

In the following chapter, this understanding is enriched and developed through the exposition of the theoretical framework this study is based upon. In accordance with these arguments, an anthropological approach is seen as one of the most effective ways to analyse how power struggles between different and competing narratives are articulated in civil society. In other words, the process of re-Islamisation of the public sphere becomes evident when observing phenomena located in the sphere of 'culture', classically defined by Edward Tylor as 'that complex whole which includes knowledge, belief, arts, morals, law, custom, and any other capabilities and habits acquired by man as a member of society' (Tylor, 1994: 1). Hence, economic anthropology will be seen as one of the best methodological tools to observe this vast process of Islamisation, or re-Islamisation, of society.

2 Understanding Islamism
Theoretical and conceptual framework

Introduction

In the previous chapter, the development of Islamism is analysed in its dynamic and dialectical relation within the framework of political economy, following a line of reasoning which interprets the rise and development of Islamism related to socio-economic transformations of society. However, it is stressed that a focus on political economy should not lead to deterministic approaches regarding the relations between economy and culture, thus neglecting the creative role of agency of social actors. As Wickham (2002: 8) states in the introduction to *Mobilizing Islam*:

> the rise of Islamic activism in Egypt – and, by implication, in other settings – was contingent on a deliberate process of mobilization initiated and sustained by Islamic counterelites. By granting center stage to the question of how oppositional leaders mobilize support, this book introduces an element of agency that is missing from – or at least underdeveloped in – most accounts of Islamic activism in Egypt and beyond.

Indeed, acknowledging the creative role of the agency of social actors is essential in order to understand the process of Islamisation *qua* production and reproduction of symbolic and interpretive frames. Following this approach, this chapter analyses theoretical lines useful to conceive social action and mobilisation as processes of 'articulation', defined by Laclau and Mouffe (2001: 105) as 'any practice establishing a relation among elements such that their identity is modified as a result of their articulatory practice'. The articulation of the Islamist project, hence, needs to be read in its socio-economic contexts; this very articulation has contributed to a profound transformation of this context, and in turn Islamist identity itself has been subjected to change. To put it differently, an analysis that takes into consideration both economy and ideology, seen in their autonomy and interdependence, reveals the complexity of their dialectical relationships, allowing for the elaboration of a more sophisticated topography of the social (Robinson, 2005: 16).

This chapter, hence, attempts to locate Islamism in social theory, conceptualising the relationships between economic practices and cultural representations as dialectical processes, of which the social construction of identities and ideologies by social movements is an integral part. In fact, the critique of essentialism and of economic determinism should not, as argued by this study, lead to theoretically agnostic accounts of 'facts': facts themselves need, indeed, to be studied as social constructions, since they are the products of a multiplicity of discourses and practices that need to be unfolded.

The theoretical undertaking of this study, thus, aims at contributing to the articulation of an analytical perspective by conceptualising the role played by economy and culture in the construction of forms of social consciousness and in the interdependent processes of reproduction of social formations (Postone, 2004: 78–79). The theoretical framework that informs this study is highly indebted to a post-Gramscian understanding, since it identifies in Gramsci's concept of hegemony, critically examined, an attempt to analytically bridge the gap between political economy and the cultural analysis. Therefore, this research refutes essentialist interpretations of Islamism, which focus on fixity and identity, instead proposing to conceptualise Islamism as a contingent and shifting nexus of 'historico-discursive formations' (Laclau and Mouffe, 2001: 114). As Piscatori (1986: 33) concisely and effectively puts it: 'just as Islam can be used to legitimate, so can it be used to express opposition'. Following this line of reasoning, the articulations of historico-discursive formations through the adoption of Islamic frames constitute the subject of this research, whose theoretical underpinnings are provided in this chapter. Laclau and Mouffe (2001: 7) underline the importance of the concept of hegemony in interpreting social reality: 'with Gramsci, the term [hegemony] acquires a new type of centrality that transcends its tactical or strategic uses: "hegemony" becomes the key concept in understanding the very unity existing in a concrete social formation'.

This dimension constitutes the focus of the present research: the use of the concept of hegemony to comprehend the articulation of hegemonic and counter-hegemonic ideologies, discourses and practices. Consequently, in the first part of this chapter, the Gramscian concept of hegemony *qua* articulation is proposed as a category of political analysis, inasmuch as it stresses the significance of the cultural and ideological dimensions of power and their dialectical relationships with political economy. The second section examines social constructivism, as a premise to analysing Islamism as the outcome of processes of interaction between different social actors, thus challenging the idea of the existence of an abstract nature of Islamic movements. Moreover, it introduces social movement theory and the framing perspective as valuable analytical tools to scrutinise the dynamics through which social movements produce their ideas, shape and are shaped by the social world around them. The conclusion reviews the arguments of the chapter, highlighting their relevance for the exploration of the articulations of Islamism in Jordan, which will be conducted in the following chapter.

Hegemony as a category of political analysis

Overcoming economic determinism

Gramsci is considered the first Marxist thinker to address the problem of the superstructure, stressing the importance, and the autonomy, of the ideological sphere of society (Bobbio, 1979: 30); Laclau and Mouffe (2001: x) consider his concept of hegemony 'the central category of political analysis'. Gramsci's novelty can be fully appreciated when compared with what is generally called 'orthodox Marxism', that is to say the interpretations of Marxism prevailing among the Socialists of the Second International (1889–1916). Orthodox Marxism interpreted dialectics as a necessity and adopted a positivistic epistemology, postulating deterministic relations between the economic base, 'the material conditions of life', and the ideological superstructure. These readings arguably abandoned the original Hegelian monism, which inspired Marx's early thought, introducing a marked Kantian dualism between object and subject, in the form of a sharp distinction between an 'objective' economic base and a 'subjective' superstructure (Postone, 2003: 80) to reveal the extent to which the ontologically monistic Hegelian inspiration of Marx had been superseded by a post-Kantian dualism between subject and object. The dualism between economic base and ideological superstructure has led to an 'economic determinism', where cultural, political, legal and religious forms are seen as reflections of the on-going tensions between forces of production and relations of production.

The faith of orthodox Marxism in the economic constitution of the social has been challenged, within Marxism, by Gramsci's crucial acknowledgement of the 'symbolic constitution of the social' (Laclau and Mouffe, 2001: 86) through the development of the concept of hegemony. The new importance attributed to ideology and culture as autonomous domains of the social formation led thinkers such as Lukács, Korsch and Gramsci to conduct vigorous critiques of economic determinism. Their Hegelian readings of Marx stressed the dialectical interdependence between base and superstructure, criticising those who merely see the latter as a by-product of economic processes and ideologies, mere masks of underlying economic interests. In fact, if ideologies are likely to be seen by orthodox Marxists as by-products of the interplay between forces of production and relations of production, for Lukács (1971: 58) 'ideological factors do not merely "mask" economic interests, they are not merely the banners and slogans: they are the parts, the components of which the real struggle is made'. Gramsci and Lukács therefore proposed readings of Marxian thought that emphasise the creative role of social actors in the historical process. By doing so, they managed to integrate within the Marxist tradition the importance attributed to creative will by non-Marxist thinkers such as Nietzsche and Bergson. The main contribution of Gramsci and Lukács therefore consists in recognising the autonomy of ideology and culture, while affirming their interdependence with socio-economic forces and practices. The critique of economic determinism leads Laclau and Mouffe (2001: xviii) 'to acknowledge that any form of consensus is the result of a hegemonic articulation'.

Articulations of Gramscian conceptualisations

Gramsci's concepts have been widely used to understand social movements in different environments, including Arab societies. Simms (2002) applied a Gramscian framework to analyse the history and ideology of the Muslim Brotherhood of Egypt from 1928 until 1953. According to Simms (2002), the emergence of the Muslim Brotherhood has to be understood as a reaction against hegemonic power, then represented by British colonialist ideology. While Simms' contribution is undeniably remarkable in applying Gramscian categories to explain the rise of the Muslim Brotherhood, it risks being too deterministic in considering Islamist ideology as a mere reaction to imperialism.

The concept of 'passive revolution', seen as a way in which the ruling classes react by annihilating the counter-hegemonic potential of subversive groups through a selective policy of co-optation and coercion (*trasformismo*) offers extremely valuable insights in understanding how the Egyptian government reacted, under Mubarak, to the challenge represented by Islamism. Once more, approaches that focus exclusively on the political sphere, narrowly defined, tend to merely dismiss as a failure what they perceive as the Islamist attempt at conquering the state. On the other hand, a more sophisticated perspective, such as Bayat's (2007), can help to highlight how the counter-hegemonic Islamist attempt was defused by the state through a 'passive revolution' that led to a profound Islamisation of Egyptian society, a process which culminated in what Esposito and Voll (1996: 96) call Mubarak's 'institutionalization of Islamic Revivalism'. In other words, the Gramscian perspective offers Bayat the tools to conceptualise complex dynamics that invested Egyptian society. It can be argued that the concept of passive revolution helps to explain the degree to which the boundaries between the hegemonic and counter-hegemonic social actors can become blurred. Not only counter-hegemonic elements and agendas can penetrate hegemonic social formations such as the state, but also counter-hegemonic forces can be co-opted into the ruling bloc. Such a phenomenon will be observed, in the next chapter, regarding the case of Islamism in Jordan. Notwithstanding the heuristic potential of the concept of passive revolution, this very concept reveals the extent to which postulating a static dichotomy between hegemony and counter-hegemony runs the risks of offering an inadequate topography of the social. Undoubtedly, Gramsci's thinking suffers because of its own success, which led to a sort of theoretical overstretching of his philosophy, since it risks becoming a recipe for explaining everything. Social constructivism seems to offer a sophisticated theoretical approach in order to overcome the rigidities of a Gramscian perspective. In the following section, the extent to which social constructivism and social movement theory can offer analytical tools to provide a more refined approach to social reality, engaging in a dialogue with Gramscian categories, is analysed.

Social constructivism and social movement theory

In this section, building on the preceding section, the philosophical underpinnings of social constructivism will be briefly revealed. The contribution of social constructivism can be valuable in enriching a Gramscian framework with a more nuanced approach to the analysis of the dynamics of social movements. Indeed, a rigid adherence to Gramsci's conceptualisations may lead to postulating a dualism between two static actors such as the hegemonic bloc and counter-hegemonic forces. The risk inherent in this position is that of ignoring how deeply hegemonic and counter-hegemonic forces continuously cross-fertilise each other. In other words, Gramsci's analysis of the dialectic of hegemony and counter-hegemony may still provide valuable analytic tools, but a Gramscian framework can highly benefit from a theoretically informed approach, which fully takes into account the socially constructed nature of social movements.

Social constructivism

Social constructivism, as a trend in the social sciences, upholds a critical approach towards knowledge, relying on the idea that knowledge itself is a social process (Burr, 1995: 3–5). In other words, social interaction produces movements and institutions, which become 'opaque' when social actors do not perceive them anymore as socially constructed, since processes of reification and objectification make them appear self-evident and natural. For social constructionists, knowledge and social reality are the products of on-going processes of interaction among different subjectivities. To put it differently, 'knowledge is therefore seen not as something that a person has (or does not have), but as something that people do together' (Burr, 1995: 6). Social constructivism rejects assumptions merely based on common sense, but also rejects the worldview of social sciences such as psychology and anthropology, when they claim to identify underlying patterns and structures that are supposed to exist in the individual psyche or in society (Burr, 1995: 4–6).

The philosophical underpinnings of social constructivism can be identified in a vast and diverse corpus of literature, which includes Vico, Wittgenstein and Foucault. However, a minimum common denominator, the concept of socially constructed reality, is rooted in the Marxian distinction between substructure (*Unterbau*), the economic basis of the society, and superstructure (*Überbau*), the ideological sphere. Such a concept inspired sociologists such as Berger and Luckmann (1967: 18) to critically analyse the relationship between 'human activity and the world produced by that activity'. Their concept of 'human activity' reveals indeed their debt to the Marxian notion of substructure, while 'the world produced by that activity' (Berger and Luckmann, 1967: 18) is linked to the superstructure. The main undertaking of social constructionists can be considered as a critical analysis of social reality, with the aim of understanding institutions as human products. Social constructivist ontology has provided, in the last decades, the theoretical underpinnings for the articulation of new frameworks to understand and explain social reality. Stemming from social constructivism, social movement theory has attempted to explain social reality overcoming both essentialism and economic reductionism. The next part of this study will critically analyse social movement theory, highlighting its relevance for the present study.

Social movement theory

The social movement approach, when nurtured by the theoretical acquisitions of the social constructivist school, seems to provide remarkable analytical tools to shed light on the 'mechanisms of collective action' utilised by Islamic movements. Indeed, the social constructivist approach helps to refute the concept of an inherent nature of Islam and of Islamic movements, leading us to a more pragmatic approach to the processes through which social movements construct their identities, mobilise their resources and pursue their goals. Early approaches to the study of social movements identified the main factors of mobilisation, but relied on a static conception of the movements themselves (McAdam *et al*., 2001: 41, 42).

The contribution of social constructivism has enriched social movement theory through the recognition of the central weight of the processes of identity construction in determining political mobilisation (McAdam *et al*., 2001: 56–58). The focus on the social construction of identity provides dynamic accounts of political mobilisation, since the process of identity construction happens through continuous social interaction. The actors involved in social interaction are constantly creating and negotiating new identities, whose social construction is, thus, identified as a crucial factor in originating contentious politics.

To highlight the importance of the contribution of social constructivism to social movement theory, the major contributions of the early approaches to the study of social movements will be analysed. The four major concepts, which McAdam *et al.*, (2001: 14) define as the 'classical social movements agenda' are political opportunities, mobilising structures, collective action frames and repertoires of contention. The formulation of these concepts in the 1960s and 1970s offered a theoretical background to explain contentious politics, whose new perspectives challenged the focus of most historians on elites as the only agents of mobilisation (McAdam *et al.*, 2001: 15). These new conceptual frameworks aimed at explaining social change, refuting the idea that the 'masses' were passive objects in the hands of the elites. These theoretical acquisitions undoubtedly reflected the political atmosphere of the 1960s and the 1970s. New generations of scholars and academics proposed new concepts to understand and explain social reality. These reflections often sprang from the observation of, and sometimes from the participation in, the process of social and cultural change, which characterised that period. Undoubtedly, these theoretical acquisitions recognised the importance of factors, which had been neglected by earlier generations of historians and social scientists, but even their contribution relied on conceptions that implied a static nature of social movements, failing to acknowledge the dynamic features of social movements. The contribution of social constructivism has been crucial in reviving this field of study, introducing a new dynamic perspective through which to analyse social movements. As McAdam *et al.* (2001: 51), who have led this paradigm shift, affirm: 'The most important implication of our agenda is to stress development of contention through social interaction and to place social construction at the center of our analysis'.

The key acquisitions of classical social movement theory, hence, have been reinterpreted according to this new conception of the importance of the role of social construction of identity in influencing collective action. The concept of opportunity structure, articulated in 'opportunities' and 'threats', has been reformulated in favour of 'attribution of threat and opportunity' (McAdam *et al.*, 2001: 46–47). In fact, postulating the existence of objective opportunities and threats risks leading to assumptions of deterministic connections between political economy and social movements, thus downplaying the creative role of the agency of the social actors.

The new approaches, which analyse social movements through the lenses of social constructivism, focus on the subjective perception of social reality by social actors, thus highlighting the centrality of interpretation processes. The concept of frames, seen as peculiar perspectives of social actors in representing social reality, is acknowledged as a crucial factor in the articulation of politics. Similarly, the new approach to social movement theory implies a more dynamic outlook of mobilising structures. The new focus is on the social appropriation of mobilisation sites, such as in the case of the transformation of the black churches of the South of the USA into 'vehicles of collective protest' (McAdam *et al.*, 2001: 47) during the Civil Rights Movement, or in the case of private mosques, as mobilisation sites against the government in Egypt (Kepel, 1985). Following this line of reasoning, collective action frames become key elements to interpret social movements' dynamics. As McAdam *et al.* (2001: 48) hold:

> We do not see framing as a distinct 'box' or variable in the onset of contentious politics; for us, framing and interpretation go well beyond how a movement's goals are strategically formed to a much broader set of interpretive processes. ... In short, like all of social life, mobilization is suffused throughout with collective efforts at interpretation and social construction.

Social movements can, therefore, be described as producers of knowledge and meanings (Eyerman and Jamison, 1991), according to whom social movements are to be conceptualised as 'cognitive praxis', used to describe 'the creative role of consciousness and cognition in all human action, individual and collective' (Eyerman and Jamison, 1991: 3). To put it differently, social movements are embedded in a social reality that they contribute to create and shape through their actions. Hence, according to Eyerman and Jamison (1991: 4), 'social movements are thus best conceived of as temporary public spaces, as moments of collective creation that provide societies with ideas, identities and even ideals'.

The concept of 'collective creation' is employed to explain the ongoing process of production of knowledge that is identified as the main characteristic of social movements; a collective creation which is the objectification of the interaction of the subjectivities of both the activists and the opponents of the social movements (Eyerman and Jamison, 1991: 4). In this collective creation, a crucial role is played by the movement intellectuals, conceptualised with reference to Gramsci's landmark contribution.

In Marxist thought, the new consciousness developed by the proletariat is a crucial step to replace the 'false consciousness' imposed by the bourgeoisie: the new consciousness achieved by the proletariat is therefore labelled as 'true'. Abandoning this binary value judgement, the new consciousness, when relating to a counter-hegemonic social movement, is approached through the notion of 'insurgent consciousness', used by McAdam (1999) in his analysis of the black protest movement in the USA. In other words, the development of the insurgent consciousness is seen as a process of collective identity construction, in which the social movement increasingly considers and structures itself as radically opposed to the *status quo*.

Christian Smith (1991: 62), whose work has inspired a great deal of research, has applied the notion of 'insurgent consciousness', which he defines as 'a collective state of understanding which recognises that social change is both imperative and viable', to the Catholic liberation theology movement. Smith challenges the common-sense prejudgement that religion is always an element of social cohesion, arguing that in most cases religions can foster revolution and subversion (Smith, 1991). Indeed, his analysis focuses on the 'change in consciousness' (Smith, 1991: 62) inducted by the liberation theology movement. This redefinition of the identity is obtained through a process of reframing, the creation of new meanings, which are products of subjectivities that, being shared and objectified, acquire the status of collective creations, in this case aimed at disruptive social change.

Snow (2004) provides a thorough elaboration of the framing perspective, which takes into account the intellectual traditions of both social constructivism and symbolic interactionism. His study on frames contributes to explaining how socially constructed ideas can stimulate collective action. Snow's approach challenges essentialist approaches, since it does not consider social movements as merely 'holding' ideas and beliefs, but sees them as primarily involved in the process of social construction of meanings (Snow, 2004: 384). Thus, this approach allows identification of one of the main functions of social movements in the social construction of mobilising ideas.

Following this line of reasoning, it is therefore possible to take into account the role of social movement leaders and activists, but also of antagonists and bystanders, in the process of social production of frames. Gamson (1992: 7) argues that frames need to be analysed with regard to three dimensions: injustice, agency and identity. Regarding injustice, Turner (1969: 391) pointed out that a social movement needs to successfully re-interpret what previously defined 'misfortune' as 'injustice'. In order to promote collective action, a movement therefore needs to reframe an existing situation in new terms, thus operating a 'symbolic transformation' of previous meanings, especially those pertaining to the spheres of 'just' and 'unjust' (Snow, 2004: 383). Moreover, a clear target has to be identified as responsible for the perceived injustice, in order for moral indignation to be organised and channelled in the social construction of the enemy.

The agency frame refers to the fact that activists need to be persuaded that collective action can be effective in changing the *status quo* (Gamson, 1992: 7). Indeed, a shared mental framework, which assumes that social change is impossible and that society is immutable, leads to attitudes of quiescence that are major obstacles for the development of collective action. Moreover, discourses that explain social problems as rooted in human nature are seen as the outcome of processes of reification; in other words, social problems cease to be perceived as socially constructed, acquiring the same immutable status attributed to the natural world. Thus, the mobilisation of collective action presupposes challenging this assumption, showing social problems as socially constructed and thus potentially subject to change. Finally, the notion of identity implies the formation of a collective will, the social construction of 'we' (Gamson, 1992: 7). As Gamson (1992: 85) argues 'the same sociocultural forces that discourage a sense of collective agency also discourage thinking about issues in collective terms'. The perception of bonds, which extend beyond the individual, connecting him with a broader group of people, is essential in creating a social movement.

The process through which a common identity is forged has been studied in some of the earliest approaches to social movements, based on social psychological approaches. In particular, the *esprit de corps* has been studied by Blumer (1969: 15). Blumer maintains that the development of *esprit de corps* is articulated through the development of several mechanisms. Firstly, the creation of an in-group versus an out-group dynamic strengthens the perception of 'we' and 'they' as two separate and contending entities. It should be clear that the very act of framing, of interpreting the social world in terms of two different and competing camps contributes to the rise and development of a social movement. The construction of the group identity and of the enemy are two concomitant processes, since both of them influence each other. These processes of framing, of symbolic transformation, are *conditiones sine qua non* for the creation of a social movement, since frames are crucial in persuading people to carry out social action.

It should be noted that the framing perspective challenges views that overemphasise the role of 'objective' grievances in persuading people to mobilise, highlighting instead inter-subjective processes of articulation of meanings. In fact, perspectives, which focus on factors such as economic and psychological deprivation as major stimuli for collective action fail to explain the innumerable historical circumstances in which people were subject to the most severe forms of exploitation and deprivation but did not react. In Gramscian terms, Snow's approach considers the cultural and ideological sphere of society, rejecting deterministic explanations of the links between political economy and collective action. Indeed, grievances are deeply rooted in the political economic sphere, but in order for these grievances to be transformed into political action it is indispensable that grievances are collectively framed as 'unjust'. In other terms, a transformation of the consciousness of social actors is necessary to convince them to mobilise.

This framing activity has to be carried out by the vanguard, by the leadership of the movement, but also by the 'intellectuals', in the broad Gramscian sense. In order for the framing process to be successful, these frames need to resonate with its intended target. In fact, frames perceived as alien and extraneous would be difficult to comprehend. An example of successful framing activity is the use of the term 'Pharaoh' by Islamists in Egypt (al-Ghazali, 1994). Using the term 'pharaoh' when referring to the Egyptian ruler allows the Islamists to associate the latter with a figure who is the archetype of the unjust and impious leader. Given the fact that the Quranic Pharaoh is part of the symbolic universe of ordinary Egyptian Muslims, this frame has a higher degree of resonance, since it conveys a powerful message understandable by all social strata, regardless of their age or level of education.

Another example is represented by the George Bush Jr's framing of the war on terror as 'a moral crusade', 'a war between good and evil'. This frame resonates with the symbolic universe of the US citizens, deeply influenced by moral, religious and eschatological frames. Another example pertains to recent Italian history. Silvio Berlusconi's promise of a 'new Italian miracle' had a double layered resonance for the Italian audience. Firstly, it was resonating with the Italian economic boom of 1963, still seen by most of the Italians as a golden age. Secondly, it was alluding, at a deeper and less conscious level, at the religious miracle, an essential feature of popular Catholicism.

The power of the frame is therefore represented by its reference to both the domain of political economy and that of religion, thus conveying the message that Berlusconi is a political leader able to provide economic wealth to the country, but also a man who can 'perform miracles'. A social constructivist approach, inspired by the most recent acquisitions of social movement theory and framing perspectives, seems to provide sophisticated analytical tools to analyse Islamic social movements and their social influence.

Understanding Islamic social movements

In this section will be highlighted the relevance of a social constructivist approach to the analysis of Islamic social movements and of the effects that their framing processes have had on contemporary Muslim societies. The framing perspective is helpful in two ways. Firstly, according to social movement theory, it explains how grievances are transformed into collective action through the production and reproduction of mobilising ideas and beliefs. In Gramscian terms, the framing perspective offers a more sophisticated theoretical framework through which to analyse the counter-hegemonic Islamist challenges. Secondly, this approach contributes to explaining how the meanings produced by Islamist movements influence society at large. Indeed, if the market provides opportunity spaces for the Islamists, in turn the actions of the Islamists have an influence on market practices, thus determining the emergence of new symbolic forms. So, following this line of reasoning, it becomes possible to appreciate the complexity of the process of Islamisation. The symbolic worlds of Islam demonstrate their capacity of offering tools to interpret society. Thus, Islamist movements can be seen in their creative function, which is to say in their function of production and reproduction of frames, through which it becomes possible to confer meanings on social life. Frames, thus, become tools for the articulation of collective action, but they also offer coherent explanations of the meaning of life and account for social change and transformations. In other words, these frames do not merely mobilise, but also interpret, explain and contribute to shape society. This all-encompassing and coherent nature of the frames produced by Islamic social movements justifies the adoption of the term 'ideology' used to define Islamism. As the existing body of knowledge identifies, social movement theory has already been used to analyse Islamic movements, overcoming the tendency to keep Muslim societies isolated from the theoretical developments of sociology by virtue of an alleged 'Islamic exceptionalism'. Social movement theory provides indispensable theoretical frameworks to conceptualise Islamism, dismissing the tendency to merely describe the history of Islamic groups, without a clear and deep understanding of their inherent dynamics and processes.

In 1988, an influential volume by Edmund Burke III and Ira Lapidus, *Islam, Politics and Social Movements* advocated the adoption of a new conceptual framework, by suggesting studying Islamist movements as social movements. In recent years, several ground-breaking studies have led to the opening of new areas of research, leading to a re-conceptualisation of Islamism. In particular, studies conducted by Clark (2004), Wiktorowicz (2001, 2004) and Yavuz (2003, 2004) are seminal. In this respect, Wiktorowicz (2001, 2004) proposes the integration of the analysis of Islamic movements in social movement theory, challenging essentialist readings of Islam that postulate its unique nature. On the contrary, he points out that Islamism can be better comprehended utilising a comparative approach (Wiktorowicz, 2004: 3). Indeed, Islam may differ from other religions and ideologies with regard to its ideas and to the content of its faith; nevertheless, Islamic movements do not differ substantially from other social movements in their praxis. Thus, their mechanisms of actions and their strategies can be explained with the analytical tools developed by social movement theory. In turn, the inclusion of Islamism into the social movement approach can encourage developments in social movement theory itself (Kurzman, 2004: 295–298). Islamic activism is defined by Wiktorowicz (2004: 2) as 'the mobilisation of contention to support Muslim causes ... including propagation movements, terrorist groups, collective action rooted in Islamic symbols and identities, explicitly political movements that seek to establish an Islamic state, and inward-looking groups that promote Islamic spirituality through collective efforts'. This definition focuses on characteristics shared between Islamic social movements and the other social movements. In particular, the concept of 'mechanisms of collective action' (Wiktorowicz, 2004) is identified as the focal point of the research, the emphasis being on the strategies of the movement, and not on their nature. Analyses based on the nature of Islam or of Islamic groups are criticised for their inherent tendency of considering human institutions as permanent, and not as socially constructed. Kepel's (1994) comparative approach to Islamic, Christian and Jewish fundamentalism is also criticised for its emphasis on the comparison of ideas, while neglecting the 'mechanisms' of collective action. On the contrary, social movement theory is seen as the most effective way to provide an organic framework to the study of Islamism.

In order to establish his stance, Wiktorowicz critically analysed the development of the study of Islamic activism. At first, socio-psychological approaches were prevalent in the discipline. The basic assumption was that involvement in Islamic movements was mainly due to the incapacity of individuals to integrate into modern societies. Islamic activism was seen as a sort of anomie, a social pathology, or as a reaction against Western cultural imperialism (Wiktorowicz, 2004: 9). A common feature of this trend was the relevance attributed to structural strains in driving individuals into Islamic movements. A different approach, based on the resource mobilisation theory, went beyond the alleged shortcomings of the socio-psychological approach, stressing the rationality of the social actors and refusing to regard the masses as irrational and merely determined by social structures (Wiktorowicz, 2004: 9–13). Wiktorowicz (2004: 10) argues that:

> For RMT [resource mobilization theory], resources and mobilizing structures ... are needed to collectivize what would otherwise remain individual grievances. Movements are not seen as irrational outburst intended to alleviate psychological distress, but rather as organized contention structured through mechanisms of mobilisation that provide strategic resources of sustained collective action.

The interest in the mobilising structures developed by the resource mobilisation theory has been useful in explaining the strategies of Islamic non-governmental organisations and professional associations (Wiktorowicz, 2004: 11). In particular, Islamic non-governmental organisations have been explored in their functions of both providing social services and recruiting new followers. Wiktorowicz (2004: 12) distinguished between formal organisations, such as parties, informal institutions and social networks.

Resource mobilisation theory offers a framework in which each of those movements can be understood in its specific context. However, one of the most promising developments of the research on Islamism concerns the concept of frames analysed above, which was inspired by the social constructivist perspective. Frames are considered by Wiktorowicz means to interpret and understand reality, but also to promote collective action. Therefore, the function of frames, seen as 'interpretative devices', is to transform grievances and perceived opportunities into collective action (Wiktorowicz, 2004: 19). Indeed, Wiktorowicz invites scholars to consider Islamic movements in their essential function of producers and constructors of meanings (Wiktorowicz, 2004: 15). Such an approach helps also to critically analyse the Islamist task of taking over the state as instrumental in achieving control over the social construction of reality. Therefore, dominion over civil and political society can be conceptualised as aimed at guaranteeing a pervasive control over meaning production, which will subsequently pave the way to the implementation of *shari'a* in the social realm (Wiktorowicz, 2004: 16). To sum up, taking over the state is not an end in itself, but it is instrumental for a counter-hegemonic movement in order to control the production of meaning (Wiktorowicz, 2004: 16). The social movement approach, according to Wiktorowicz, also provides the perfect synthesis between theory and the praxis of fieldwork.

An essential contribution of the social movement approach to the conceptualisation of Islamism is provided by Yavuz (2003, 2004). Indeed, Yavuz (2004: 270) introduced the concept of 'opportunity space', defined as 'social sites and vehicles for activism and the dissemination of meaning, identity, and cultural codes' and 'a forum of social interaction that creates new possibilities for augmenting networks of shared meaning and associational life' (Yavuz, 2003: 24), since 'Islamic groups strategically use new economic and political opportunities to create counter-hegemonic spaces and discourses' (Yavuz, 2003: 25). In particular, Yavuz focused on the market as an opportunity space and studied the impact of market liberalisations on two categories of movements, the 'society-oriented movements' and the 'state-centred groups' (Yavuz, 2003: 28–31). Yavuz's conclusion is that changes in the opportunities domain generate diverse effects on social movements. Exploring market liberalisation in Turkey, he argues that it caused a profound rupture in Islamic groups, clearly separating state-centred movements, which strenuously opposed privatisations, from society-oriented ones, which greatly benefited from it. Indeed, the latter have been remarkably successful in taking advantage of the opportunity spaces provided by the withdrawal of the welfare state institutions through the expansion of a thriving Islamic private sector. In Yavuz's (2004: 277–278) understanding, the marketplace has been the space where some Islamic movements have managed to carry out their victorious counter-hegemony struggle for gaining hegemony through the conquest of civil society.

Indeed, Islamic movements have always claimed their commitment to producing structural changes in the socio-political system. According to Mawdudi, the change that Islamists aspire to is not the mere conquest of political power, but rather the creation of a whole new civilisation that could reactivate the golden age of the origins of Islam. The social, economic and cultural domains were deemed crucial loci of action for the implementation of Mawdudi's agenda. This struggle, whose main battleground is civil society, is seen not merely as tactically more efficient, but as the most comprehensive way of realising a new integral and holistic Islamic civilisation. According to Mawdudi (1955: 21–22):

> An Islamic state does not spring into being all of a sudden like a miracle: it is inevitable for its creation that in the beginning there should grow a movement having for its basis the view of life, the ideal of existence, the standard of morality and the character and spirit which is in keeping with the fundamentals of Islam.

Islamisation of civil society is a common feature of various Islamist trends, such as the Muslim Brotherhood.

It can be argued that, given the presence of strong authoritarian states, a frontal challenge to the Arab regimes was, for Islamist movements, a solution doomed to failure. Islamist strategies have indeed been shaped by the opportunity spaces available. In Iran, the revolutionaries took power by force, establishing an Islamic state following a top-down method. However, deeply intertwined ideological and tactical motivations led the Islamist movements of the Arab world to discard this option, opting for a 'war of position' through a work of *da'wa*, instead of a 'frontal attack' against the state. As Bayat (2007: 136–137) affirms with regard to the Muslim Brotherhood:

> The limits of 'frontal attack', or insurrection, to produce social change forced leaders to adopt a different strategy, a 'war of position', or a campaign for gradual social and political change in the hope of producing structural transformation and 'religious democracy' in the long run.

Bayat's (2007: 137) analysis underlines how the 'socio-religious change through *da'wa*' transformed society, thus challenging the ruling elite. The Islamisation of society through the formal and informal networks of the Muslim Brotherhood in Egypt is a central example of how effective the bottom-up approach has been in promoting social change. Through the establishment of welfare activities, movements such as the Muslim Brotherhood aimed to demonstrate that they could carry out these functions better than the regime (Tripp, 1996: 62–63).

The success of the counter-hegemonic strategy of Islamism in spreading Islamist consciousness throughout society should not be merely judged by its ability to establish a whole socio-economic Islamic sector, but also on its capacity to penetrate the state itself. In this respect, Wickham's analysis of the Egyptian experience is paradigmatic. According to Wickham (2002), the Egyptian regime under Mubarak had been extremely weak in coping with the challenge of Islamism. Despite a strategy of discriminating between moderates and radicals, the public sector, in theory the stronghold of the official hegemonic narrative, had been deeply penetrated by the *Weltanschauung* and by the networks of Islamic movements. In this case, the promotion of economic and political change occurred through the conquest of the bureaucratic apparatus of the state itself. To make the point in another way, if Islamism had not been able to take over the state by force or through the democratic process, nevertheless it did not completely renounce achieving this goal. Instead of frontally attacking the state apparatus or openly challenging it, Islamists opted for a more sophisticated, 'Trotskyist' tactic of entryism, i.e. entering into other institutions with the goal of increasing their influence.

In the following chapters, the Jordanian case is used to explore to what extent Islamists have penetrated what Althusser (1971) calls the 'ideological state apparatuses'. The secular regime of Mubarak was still in control of the political power, while society was deeply imbued with Islamic values and Islamist ideology. Indeed, the regime had chosen to counteract Islamist movements promoting trends of conservative Islam, which represented a blend of counter-hegemonic Islamist discourse and the hegemonic Islamic narrative of the state. That is why the counter-hegemonic Islamist discourse and the hegemonic narrative of the state cannot be understood as a dichotomy, but as a living dialectic process, the outcome of on-going processes of cross-fertilisation. The process can be described as an Islamisation of civil society that did not challenge the ruling elite. As Ismail (2006: 71) recapitulates, 'the state's desire to recapture positions of authority recreated and appropriated by the Islamists has necessitated that it moves into their territory'. This process can be conceptualised in the light of Gramsci's notion of 'passive revolution'.

The outcome of this process was the hegemony of Islamist ideology. While the Islamist vanguard lost the monopoly over the production and articulation of this discourse, influential Islamists were co-opted by the state in order to contain the Islamist movement. On the one hand, this could seem a victory for the establishment. On the other hand, official policies became growingly permeated by Islamist values. Regarding the Egyptian case, Wickham (2002: 110) notes the 'Islamists' direct appropriation of public offices and resources to advance their own agenda'. Wickham (2002: 111) argues that 'it is not difficult to envision a long-term scenario in which Egypt's authoritarian regime retains control of the security apparatus but gradually loses control of its social and ideological levers of domination' (Wickham, 2002: 111). This is a consequence of the fact that the Islamist influence is particularly evident in sectors such as education and services, Althusser's 'ideological state apparatuses', which allow the Islamists to be close to the masses. Again, the aftermath of the so-called Arab Spring reveals the extent to which such an analysis was gauging the pervasiveness of Islamist movements. In Gramscian terms, there is a risk of separation between the coercive apparatus and the moral and intellectual sphere. A state deprived of its *dominazione* (domination) is a social formation which does not exert any hegemonic power, and is therefore extremely fragile. Such an outcome is the product of a vast Islamisation of the political language in Egypt. In its attempt to counter-balance Islamism, the regime heavily employed the language of conservative Islam. Hence, both hegemonic and counter-hegemonic narratives adopted similar frames and symbols. This has been, undoubtedly, a crucial political change carried out by the Islamic socio-economic sector: permeating Egyptian, and to a certain extent Arab, society with its own worldview.

Conclusion

The purpose of exposing Gramsci's social thought, social constructivism and social movement theory is to provide a conceptual framework for the analysis of social movements, and in particular of Islamism. This chapter has proposed a post-Gramscian approach. It adopts Gramscian categories, while taking into account social constructivism and social movement theory. Gramsci's thought, critically adopted, is used to conceptualise Islamism as a counter-hegemonic challenge to the *status quo*. As Ayubi (1991: 175) states:

> The Islamic language therefore represents a broad alternative system of meaning and power to the hegemonic system represented by the existing socio-political order, which inevitably marginalises and/or alienates certain individuals and certain social groups. To an extent, the details of the Islamic thesis become less important than the fact that it is a very *different* thesis from that advocated by the State.

As is demonstrated in the following chapter, Islamic movements such as the Muslim Brotherhood of Jordan opted for a bottom-up method of Islamisation of civil society. In the previous chapter, this strategy has been explained in terms of openings in the political and economic structures. The theoretical framework provided in the present chapter conceptualises this process in terms of a struggle between the hegemony of the state and the counter-hegemonic force represented by Islamic movements. This struggle can be understood according to Gramsci's notion of 'war of position'. Moreover, Gramsci's contribution allows appreciation of the role of the 'intellectuals', broadly defined, in constructing an organic counter-hegemonic ideology.

Social constructivism focuses on this process of construction of knowledge. Highlighting the socially constructed character of knowledge leads to considering Islamic movements primarily in their function of producers of meanings. Social movement theory accounts for the mobilisation of contention through the articulation of frames which resonate with the living symbolic worlds of Islam. Social movement theory has been widely used to interpret social movements, and it has had relevant impact on methodology: indeed, postulating a performative role of language, discourse analysis becomes the best way to analyse social movements, since the production of knowledge undertaken by those movements is a crucial way of carrying out social action. Social constructivism, thus, offers interpretative schemes to understand social movements in profoundly different social contests and in widely different circumstances. Moreover, social constructivism facilitates the overcoming of some of the limitations of a Gramscian framework, which mainly consist of its tendency to postulate the existence of static actors, such as the hegemonic bloc and the counter-hegemonic forces. Furthermore, social constructivism explains to what extent, through the process of acquiring hegemony, Islamist ideology, strategies and languages have significantly changed. Indeed, since the production and reproduction of Islamism did not happen in a vacuum, nor has Islamism been the agent of this process, the political and economic circumstances in which these developments took place have significantly contributed to shaping Islamist discourse and practices. Social movement theory is indeed aware that this process of framing, of producing and reproducing categories for interpreting reality, also contributes to shaping social reality and influences the producers of meanings themselves. For example, the focus of a remarkable segment of the scholarly literature on the theme of the 'Islamic state' leads to underestimating the broader phenomena of Islamisation of the cultural and ideological domains, as well as processes of contamination, which change Islamist movements themselves. This is especially true in the case of Islamic movements; lacking a central spiritual or religious authority which monopolises the production of frames, the process of interpreting social reality according to Islamic frames is increasingly individualised. The next chapter attempts to apply the theoretical framework proposed here to the study of Islamism in Jordan. The conclusion of this study assesses to what extent such a conceptualisation is still useful in providing a theoretically informed, yet valid and accurate, topography of the social, with reference to the case study that constitutes the empirical object of this research.

3 Articulations of Islamism in Jordan

Introduction

The previous chapter attempted to provide a theoretical framework in order to conceptualise processes of re-Islamisation, that is to say of Islamic revivalism, as articulations of Islamism *qua* historico-discursive formation to be read as 'contingent on a deliberate process of mobilization initiated and sustained by Islamic counter-elites' (Wickham, 2002: 8). The present analysis is informed by the theoretical framework presented in the previous chapter in order to gauge processes of social construction of Islamic identities. Indeed, the Jordanian case seems to epitomise the changing faces of Muslim identities at the dawn of the twenty-first century as outcomes of these articulations, which take place in the context of globalisation. Overall, this chapter rejects the interpretation based on an alleged nature of Islamist movements. In fact 'the Jordanian Muslim Brotherhood developed its discourse in terms of the obstacles and opportunities that were present in its immediate social environment' (Moaddel, 2002: 95). Such an approach is grounded in social movement theory, seen as the most sophisticated analytical tool to analyse social movements taking into consideration both their ideological and their organisational aspects. Moreover, Gramsci's framework is used to analyse and interpret the political economy strategies deployed by the Muslim Brothers in Jordan in what will be read as a quest for hegemony over Jordanian society. An analysis of the Jordanian context, from a social, economic and historical point of view, is central to gauge the development of the Islamist movement and its relationships with the social construction of identities.

This chapter falls into three sections. The first section concerns the crucial issue of Jordanian identity, analysed in historical perspective. The second section deals with the role played by the Muslim Brotherhood of Jordan in the social construction of Jordanian identity. The third and final part concerns the position of Islamic social institutions in Jordanian society.

The elusive issue of Jordanian identity

The deep transformations experienced by Jordanian society have contributed to the elaboration of original ways of coping with the challenges of globalisation and with the construction of new Islamic identities. These processes are making obsolete any contraposition between Islam and an alleged 'Western-style modernity'. Indeed, both the worldview of Islamism and that of globalisation permeate, to different degrees, Jordanian society at large. The cross-fertilisation between the two paradigms has developed to such an extent that the formulation of a dichotomy between them is highly problematic.

It is important to highlight the main elements that contributed, from a historical point of view, to the social construction of new Islamic identities in Jordan. These new Islamic identities may be conceptualised, at the same time, as responses of contemporary Jordanian Muslims to the challenges of exogenous historical contingencies and as an active contribution of the same social agents to the social construction of what we term here 'Islamic modernities'. These phenomena cannot, obviously, be read in isolation from wider global changes in the processes of self-construction of the Muslim *ummah* (community). Indeed, the emergence of Islamic modernities in Jordan is merely a chapter in the larger history of what Roy (2004) has designated 'globalized Islam'.

The Jordanian experience, however, has its own characteristics, because of the peculiar interactions between social and ethnic stratifications that characterise the landscape of Jordanian society. In particular, two factors need to be underlined. The first is the complex relationship between the official narrative of the regime and the narrative of the Muslim Brotherhood. The working hypothesis of this study is that these may be conceptualised through a Gramscian framework; however, the findings of this study seem to suggest that Gramscian categories need to be read in the context of the acquisitions of social constructivism and social movement theory. Indeed, contemporary Islamic identity seems to have certainly been influenced by the processes of re-articulation promoted by the Muslim Brotherhood, but it also appears to be the result of cross-fertilisation and overlapping between the official Islamic narratives of the regime, the narratives constructed by the Brotherhood and other Islamic groups such as the Salafis, as well as traditional and tribal identities.

Another important factor is the relationship between the two main ethnicities of the Hashemite Kingdom of Jordan, the so-called Transjordanians (or East-Bankers) and Palestinians. Transjordanians are called the inhabitants and the descendants of the inhabitants of the East Bank of the River Jordan, while Palestinians are the inhabitants and the descendants of the inhabitants of the West Bank of the river Jordan, who fled to Jordan in hundreds of thousands after the two conflicts with Israel in 1948 and 1967, finally constituting about half the population of Jordan (Milton-Edwards, 2009: 46). Exact estimates are lacking because of the political sensitivity of the topic. As Milton-Edwards (2009: 2) points out, the 'great majority' of the Palestinians living in Jordan 'were more concerned with regaining their birth-right than with making a contribution to their country of exile'. Milton-Edwards (2009: 2) also describes the mutual behaviour of Palestinians and Jordanians towards each other as 'ambivalent', identifying in this issue 'the great fault line in Jordanian society'. Indeed, after the 1967 Arab defeat against Israel, Jordan became the main base of the Palestine Liberation Organisation (PLO), which created a 'state within the state' in Jordan (Milton-Edwards, 2009: 41); the complicated relationships between King Hussein and the PLO led in 1970 to a civil war, known as Black September, between the Jordanian army and the Palestinian militias, which risked becoming a full-scale conflict between Transjordanians and Palestinians. Such a fault line in Jordanian society had a huge impact, as is discussed later, not only on Jordanian society, but also on the Islamist movement.

It goes beyond the limited purpose of this study to assess to what extent Transjordanians and Palestinians can be really conceived as two distinct ethnicities. This issue is too complex and too politically sensitive, on both sides of the river Jordan, to be treated here. What matters here is that many contemporary Jordanians perceive the relevance of these categories as conceptualising the ethnic landscape of their society. What is interesting is the extent to which ethnic categories overlap with social classes in Jordanian society. As Marger (2012: 28), evidently influenced by Gramsci, points out: 'The power of a dominant class or ethnic group is not simply the power of force but also the power to propound and sustain an ideology that legitimizes the system of inequality.' Marger (2012: 38) highlights that ethnicity and social class are always 'closely interrelated'. It is, therefore, of the utmost importance to analyse the interdependencies between ethnicities, social class and ideologies that legitimise power. Jordanian society presents an interesting interdependency of class and ethnic stratification. What is particularly relevant for us is to analyse the extent to which social class and ethnic stratifications interacted with the other processes that shaped the social, economic and cultural landscape of the country, together with the forced Palestinian migrations of 1948 and 1967.

The first process is the re-Islamisation of Jordanian society carried out by the Muslim Brotherhood since its inception in the 1940s. It is argued here that in an initial phase, which lasted from the establishment of the Brotherhood in the 1940s to the 1970s, the Brotherhood operated in accordance with the regime. In this period, the hegemonic discourse was a joint product of the collaboration of the Hashemite regime and the Islamist movement, since both were sharing a similar social basis, constituted of merchants and landowners. In a second phase, which started in the 1970s and is still on-going, the two discourses started to diverge, even if the cross-fertilisations between them continued. It is argued in this study that the Muslim Brotherhood increasingly came to represent a new middle class, whose social and political aspirations were frustrated by the regime. Thus, Islamic frames were reframed more and more to convey oppositional and confrontational meanings. Moreover, after the failure of the struggle of the PLO, the Islamist discourse of the Brotherhood became more appealing to large segments of the Palestinian-Jordanians (Clark, 2004: 17). These developments significantly interact with the second important factor, which is the advent of globalisation that triggered profound transformations in Jordanian society.

The thesis of this study is that these two processes have played an important part in influencing contemporary Islamic identity in Jordan, transforming 'traditional' Islamic discourses into 'modern' ones. To put it simply, Jordan did not become modern through secularisation, as the theory of modernisation maintains, but through processes of articulation and re-articulation of frames pertaining to the symbolic world of Islam. These re-negotiating processes conducted by the social agents often took place in a subaltern manner, accepting 'foreign' world views, even when articulated through the frames of Islam. These processes have variously been articulated by different social actors, such as the regime, the Muslim Brotherhood and Salafi groups. Thus, contemporary Islamic identities in Jordan appear as a nexus of multiple and changing relational and social identities, which include social class, ethnicity, tribe, religion and politics.

As already highlighted, contemporary Islamic identities cannot be merely seen as contemporary facets of Islam, as if Islam developed in isolation. On the contrary, contemporary Islamic identities need to be read in the specific and historically situated contexts in which they developed. This is precisely the aim of this research: historically locating the process of social construction of contemporary Islamic identities in the context of Jordanian society. A landmark study in this sense is represented by Massad's (2001) analysis of the social construction of a national identity in Jordan. His study begins with the premise that, before the establishment of Transjordan by the British in 1921, there was not an entity such as 'Jordan'. The Jordanian state is a recent and artificial historical product, a consequence of the collapse of the Ottoman Empire during the First World War and of the reorganisation of the Middle East under the aegis of France and Great Britain (Salibi, 1998: 73–91).

The process through which the European colonial powers, and in particular Great Britain, decided to establish Transjordan, which later became Jordan, is examined by Salibi (1998) and Milton-Edwards (2009). A fact often stressed is that the land which is now Jordan lacked any historical or geographical continuity (Robins, 2004: 16–34). The creation of Transjordan was instead the expression of a nexus of geopolitical factors, such as the necessity, for the British, to reward Abdullah Ibn Hussein (who later became Amir of Transjordan and later the first King of Jordan) for his participation in the war against the Ottomans. There was also the need, again for the British, both to counter-balance the newly established French presence in Damascus and to manage the Jewish 'national home' on the other side of the river Jordan. The area on the East Bank of the river Jordan had been allotted to Britain by the Sykes-Picot secret agreement of 1916, and this decision was later confirmed by the San Remo conference of 1920 (Milton-Edwards and Hinchcliffe, 2009: 18). Abdullah Ibn Hussein, considered the 'founder' of the Jordanian state (Salibi, 1998: 73) was the second son of Husain, the Sharif of Mecca, who claimed descent from the Prophet Muhammad. Abdullah played, together with his brother Feisal, a significant role in the Arab revolt of 1916–1918 against the Ottoman Empire; according to Salibi (1998: 79), Abdullah was its 'chief engineer'. At the Cairo Conference of 1921, chaired by the British Secretary of State for the Colonies Winston Churchill, Feisal was recognised as King of Iraq, while Abdullah as 'responsible for an Arab government in Transjordan' (Milton-Edwards and Hinchcliffe, 2009: 19). His role of Amir of an 'independent constitutional state' under British tutelage was recognised two years later, in 1923 (Milton-Edwards and Hinchcliffe, 2009: 19). The difficult circumstances in which Transjordan was born led the Amir to structure his power basis through the co-option of merchants and tribal leaders, giving birth to neo-patrimonialistic assets, which relied on clientelism and on tribalism, especially emphasising personal loyalty to the monarch (Robins, 2004: 23–27). These were due to become features of Jordanian society for decades to come.

From the beginning, Great Britain played a crucial role not only in the establishment of Jordan as a country, but also in its national identity. Massad has studied the extent to which colonial practices have not only been 'repressive of a range of cultural material' but also 'productive' (2001: 7). Massad is indeed persuaded that the 'law and the military are central to the production of the nation and are generative of other discourses that infiltrate other state agencies and society at large in their defining of national culture' (2001: 15). While, at first, British colonialism had a huge impact on moulding Jordanian national identity, in a second phase, which coincided with decolonisation, Jordanian identity developed against the coloniser.

In particular, according to Massad, Jordanian identity has been moulded by its relationship with the 'other': firstly, the external other, represented by the British colonisers, and then by the internal other, represented by the Palestinians after their mass exoduses of 1948 and 1967 (2001: 21). On the whole, Massad recognises the crucial importance played, in all these phases, by the state agencies conceived, according to Althusser, as 'ideological state apparatuses'. Following Anderson (1983), Massad (2001: 15) is persuaded that all national identities are artificial and socially constructed; in Jordan, since these processes of social construction are, at the same time, recent and controversial, it is arguably easier to study them, because they are more evident and transparent. A point highlighted by Massad (2001: 41), which is particularly relevant to the present study, is the 'privileging of Arabic, Arabness and Islam' in the 1952 Jordanian Constitution to define what being Jordanian means. Even if other segments of Jordanian society, such as Arab Christians and Muslim Circassians, are guaranteed equal status in front of the law, Arabness and Islam are recognised as fundamental elements in constituting the Jordanian subject. Another crucial factor defining the Jordanian idea of nation is, for Massad (2001: 50), the 'dyad of modernization and tradition' upon which 'anticolonial nationalism' is based. Such a dyad is extremely influential in defining the position of, for example, women and Bedouins regarding national identity (Massad, 2001: 50).

The dyad of modernization and tradition had a remarkable influence on Islamic identities, on defining what it means to be, at the same time, Muslim and modern. But, Massad (2001) argues, identifying the Bedouins, Transjordanians par excellence, as the authentic repository of Jordanian national identity, as the very embodiment of Jordanian tradition, had been fundamental in defusing the Palestinian challenge, especially in the aftermath of the 1970 civil war between the Jordanian regime and Palestinian militias. Thus, 'consolidating Jordanian national identity' has been implemented through 'the inclusive project of Bedouinizing all Jordanians' (Massad, 2001: 77). Massad's (2001: 50) intuitions regarding both the role of state agencies in producing the Jordanian subject and the importance of the 'dyad of modernization and tradition' offer precious insights to understand contemporary Jordanian society. The next section examines to what extent the relationships between the Hashemite monarchy and the Muslim Brotherhood have contributed to the social construction of Islamic identities in Jordan.

The Muslim Brotherhood between hegemony and counter-hegemony

Islamism and hegemony

The daily life of the Jordanians, their symbolic words and their patterns of consumption are strongly influenced not merely by Islam as a traditional religion, but by modern Islamism or, more correctly, modern Islamism. Islamisms, as social, economic and political ideologies are in complex relationships with socio-economic formations. Since the 1970s, a multi-faceted process of Islamisation of society and politics spread all over the Arab countries. In Jordan, this phenomenon has been particularly evident. The defeat of Nasser's Arab socialism against Israel paved the way, throughout the Arab world, for the spread of Islamism, which engaged in a successful 'cultural war' against the secular leftists (Bar, 1998: 32).

The Muslim Brotherhood of Jordan was established in 1945 with the help of the Egyptian Muslim Brotherhood by Abu Qurah, a merchant from the northern city of Salt (Boulby, 1999: 37). The foundation of the movement was supported by King Abdullah himself (Kazem, 1997: 15). Boulby (1999: 37) defines the Brotherhood of those days as 'a loose-knit coalition of merchants whose primary goal was to support the *jihad* in Palestine'. Not surprisingly, this was the same social group that constituted the basis of the Hashemite state (Moaddel, 2002: 67–70). However, reflecting the development of a state bureaucracy, by 1952 a new leadership of professionals took control of the Muslim Brotherhood, transforming it into 'a political organization which could compete with secularist parties' (Boulby, 1999: 38). From a legal point of view, it evolved from simply being considered a charitable and philanthropic society to a 'general multifunction Islamic body' (Kazem, 1997: 15). While its ideology was vague, mainly focusing on opposition to the penetration of Western values and British colonialism (Kazem, 1997: 18–19) an important feature of its political agenda was the loyalty to the Hashemite monarchy (Boulby, 1999: 38). As Moaddel (2002: 34) points out, the Hashemite monarchy and the

Muslim Brotherhood did not just develop an 'alliance' against their common enemies, such as Pan-Arab nationalism and Communism throughout the decades, but shared a 'cultural bond' from the beginning.

Indeed, King Abdullah's 'traditionalist approach' (Moaddel, 2002: 34) led him to identify a partner in the Muslim Brotherhood, since its establishment in Amman in 1945. The terms of this partnership have often changed over time, since 'the Hashemites have also been consistent in dealing with the Muslim Brothers by combining a policy of conciliatory gestures toward the movement and its supporters with a strict monitoring of their activities' (Moaddel, 2002: 35). In particular, members of the Muslim Brotherhood enjoyed a privileged status in two state apparatuses, the Ministry of the *Awqaf* (Islamic Affairs) and of Education. Arguably, these two ministries were crucial for the movement, since they granted it a control on the institutions where official Islam was produced and reproduced. That is why a clear-cut distinction between the official Islam discourse constructed by the state and a counter-hegemonic discourse is untenable, since these discourses overlap considerably. As Moaddel (2002: 108) reports, the co-option of members of the Brotherhood into the state apparatuses, in particular of the two afore-mentioned ministries, also led to two important leaders of the Brotherhood reaching the office of Minister. Kamil Ismail al-Sharif, who was one of the leaders of the Muslim Brotherhood in Egypt in the 1950s, became Minister of the *Awqaf* (Islamic Affairs). However, the influence of the Muslim Brotherhood has traditionally been strong in the Ministry of Education, whose influence in shaping the contemporary Muslim subject in Jordan can hardly be over-estimated. Several of the members of the executive bureau of the Muslim Brotherhood were working in the Ministry of Education, especially the influential Ishaq Farhan, who can be singled out as one of the 'architects' of Islamist hegemony. Farhan was Minister of Education from 1970 to 1973, president of the University of Jordan, the most important university of the country, from 1976 to 1978 and later on leader of the Islamic Action Front (Moaddel, 2002: 35). As Moaddel (2002: 35) states: 'The Muslim Brothers naturally used their influence in the ministry to ensure the conformity of its policies with Islam and restrict the cultural and educational desires of religious minorities'. However, instead of 'conformity' with Islam, it may be argued that the influence of the Brotherhood in the Ministry of Education has been crucial in the production of official Islam.

Relying on the same social groups, the Hashemite state and the Muslim Brotherhood had the same enemies. The Muslim Brotherhood was contributing to producing, through its influence on the state and society, the official Islamic narrative which legitimised the regime against its enemies. The outcome of this collaboration has been, as has been said, the profound re-Islamisation, intended as re-articulation of 'traditional' Islamic frames, of Jordanian society. The Hashemite monarchy bases its legitimacy upon its descent from the Prophet Muhammad (Shimada, 1993: 83–85; Moaddel, 2002: 33; Kazem, 1997: 14), and it used the Muslim Brotherhood, since its establishment in 1945, to reinforce the Islamic character of Jordanian society, especially against common enemies such as the leftist forces. As mentioned previously, the Brotherhood could be conceptualised, in this period, as a sort of Althusserian 'ideological state apparatus'. It can be argued that the Muslim Brotherhood played an important role in the process of national identity building: mainly, this happened because of their constant action, throughout the decades, against all the ideologies, such as Pan-Arab nationalism and Communism, which were explicitly or implicitly threatening the narrative of the Hashemite Kingdom of Jordan (Wiktorowicz, 2001: 96). In this context, supporting an Islamist discourse also contributed to bringing together Palestinians and Jordanians, highlighting the common heritage of Islam, downplaying traditional tribal allegiances and partially defusing ethnic tensions. Indeed, such an effort has been remarkable in welding the two major groups, the Transjordanians and the Palestinians. While the Muslim Brothers often criticised Jordanian governments, their criticism never touched the legitimacy of the Hashemite monarchy and the assumptions upon which Jordanian state and identity are based.

It should be noted that from its foundation in Jordan in 1945, the Muslim Brotherhood decided not to challenge the legitimacy of the Hashemite Kingdom and adopted a mainly collaborative approach (Boulby, 1999: 52–53). Thus, the moderate attitude of the Brotherhood needs to be read in the context of what Kazem (1997: 21) defines as a 'tradition of cohabitation and collaboration' between the Brotherhood and the Jordanian state, to the extent that Boulby calls their relationship 'symbiotic' (Boulby, 1999: 1). The Brotherhood competed in the elections, always shaping its strategies in relation to the opportunity spaces available, adopting a gradualist agenda to realise its goals. Such an attitude has allowed them, throughout the years, to take full advantage of the opportunity spaces provided by the regime, establishing their institutions and permeating society with their values, whilst combating the penetration of Western values seen as threatening the social fabric of an Islamic society (Wiktorowicz, 2001: 685). It can therefore be maintained that the Muslim Brotherhood's strategy has been largely shaped by the convergence of interests between the Hashemite monarchy's legitimacy claims and the discourse of the Islamist movement. To put it differently, the Hashemite monarchy identified a precious ally in the Muslim Brotherhood, a bulwark against legitimacy challenges, and this afforded the Islamist movement opportunity spaces in which to expand and thrive.

The collaboration between the Hashemite monarchy and the Muslim Brotherhood was based, since the establishment of the latter in the 1940s to the 1970s, on the fact that the two shared a similar social basis. Merchants and landowners, who constituted the stronghold of the regime, were also 'the predominant group among the Brothers' activists in this period' (Moaddel, 2002: 97). The interests of the Hashemite monarchy and of the Brotherhood coincided also because the two were expressions of the same social groups. It is therefore not surprising that the merchants and landowners funded the Islamic College in Amman, which was established in 1947 by Abu Qurah, the merchant of Salt who funded the Muslim Brotherhood in 1945; the Islamic

College became the school were Jordanian elite, including King Hussein, studied (Moaddel, 2002: 98). It is in the light of the social basis of the Muslim Brotherhood that what Boulby (1999: 1) terms 'symbiotic relations between the Brotherhood and the regime' and what Kazem (1997: 21) calls a 'tradition of cohabitation and collaboration' can be understood. It is in this sense that the Brotherhood was providing ideological support to the regime, contributing to make the discourse of the regime hegemonic through the adoption of Islamic frames.

According to Milton-Edwards, the abstention from opposition to the regime was the *conditio sine qua non* for the survival of the Brotherhood (Milton-Edwards, 2009: 52). Moreover, as Bar maintains (1998: 6):

> As of the 1950s, the regime cultivated the movement and allowed it a wide range of religious, political and economic freedom in striking contrast to the ban on other political parties. The *raison d'état* behind this policy was the need to provide a counterweight to the clandestine political parties which denied the very legitimacy of the 'Jordanian identity': the Communist Party, various Nasserist groups, the pro-Syrian and pro-Iraqi Ba'th parties, and later on, the Palestinian fida'i organizations.

Bar (1998) highlights the fact that the Muslim Brotherhood was one of the few political forces to recognise the legitimacy of the Hashemite discourse on 'Jordanian identity'; in social constructivism terms, it can be said that the Brotherhood actively took part in the social construction of such an identity. Indeed, in the 1950s, the Pan-Arab nationalist ideology was growing in popularity in Jordan, posing a serious threat not only to the Islamist movement, but also to the Hashemite dynasty (Moaddel, 2002: 102). In Jordan, Pan-Arabism was embodied by the charismatic Suleiman al-Nabulsi, leader of the National Socialist Party and Prime Minister in 1956–1957. His pro-Egyptian policies contributed to irritating the Muslim Brotherhood, given the harsh persecutions experienced by the Muslim Brotherhood in Egypt under Nasser. Indeed, the Muslim Brothers of Jordan were experiencing a degree of freedom uncommon in the Arab states ruled by leftist and secular governments. As Mandaville (2007: 131) concisely puts it: 'the palace left the Brotherhood to get on with its work so long as it did not interfere with regime policies'. In this decision, we can begin to see the fracture between a political society, firmly in the hands of the ruling elite, and a civil society, growingly influenced by the Muslim Brotherhood. Such a distinction may not be relevant for the period in which the Muslim Brotherhood was operating as an 'ideological state apparatus' of the regime, but becomes increasingly so in a later period. Indeed, the latter will be, in the following decades, the embryo of the counter-hegemonic attempt of the Brotherhood. The anti-monarchical and anti-Western leanings of the nationalists were a constant reason for apprehension for King Hussein, who rose to the throne in 1953, after the murder of King Abdullah and the short rule of King Talal. The King was anti-Communist and persuaded of the necessity for Jordan to remain aligned with the West (Moaddel, 2002: 102). Thus, an alleged attempted coup of the nationalists against the regime consolidated the alliance between the Hashemite monarchy and the Muslim Brotherhood of Jordan, as the interests of the latter coincided with the monarchy, since both identified in the spread of nationalism, socialism and communism a threat to their own survival (Moaddel, 2002: 102).

The movement, therefore, did not have any interest in waging frontal war against a regime that was so benign towards it. From 1945 to the 1990s, the Muslim Brotherhood contributed to the process of nation building, trying to merge Transjordanians with Palestinians in one single nation under the banner of Islam. Overall, in Gramscian terms, the Muslim Brotherhood supported the hegemonic narrative of the Hashemite regime. This project enjoyed the support of the monarchy, especially under King Hussein. According to Wiktorowicz (2001: 93):

> The historical relationship is predicated upon a balance between the ideological objectives of the Brotherhood and the need to assuage the survival imperatives of the Hashemites. The result is a symbiosis in which the regime allows the Brotherhood to organize and promote its objectives, while the movement upholds the regime's right to rule and refrains from challenging Hashemite Islamic legitimacy.

It can be argued that the Muslim Brotherhood of Jordan pursued a strategy of creating, in Gramscian terms, a 'historic bloc' between Transjordanians and Palestinians, welding together the religious bourgeoisie and the Lumpenproletariat, to forge a national-popular will cemented by Islamism. In Jordan, the Muslim Brotherhood have always operated as legal opposition, never being violently persecuted as in Ba'athist Syria or in Nasser's Egypt (Kilani, 1993: 7–16). The main feature of the Jordanian exception has been an Islamist movement that was integrated into the political life of an Arab country and that showed a mainly non-confrontational attitude towards the state (Moaddel, 2002: 1–3). Indeed, the Muslim Brotherhood of Jordan developed what could be termed as an 'Islamo-nationalist' discourse, outcome of a 'pragmatic' and 'reformist' approach (Boulby, 1999: 37).

Arguing that the two developed a 'symbiosis' should not lead to conflating their discourses into a single discourse, since with time the two began to differentiate. In developing the argument further, the next section argues that, since the 1970s, the strategy of the Muslim Brotherhood can be increasingly conceived as counter-hegemonic.

Islamism and counter-hegemony

Islamist movements are often conceptualised, and often conceptualise themselves, as an alternative to the Arab state, and to its secular and nationalist credentials. Chapter 1 has highlighted the extent to which the emergence of

Islamist movements can be read against the background of the failure of the Arab state to deliver its promises. It will therefore be considered whether the Gramscian category of counter-hegemony may be useful to conceptualise the process of mobilisation activated by the Muslim Brotherhood of Jordan. This section argues that, since the 1970s, the Muslim Brotherhood have gradually abandoned their 'symbiotic relations' (Boulby, 1999: 1) with the regime, developing counter-hegemonic features. Such a process reveals a wider process taking place in the political economy of the Arab world. Also in Jordan, during the 1970s, a new middle class started to develop. Its emergence entered on a collision course with the interests of the merchants and landowners, who used to dominate the Jordanian state. Islamic frames became the most effective tools available to express the social critique of this social class against the establishment, and the Muslim Brotherhood began to express the frustrations of this social group. Furthermore, in Jordan the discourse of the Brotherhood became more and more appealing for a large number of Palestinians, disappointed by the failure of the secular and socialist option represented by the Palestine Liberation Organisation (Clark, 2004: 89).

Several scholars on Jordan postulated that the goal of Islamist movements is what Boulby (1999: 1) labels a 'theo-democracy'. As Clark (2004: 15) maintains in her study on Islamism in Jordan and Yemen: 'both moderate and radical Islamism share the same loosely defined ultimate goal of a society and state governed by Islamic law'. In this view, what differentiates Islamist movements are merely the strategies to achieve such an outcome. Also Boulby's (1999: 130) research on the Jordanian Muslim Brotherhood suggests that parliamentary democracy is merely a 'transition to Islamic rule'. Similarly, in his essay on the Jordanian Muslim Brotherhood, Kazem (1997: 27) states that the goal of the Muslim Brotherhood is 'setting up an Islamic state that rules by God's laws'. Indeed, the concept of popular sovereignty seems not to appear compatible with the Muslim Brotherhood's world view, as the sovereignty belongs only to Allah, and not to the people (Boulby, 1999: 132). Their long-term objective, therefore, has been described as a 'theocracy', intended by Bernard Lewis (2010: 66), 'not in the Western sense of a state ruled by the Church and the clergy, since neither existed in the Islamic world, but in the more literal sense of a polity ruled by God'. However, these frames, which develop a confrontation against the secular character of the Arab state, developed out of social transformations. It is in this overlapping between ideology and social formations that the Muslim Brotherhood may be defined as a counter-hegemonic movement, since its goal appears to be beyond the boundaries of the Arab state.

Since the 1970s, a new social group has developed its influence over the Islamist movement. By then, Arab nationalism was experiencing a deep crisis after Nasser's defeat. The economic developments of the 1970s, and in particular the remittances of the 400,000 Jordanians employed in the Gulf as a consequence of the oil boom and the emergence of Amman as a regional economic centre during the Lebanese civil war benefited the Jordanian economy (Moaddel, 2002: 106). Moreover, new opportunities for education contributed to the rise of a new middle class of professionals, while at the same time the Jordanian Muslim Brotherhood attracted large numbers of young people, fascinated by the radical message of Sayyid Qutb: future leaders of the 'hawk' faction of the Brotherhood grew up in that milieu (Moaddel, 2002: 106). At the end of the 1970s, the success of the Iranian revolution further fuelled the emergence of an insurgent consciousness within the Muslim Brotherhood. Indeed, the aftermath of the Iranian revolution has been marked by the attempt of Islamist groups at taking power by force. Khomeini demonstrated the possibility of an Islamic revolution and the struggle of the *mujahidin* against the Soviets galvanised segments of the Islamist movement all over the world. In particular, Abdallah Azzam, a Palestinian-Jordanian who became a warrior in Afghanistan, also became an idol for the radical Islamists (Bar, 1998: 35).

These concomitant processes had a long-term influence on the movement. As Boulby states, 'by 1993 two groups were particularly significant in the Brotherhood's support base: Palestinians disenchanted with the peace process and a new generation of educated Transjordanians demanding greater political freedoms and more economic opportunities' (Boulby, 1996: 3–4). The new generation of Palestinians who had joined the Muslim Brotherhood since the middle of the 1980s are so described by Bar (1998: 46):

> The Palestinians who joined the ranks of the Brotherhood saw themselves as representatives of the refugee and displaced Palestinian population and champions of the social, economic or political 'underdogs' of Jordanian society – though they themselves came mainly from educated, socially mobile Palestinian families. These trends added undercurrents within the movement calling for more militant positions toward the regime and for a younger and more activist leadership.

Thus, since the 1970s, the Muslim Brotherhood can be conceptualised as a social movement which, in order to achieve its goals, attempted to achieve its hegemony over Jordanian society. In the previous phase, from the 1940s to the 1970s, the Brotherhood seemed instead to collaborate so closely with the regime to the point that the goals of the two seem indistinguishable.

The main advantage of the use of a Gramscian framework to interpret the strategies of the Muslim Brotherhood is that it allows consideration of the social and economic realms as the main loci in which to carry out its struggle to promote conformity with Islamic values. Undoubtedly, the political domain represented another locus in which the Muslim Brothers carried out their action; but politics, narrowly defined, has never been the major focus of the movement. Following this line of reasoning, the strategy of the Muslim Brotherhood can be defined as presenting counter-hegemonic features. The use of this term presupposes that there is a hegemonic power that the Muslim Brotherhood is challenging: but this power is not primarily, in the Jordanian case, the power of the state. Indeed, the relationship between the Muslim Brotherhood and the Hashemite monarchy has been characterised, for decades, by a non confrontational attitude of the Islamists. Thus, the counter-hegemonic challenge of the Islamist movement has not been substantiated in a revolutionary or violent approach aimed at overthrowing the monarchy. Indeed, the Brotherhood mainly strived to counter Western and secular influences, without challenging the legitimacy of the Hashemites. The Jordanian governments have only been attacked and criticised when they have been perceived as threatening the idea of Islam embodied by Islamists.

Broadly speaking, the Muslim Brotherhood managed to express, in an effective language easily understandable by everybody, the necessity of 'returning' to Islam in order to solve the social and political problems of Jordan, where the concept of return pre-supposes that there had been a golden age in which utopia and reality coincided. This belief can be identified as the core of the Brotherhood's Islamist ideology. Indeed, the causes of the problems of Muslim societies have been identified by the Islamists in the abandonment of Islam (Clark, 2004: 13–14).

In this opposition to the alleged secular character of society and to Western influences, and not in their challenge to the ruling dynasty, lie the counter-hegemonic features of the Islamist project. In Gramscian terms, the Muslim Brotherhood did not wage a 'war of movement' against the monarchy. In fact, the strategy of the Muslim Brotherhood has been aimed at the re-Islamisation of Jordanian society. Such an endeavour has been primarily carried out through *da'wa* (call to Islam): this *da'wa* is here conceptualised, in Gramscian terms, as a 'war of position', aimed at conquering hegemony, winning the hearts and minds of the Jordanians. The hegemonic ideology to be countered has been primarily the Western secular discourse and its multi-faceted influence on Jordanian society. The counter-hegemonic effort has mainly been conducted by a vanguard, that is to say the leadership of the Muslim Brotherhood. Gramsci recognized the vanguard as an essential factor in 'awakening' the masses, who, in a Marxist framework, are supposed to be victims of a 'false consciousness' that prevents them from being aware of their state of submission to the bourgeoisie. This idea of false consciousness bears striking similarities to the Islamist concept of *jahiliyya* (ignorance), especially as developed by Sayyid Qutb. The masses appear to be unaware of their true needs and aspirations: the vanguard has the duty to awaken them, making them conscious of their present state of exploitation and leading them to challenge the ruling classes and their unfair system. This undertaking is the kernel of the counter-hegemonic project.

In a Marxist framework, educating and regimenting the masses is a crucial duty of the vanguard. Similarly, the Islamist emphasis on education has to be read as a conscious effort of 'reforming' the Muslim individual and as an essential step to reform society as a whole. To put it differently, education is necessary to spread 'insurgent consciousness' (McAdam, 1999: 49) throughout society, to persuade people that social change is necessary. In a

Gramscian framework, disruptive social change aimed at overthrowing the ruling elites ought to challenge their hegemony, a hegemony that relies upon dominance, exerted through state coercion, as well as intellectual and moral leadership exercised throughout the ganglia of civil society (Joll, 1977: 8). The revolutionary group, in order to topple the ruling class, must therefore establish its own counter-hegemony, composed by its own dominance and intellectual and moral leadership. This consensus has to rely on an organic alliance of social forces, a 'historic bloc', led by professional revolutionaries able to forge a 'national-popular will' (Femia, 1981: 130–164). It can be argued that the endeavour of the Muslim Brotherhood has been aimed exactly at establishing their intellectual and moral leadership over Jordanian society through the construction of a 'historic bloc' that tied together different ethnicities and social classes. The message of the Muslim Brotherhood cemented sectors of the Islamist middle class with the masses in the name of an Islamic identity largely shaped by Islamism. Islamism, interpreted as a modern ideology, acted as glue for this bloc. Thus, in this context, the intellectuals of the revolutionary movement should play the role of 'organizers of hegemony' (Sassoon, 1980: 134), transforming individual frustrations into political action, spreading insurgent consciousness and leading the masses towards change. This theoretical framework may be applied to the strategies of the Muslim Brotherhood through the use of the Gramscian concept of 'war of position', seen as the peculiar way in which the Muslim Brotherhood articulated its counter-hegemonic project. Introducing this notion may be useful to understand the implications of the notion of *da'wa* (appeal or invitation to Islam) in the context of the strategies of the Muslim Brotherhood. The strategy of the Muslim Brotherhood in Jordan has been defined in one of its statements, clearly inspired by Hasan al-Banna, as follows (Boulby, 1999: 94):

> Islam is the solution to all the nation's political, social, economic and moral problems. Its course is: reforming the Muslim, then the Muslim family, then the Muslim people, then the Muslim government will apply God's *shari'a*, demand what is right and forbid what is wrong.
> (Boulby, 1999: 94)

Abdul Majid Thunaybat, former leader of the Jordanian Brotherhood, has spoken in a similar vein (Wiktorowicz, 2001: 93):

> Our approach to education is to begin with the individual and then move to the family and then ultimately the Islamic government that rules as provided for in God's *shari'a*. Our mission does not envisage an overthrow of the regime in the sense of holding the reins of power regardless of people's temperament or whether they approve of this regime or not. We seek the creation of faithful grassroots that receive these instructions and this order, and government by Islam comes later.

Thunaybat indicates a reformist, gradualist approach aimed at the establishment of an Islamic state. In a similar vein, Ishaq Farhan, one of the most significant leaders of the Brotherhood, has also expressed a preference for a reformist approach 'in order to shift towards the application of the Islamic *shari'a* in society' (Wiktorowicz, 2001: 94). The concept of *da'wa* (appeal to Islam or invitation to Islam) is indeed crucial to understand the strategies of the Brotherhood (Hammad, 1997: 169). The Islamist notion of *da'wa* is so defined by Clark (2004: 14):

> Beyond simply proselytizing or preaching (as traditionally operationalized), *da'wa* becomes the very act of 'activating' Islam through deed in all spheres of life. ... The Islamist project, therefore, is an attempt to create a seemingly seamless web between religion, politics and charity and all forms of activism. ... Islamic social institutions are thus a form of putting *da'wa* into practice.

The notion of *da'wa* as the 'activation' (or re-activation) of Islam in 'all spheres of life' could be also defined as a re-articulation of the Islamic discourse *qua* integral project for the renewal of contemporary Muslim societies. The activation of Islam pursued by the Muslim Brotherhood is a holistic project that goes far beyond the boundaries of 'politics', narrowly defined. Following Gramsci's framework, *da'wa* resembles a sort of war of position, or 'jihad of position', an effort to gradually implement God's will through the promotion of conformity with Islamic values in the political domain. The strategic goal of achieving hegemony on Jordanian society has been carried out, according to one of the most prominent leaders of the Jordanian Muslim Brotherhood, Ishaq Farhan, in four phases (Wiktorowicz, 2001: 97):

> In the 1950s, the movement focused on *da'wa* (call to Islam). As a broad religious committee, the Muslim Brotherhood enjoyed access to the mosques and other religious institutions and used these opportunities to support missionary work. In the 1960s, the movement promoted Islam through education. In the third stage during the 1970s, the movement formed grassroots charitable organizations and became active in professional associations. In the 1980s and 1990s, particularly after political liberalization, the Brotherhood became more directly involved in politics by participating in parliamentary elections, briefly joining the government's cabinet, and forming the IAF [Islamic Action Front, the political wing of the Muslim Brotherhood].

Here we can observe, in the words of Farhan, the breadth and the depth of the Muslim Brotherhood's holistic counter-hegemonic project. Without challenging the government, but in fact taking advantage of the opportunity spaces available to them in each historical period, the Muslim Brotherhood pursued a coherent and organic counter-hegemonic strategy through the articulation and re-articulation of Islamic frames. In Farhan's reconstruction, during the first tactical phase, the Muslim Brotherhood attempted to control the mosques, crucial loci of production and reproduction of Islamic discourse (Bar, 1998: 33). In the second tactical phase, they focused on establishing a network of educational institutions to inculcate the youth with Islamist values and worldview. According to Farhan, the third tactical phase focused on establishing grassroots charitable organizations and on achieving hegemony over professional associations. The fourth tactical phase, which began with the political liberalisation signified by the end of the Cold War, has been marked by the Muslim Brotherhood's growing involvement in the political domain.

The focus is now on two of those phases, examining the attempt of the Brotherhood to control education and the private sector. Those efforts are particularly apt in showing the extent to which the project of achieving hegemony on Jordanian society has been attempted in a way that is consistent with Gramsci's theorisation, as well as with social constructivism. In other words, the school and the market have been identified as crucial bulwarks to conquer in order for them to establish their intellectual, social and intellectual leadership. The Muslim Brotherhood's strategy seems to be a long-term 'war of position' that aims to conquer civil society and, in so doing, to deprive the state of its moral and intellectual leadership. When the counter-hegemonic narrative of the Muslim Brotherhood becomes the hegemonic paradigm in society, the state will be deprived of its legitimacy and of its historical basis. A state 'deprived of its historic base' is like an empty shell, merely relying on 'the armor of coercion' (Buci-Glucksmann, 1980: 281), while the Islamists will enjoy the intellectual and moral leadership, a micro-power spread throughout the ganglia of society.

However, the counter-hegemonic strategy of the Brotherhood has had mixed outcomes. One of the factors, which probably contributed to the weakening of their project, has been the struggle within the movement between Transjordanians and Palestinians. Instead of cementing all Jordanians under the banner of Islam, the Muslim Brotherhood has been victim of the same inner strife as the rest of Jordanian society. The split between those two ethnic factions has been one of the main reasons for the failure in creating a Gramscian historic bloc. The Muslim Brothers split up in different factions, and the prevalence of pro-Palestinians radical groups determined the crumbling of the historic bloc built by the movement in the previous decades, inaugurating a period of growing marginalisation. Such an outcome represents a halt to the project of a national way to Islamism, able to cement the two groups in a common narrative and identity. The Islamist movement was indeed apparently hijacked by a radical Palestinian minority close to Hamas (Bar, 1998: 46–47).

If the failure in creating a historic bloc happened primarily along ethnic lines, the project failed also because of social reasons. As demonstrated by Clark, Islamic social institutions focused on recruiting middle-class people as well as on providing service to the poor. The choice of privileging clientelistic bonds instead of establishing an interclassist social bloc, weakened the cohesion of the movement and its possibilities to organically consolidate the 'historic bloc' (Clark, 2004: 33–34). In other words, the Muslim Brotherhood did not manage to do in Jordan what Hamas and Hezbollah did in Palestine and Lebanon, respectively. The defeat of the Islamic Action Front Party paved the way for inner strife (Bar, 1998: 46–47).

Besides, but the thaw between Jordan and Israel led the Muslim Brotherhood to adopt a more confrontational agenda, as argued by Bar (1998: 48–49). In order to assess the counter-hegemonic features of the strategies of the Brotherhood, the next section focuses on the Islamic social institutions established by the movement, which constitute the implementation of its *da'wa*.

Islamic social institutions

The counter-hegemonic project of the Muslim Brotherhood has mainly been implemented through the foundation of a vast network of institutions inspired by its ideology, engaged in spreading its values (Hammad, 1997: 169–70). Having been excluded from the heart of the state, the market became for the Muslim Brotherhood one of the main opportunity spaces. This allowed the development of a dynamic private Islamic sector that enjoyed the support and patronage of the members of the Muslim Brotherhood working within the institutions. The social influence exerted by the Muslim Brothers may have contributed in the late 1980s and in the 1990s to the social and political stability of Jordan, since it allowed the state to take away resources from welfare in times of economic liberalisations. The favourable approach of Islamist movements towards economic liberalisation has been thoroughly studied by Yavuz (2003), Utvik (2006) and Beinin (2005). In particular, the support of neoliberal policies by the Egyptian Muslim Brotherhood and the emergence of an Islamist bourgeoisie have been studied by Utvik (2006: 150) and Beinin (2005), while Yavuz (2003: 81–101) has analysed the development of a pro-market attitude among the Turkish Islamists during Özal's reforms in the 1980s.

The growing importance of Islamic social institutions in the age of globalisation in the Arab world at large was stressed by Ayubi (1991: 198):

> There is little doubt that the Islamic societies are increasingly providing an alternative social and organisational network to that sponsored by the State. They fill in the gaps created by the retreat of the State from some of its previous areas of activity, and build closer and more intimate links with the people at the grass-roots level, thus constraining the penetration of the State into society and eroding a great deal of the State's 'achievement based' claim to legitimacy.

Indeed, economic liberalisation paved the way for an expansion of the influence of Islamist oppositional groups such as the Muslim Brotherhood. Also in

Jordan, the more the state was incapable of providing basic services and a decent standard of living to the Jordanian population, the more the power of the Brotherhood grew. The Muslim Brotherhood performed welfare functions, securing its consensus through the help to the poor, but its charitable outreach also strengthened bonds among the members of the middle class who took part in these activities (Clark, 2004: 146–161).

Clark carried out ground-breaking research on Islamic Social Institutions (ISI) in Jordan, highlighting their crucial importance for the Islamist movement. She argues that (2004: 6):

> ISIs are more than just a challenge to the state's ability to do its job; they are a challenge to the secular state itself. They represent an alternative organization of state and society – a potentially revolutionary one – based on Islam.

Indeed, Clark (2004: 6) indicates the need to study the ISIs as a 'locus of social and political change', arguing that (Clark, 2004: 15):

> ISIs are thus not only an alternative to state institutions; they represent the foundations of an alternative society. They stand in direct contrast to secular states that appear to have lost their concern for the poor.

Clark's approach suggests focusing our attention on the social and economic realm in order to comprehend the breadth of the Islamist project. The mushrooming of Islamic social institutions has been nurtured and sponsored by the Islamic Centre Charity Society (ICCS), established in 1963 and whose activities boomed in the 1970s as a consequence of the oil windfall (Wiktorowicz, 2001: 101; Clark, 2004: 92). Through the ICCS, which was licensed in 1963, the Muslim Brotherhood ended up controlling a vast network of Islamic social institutions (Dabbas, 1997: 214–215), until, after the appointment of Zaki Banu Rasheed as the Secretary General of the Islamic Action Front Party, in 2006, the regime took over the ICCS from the Brotherhood (Abu Rumman, 2007: 26).

The ICCS can be identified as the engine of the process of Islamisation of civil society. It provides health care and organises several events aimed at spreading Islamic values, and Islamic ideology, throughout Jordanian society (Hammad, 1997: 171). The ICCS states that its goal is 'providing mosque facilities' but also 'education, health, income-generating and training projects, financial assistance for needy families, the care of orphans, and assisting the poor who are sick' (Clark, 2004: 92). Thus, the ICCS has been at times perceived as an alternative power centre to the state, controlling a wide range of economic activities (Wiktorowicz, 2001: 102–109).

It should be noted that the headquarters of the ICCS are in Amman, in the neighbourhood of Abdali, and four branches are located in the cities of Zarqa, Irbid, Mafraq and Ramtha (Clark, 2004: 92). As seen before, through the ICCS, the Muslim Brotherhood used to control several educational institutions, such as the Dar al-Arqum and Dar al-Aqsa schools, the Islamic Community College, the Zarqa University, the Islamic Hospital in Amman and the Islamic Studies and Research Association (Wiktorowicz, 2001: 102–09). In 1997 and 1998, the ICCS used to control a network of forty-one education institutions, composed of elementary and secondary schools and kindergartens (Clark, 2004: 93). Among them, there was the Zarqa University, which attracted students from all over the Muslim world. The ICCS also controlled 'two hospitals and fifteen medical centers housing thirty-two medical clinics and eleven laboratories' (Clark, 2004: 93). In particular, the Islamic Hospital in Amman was considered to be the cutting edge of the entire Muslim Brotherhood controlled private sector. The establishment of this hospital and of other top class Islamist institutions has to be read, according to Clark (2004: 83) as a 'conscious decision by the ICCS to build powerful symbols of the Islamist alternative to the state. They are a concrete expression of Islamist identity.'

Undoubtedly, those institutions are an expression of Islamist identity; but they are also the *fora* in which Islamist identity is incessantly produced and reproduced. Islamic social institutions, such as non-governmental organisations, have been engaged in *da'wa*, spreading Islamic values in society through welfare services, education, and the media. The aim of such endeavours has been the production and reproduction of consensus and the development of networks of solidarity and patronage in various sectors, from health care to education, from finance to publishing (Kilani, 1993: 9–10). The expansion of these Islamic charities, as well as profit-making institutions has to be read against the backdrop of what Kahf (2004: 17) terms 'the alliance of wealth and *sharia* scholarship', of which the birth of the international Islamic financial system is a direct consequence.

As is well known, education is one of the primary activities of the Muslim Brotherhood, which is committed to reforming the Muslim individual, an indispensable premise for the reform of society. Indeed, Hasan al-Banna, the founder of the Egyptian Muslim Brotherhood, was a teacher, and since its inception, the movement has been committed to the education of the youth, with the aim of forging a new man, the *homo islamicus*. As the Muslim Brotherhood bylaws maintain, one of the goals of the movement is 'to educate those who have embraced the Islamic faith as individuals and groups and to pool their efforts and resources so that they may become qualified to carry the banners of Islam and advance its cause and mission' (Awad, 1997: 82–83). The Islamist movement, hence, fostered the creation of an Islamist network of schools, but at the same time, it also infiltrated the state school system through the creation of patronage networks (Hourani, 1997: 268). Ishaq Farhan, notable member of the movement, was Minister of Education from 1970 until 1973 and influenced teaching programmes and teacher recruitment (Bar, 1998: 32–33). The appointment of Ishaq Farhan as Minister of Education was interpreted as a reward for the support of the Brotherhood to the regime during the Black September civil war (Bar, 1998: 33). As Bar (1998: 32–33) continues:

Control over the largest, and potentially one of the most influential ministries afforded the Brotherhood the opportunity to build up the educational system as an important power base. Hundreds of education ministry officials, at all levels, were identified with the Brotherhood, as were many of the school principals, one of the more secure expressions of Brotherhood power within Jordanian society.

The Muslim Brotherhood also established cultural and research centres, where the movement's intellectuals produced and disseminated the worldview of the Brotherhood, playing a major role in the construction of the moral and intellectual leadership of the society. New generations of Islamists have been moulded, and the cadres of the movement have been formed in these institutions with the objective of reaching the long waited aim of hegemony.

These institutions used to educate students in Islamist discourses and foster students' conformity with Islamic behaviour (Wiktorowicz, 2001: 102). In Islamic schools, Islamist ideology permeates the whole curriculum: for example, the natural sciences, such as biology, are explained in the light of the Quran (Wiktorowicz, 2001: 102). Regarding the Dar al-Arqam school, Clark (2004: 93) underlines the importance of conformity to Islamic ideals, which teachers teach to children with their lessons and with their personal example. Thus, segregation of male and female students is enforced, wearing the *hijab* is compulsory for female teachers, and young girls are invited to wear it as well; the same respect for Islamic orthopraxy is expected for what concerns prayers and fast during the holy month of Ramadan.

On the whole, the Islamist private sector aimed indeed at demonstrating the possibility of establishing an Islamic society through a bottom-up approach (Clark, 2004: 18), which as a strategy is likened to the creation of the 'society within the society' (Hammad, 1997: 169), parallel to the mainstream one. The Brotherhood also successfully attempted to gain control of professional associations in an effort to convert the middle class to its ideology and, at the same time, to combat the influence of the secular left in these bodies.

A similar struggle for hegemony took place in the universities, where the Brotherhood effectively managed to counteract the leftist and pro-Palestinian groups (Robins, 2004: 129–132). Leftist student movements were considered as posing a major threat to the government, due to their staunch support for the Palestinian cause, and curbing their influence was a central policy of the regime. Once again, the Brotherhood took advantage of the opportunity spaces provided by the government. Defending the interests of the regime, Islamists were at the same time pursuing their own objectives, namely eliminating their political competition. Overall, this bottom-up approach that aimed to overtake civil society appears to be a common feature of other Islamist movements such as Hamas and Hezbollah.

The market and the education sector have been the main opportunity spaces available to the Islamist movement in Jordan (Clark, 2004: 18). The efforts of the Muslim Brotherhood have been particularly successful in recruiting members from the middle class, especially from the banking sector, small and medium enterprises, and the professional associations. At the same time, the Muslim Brotherhood appeared as the expression of this rising new middle class. As Boulby (1999: 74) states, 'analysis of the evidence shows that the Muslim Brotherhood's membership and leadership continue to be dominated by professionals and students and that the movement reflects the hopes of an emergent professional class for political power'. One primary outcome of the development of the Islamic sector has been the construction of a specific and 'authentic' Islamist identity. In particular, the new middle class found in moderate Islamism the answer to their own frustrations, their impotence and their striving for authenticity (Clark, 2004: 17). It is not a coincidence that the cadres of the movement were mainly constituted by the educated middle class, which also comprised the main recruiting target (Moaddel, 2002: 115–122). Not surprisingly, the founders of the political wing of the Muslim Brotherhood, the Islamic Action Front Party established in 1992, were professionals and the professional associations constituted a stronghold of the Islamist movement (Boulby, 1999: 109). Socio-economic transformations provoked the rise of new social classes which, in turn, influenced the strategy and ideology of the Muslim Brotherhood.

Islamic banking as the articulation of Islamism in Jordan

Islamic banks, in the modern sense, initially emerged in the 1960s and then flourished in the post 1975 period, as part of the Islamic economics discourse that had developed since the 1940s. Islamic economics discourse aimed at constructing the Islamic alternative to the current economic system through the authentic norms and principles of Islam. Such an objective was related to the creation of an 'authentic' Islamic identity, which also required an Islamic alternative economic model to complete the Islamic system, that is to say a holistic understanding of Islam.

The first precursor of Islamic banks is considered to be the Mit Ghamr, a bank which operated in the Nile Delta of Egypt from 1963 (Warde, 2000: 73; Kahf, 2004: 19). Mit Ghamr emphasised profit-and-loss sharing contracts such as the *mudarabah*, as well as charitable purposes, in the form of raising and allocating *zakat* (Warde, 2000: 74). Moreover, as Malley (2004: 192) affirms, several members of the Muslim Brotherhood had professional and financial ties with this experiment. It could be argued that such an experience gave form to the aspirations of the Muslim Brotherhood of Egypt, which aimed at building capacity and fostering development through the provision of social credits, since in this experiment 'the social mission of Islamic banking was predominant' (Mayer, 1985: 37–38). The bank closed down in 1967, according to some because the regime became suspicious of this experiment (Warde, 2000: 74). As Mayer (1985: 39) explains, the regime of Nasser, which embraced a socialist ideology, was suspicious of such an experiment since it merged 'capitalist ideas and Islamic precepts'.

This initial and small-scale social banking oriented operation paved the way for the creation of large-scale Islamic commercial banks in the post-1974 period as part of the Organisation of the Islamic Conference (OIC) strategy, which was hegemonised by Saudi Arabia (Warde, 2000: 74). The oil boom which followed the Yom Kippur war of 1973 provided Arab Gulf countries with huge capital which was partially invested in the establishment of Islamic banks. In 1974, at the OIC Lahore summit, it was decided to constitute the Islamic Development Bank; as Warde (2000: 75) explains, 'the new institution was to promote, through direct participation, training and advice, the creation of additional Islamic institutions'. It can be argued that this project also had the function of institutionalising a project that, on an international scale, was counter-hegemonic in respect to the declining socialist-inspired pan-Arab ideology. With the birth of the Dubai Islamic Bank in 1975, the history of private, commercial Islamic banks begins (Warde, 2000: 75).

The history of Islamic finance needs to be contextualised in the historical framework proposed in Chapter 1, that is, in the context of the crisis of Pan-Arabism and the emergence of Pan-Islamism; as Islamic banks constituted the backbone of the latter. In addition, the emergence of Islamic banks in the mid-1970s needs to be explained with the rise of Islamic consciousness that essentialised an 'authentic' Islamic identity, in so doing contributing to the institutionalisation efforts of Islamic movements such as the Muslim Brotherhood. The economic liberalisation and government policies for the expansion of the private sector in the Middle East and the Muslim world provided the necessary opportunity spaces for Islamic banks to flourish (Khan, 2006). This very same process of withdrawal of the state from the economy also opened up opportunity spaces for Islamic movements like the Muslim Brotherhood. This nexus of international organisations such as the OIC, political movements such as the Muslim Brotherhood and economic institutions such as Islamic banks benefited from the crisis of Arab socialism and were at the same time one of the main forces that contributed to its erosion. Thus, a new political phase was opened by the set-back of the Pan-Arab project of Nasser in the 1967 war against Israel; however, the articulation of a new project, counter-hegemonic with respect to the Pan-Arab hegemonic project, was made possible only by the capital made available by the oil shocks, which followed the 1973 Yom Kippur war. In this light, the establishment of a network of Islamic banks all over the Muslim world was also functional to cold war strategies. After the defeat of Nasserism and the setback of Arab socialism, the bond between Saudi Arabia and the USA was further strengthened by their common opposition to both the Iranian revolution of 1979 and the consequent Iranian attempt to extend its hegemony in the region, as well as to the Soviet campaign in Afghanistan, which started in the same year (Warde, 2004: 43). As Warde (2004: 37) affirms: 'Since its inception in the mid 1970s, Islamic finance was firmly embedded within the US-centred international economic order, under the aegis of Saudi-supported pan-Islamism'.

From the point of view of local politics, the establishment of Islamic banks offered new opportunity spaces for co-operation between businessmen and Islamists. As Kahf (2004: 29) states 'Islamic bankers have not shied away from utilizing the service of 'moderate Islamists, as long as it does not disturb the banks' relations with governments. Hence, many moderate Islamists have found peaceful havens in the Islamic banks, especially in Egypt and Jordan'. Indeed, since the 1970s a new phase has opened for Islamists as well.

This process, which also took place in other countries such as Egypt, assumed particular features in the Jordanian context. In this case, it is on the one hand a continuation of the 'symbiotic relationship' (Boulby, 1999: 1) between the Muslim Brotherhood and the regime, that is to say, the need to defuse the leftist threat and the new malaise of the Palestinians in Jordan by opposing the forces that were contesting the legitimacy of the Hashemite Kingdom. On the other hand, this articulation is part of the long-term counter-hegemonic strategy of the Muslim Brotherhood, which aimed at building the infrastructure of an Islamic society. In Gramscian terms, Islamic banks have been crucial in the social construction of a 'historical bloc'; concerning several Muslim countries, Jordan included, Kahf (2004: 29) states that Islamic banks 'helped change the map of power distribution and brought about a new power centre'.

This 'historical bloc' is not limited to the upper and middle classes since, through the provision of almsgiving in the form of *zakat* distribution to the poor by the Islamic banks, it was possible to reach out also to the lower classes (Kahf, 2004: 27), in order to buy their consensus and weaken the penetration of leftist ideologies, which were criticising wealth allocation in Arab societies. Thus, the expansion of Islamic banks coincided, for example in Egypt, with the liberalisation policies (*infitah*) promoted by Sadat, also by offering credit to disadvantaged social classes who could not access it through loans (Mayer, 1985). Thus, a shift could be observed, in the Islamist discourse, from the construction of an Islamic society to the acceptance of the capitalistic system 'moderated' by Islamisation, whose stark imbalances needed to be cured. This can be further observed in the 1990s, since both the 'Washington consensus' and Islamism were in favour of the downsizing of the state (Warde, 2004: 47). It is precisely this heterogeneous environment that constitutes the cradle of the processes of cross-fertilisation between the paradigms of *homo economicus* and *homo islamicus*, as well as between the processes of globalisation and Islamisation.

The relationship between Islamic finance and Islamist movements has been studied by Malley (2004) in relation with the Jordanian case. As a consequence of the Muslim Brotherhood's support for the regime during the 1970 civil war, the Islamists were allowed to further institutionalise their presence in the Kingdom, through the expansion of their network composed of charities, schools and hospitals (Malley, 2004: 191). A crucial role in the establishment of Islamist finance in Jordan was played by the Jordanian economist Sami Hamoud, whose PhD dissertation, published in 1976 'was widely viewed as the most substantial academic piece on Islamic banking that had been written until that time' (Malley, 2004: 192). Sami Hamoud, who was working at the Jordanian National Bank, became a vocal proponent of the creation of an Islamic bank in Jordan, and for this purpose he found support in the Muslim Brotherhood; among his supporters, were Ishaq Farhan, one of the most important leaders of the movement, and the Islamist scholar and leader Sheikh Ibrahim Zaid al-Kilani (Malley, 2004: 193). From these early stages, Hamoud's project attracted the interest of Saudi Arabia's Prince Muhammad al-Faisal and businessman Sheikh Saleh Kamel, considered two of the main advocates of Islamic finance. As Malley (2004: 195) affirms, the meetings regarding the establishment of an Islamic bank in Jordan were attended by several Muslim Brotherhood members, who participated in both the Preparatory Committee and the Founders Committee. Overall, 'the Muslim Brotherhood played a decisive role in providing needed support for the initial establishment of the Jordan Islamic Bank' (Malley, 2004: 207).

Finally, the Jordan Islamic Bank was established on 26 March 1979; the Muslim Brotherhood played an important role in lobbying for its establishment, although throughout its history they took care not to be perceived as too closely connected with it. However, the relationships between Islamic banks and the Islamist private sector is still important, since the latter utilise them for all their financial operations. Moreover, the Jordan Islamic Bank funds charities close to the Muslim Brotherhood, such as the Afaaf Charitable Committee, which provides funding to couples who want to get married but have difficulties in raising the money (Malley, 2004: 208–209).

Despite their social commitments as well as their growth in profitability (Saleh and Zeitun, 2007: 59), the Jordan Islamic Bank, as well as the Arab Islamic Bank, founded in the 1990s, attracted criticism. On the one hand, with regard to the Jordanian case, Malley (2004: 196) affirms that 'the success of such banks gave concrete weight to the assertions of the Islamists that Islam as a religion was suitable for modern times in all aspects of life'. On the other hand, Islamic banks failed, also in Jordan, to fulfil their objectives in terms of development, and attracted criticism for both mismanagement and being only devoted to profit. For example, Saud Abu Mahfudh, a leader of the Brotherhood and editor of *al-Sabeel*, an Islamist newspaper, accused Jordanian Islamic banks of not being really Islamic, since they limit themselves to forbidding *riba* (interest), a necessary but not sufficient condition (Malley, 2004: 199–200). Overall, the emerging debate around 'social failure' of Islamic banking and finance (Asutay, 2012) seems to be a common discourse among Jordanian Islamists as well (Malley, 2004: 200). Islamic banks are often perceived in Jordanian society as having given up the moral economy discourse of Islam in favour of profit, thus accepting the *homo economicus* world view.

In Islamic economics literature, the initial discourse, from the 1940s onwards, sees Islamic economics in the light of development, rather than based on financial definitions of profit (Ahmad, 1980; Chapra, 1985; Chapra, 1992). In an effort to develop an Islamic authentic identity in the economic realm, the founding fathers of Islamic economics, such as Ahmad (1980) and Chapra (1985, 1992) essentialised economic development through the ontology of Islam as a response to the failure of Western inspired developmentalist theories in the Muslim world (Asutay, 2007a: 5). In other words, capitalist and socialist forms of economic development were considered to have failed, because they were based on wrong assumptions about human nature (Asutay, 2007a).

In this effort, Islamic ontology and epistemology provided the norms, but also the operational forms. This paradigm, a nexus of theory and praxis, aimed at constructing, or re-activating, the *homo islamicus*, motivated by religious incentives rather than economic and financial incentives (Asutay, 2007a: 4). Such a systemic nature is guaranteed, within an Islamic economics framework, by the concept of *tawhid* (divine oneness), on which is founded 'a general view of reality, of truth, of the world, of space and time, of human history and destiny' (al-Faruqi, 1992: 10). *Tawhid* is, therefore, the hub of a whole ontology, epistemology and value system that establishes the systemic nature of Islam. Hence, the distinction from conventional economics understanding is through constructing a new individual, at the same time the product and the producer of counter-hegemony, in a Gramscian sense. Hence, the social construction of the individual qua *homo islamicus* is to be read within the systemic framework of Islamic economics. As Asutay (2007a: 5) suggests:

> Islamic economics aims at a world order, where its ontological and epistemological sources, namely the *Qur'an* and *Sunnah*, determine the framework of the economic value system, the operational dimension of the economy and the economic and financial behavioural norms of the individual Muslims.

In other words, Islamic economics aspire to an ethical and philosophical reform (*islah*) of the economic system, as well as of the individual. The context for this reform to be realised is provided by Siddiqi (2004) who affirms that Islamic economics should not only limit itself with static adherence to Islamic rulings as embodied in *fiqh* (Islamic jurisprudence), especially for what concerns the prohibition of *riba* as interest, but adopt a dynamic approach which consists in realising the *maqasid al-shari'a*, the objectives of Islam. To put it differently, Islamic finance should not only be concerned with the form of Islam, i.e. *shari'a* compliancy, but also with its substance, thus implementing the objectives of Islam as a system (Asutay, 2012: 100). Islamic financial institutions, thus, are seen as the 'praxis' realising the 'theory' of Islamic economics, where the nexus between the former and the latter is indivisible.

However, this systemic understanding of Islamic economics was considered to be 'politically motivated' by the regimes in the Muslim world, including in Jordan, and therefore in the mid-1970s a paradigm shift was observed; from Islamic economics discourse to Islamic banking and finance. In other words, since the Islamic alternative was seen as a challenge by the regimes, suspicious of the fact that the Islamists' worldview was rooted in an ontology that considered Islam as a system, Islamic banks opted for political quietism. However, by adopting a collaborative approach with the regimes by locating Islamic banking and finance in the neoliberal economy and neo-classical economics, they also abandoned Islamic economics' plans for social reform.

This suggests that the *homo islamicus* model has been replaced by a hybrid model through the merging between *homo islamicus* and *homo economicus* represented by Islamic banking and finance, which does not necessarily share the aspirations of Islamic economics or Islamic moral economy (Asutay, 2007b: 4–5). Arguably, the problem is that the historically situated development of Islamic banking led to the emergence of financial institutions, which, though formally compliant with *shari'a*, have adopted the ontology, epistemology as well as the value system of *homo economicus*.

It is this cross-fertilisation which can be conceptualised within the framework of the emergence of multiple modernities through Islamic finance (Asutay, 2010). This shift is also parallel to the shift in the strategy of Islamic movements, as instead of developing institutions through a 'top-down model', Islamic banking and finance became an instrument of a 'bottom-up' process of Islamisation. However, the so-called Arab Spring significantly changed this landscape, by opening up new opportunity spaces for Islamist movements, which embraced again a 'top-down' model.

Islamic economics aspires to an Islamic society, regarded as qualitatively different and morally superior to the present one. However, Islamic banks and financial institutions historically developed within the current neoliberal framework. It should not be forgotten that the contemporary interpretation of Islamic norms has been criticised for allegedly hindering economic development in the Muslim world; in particular, the fact that 'healthy economic development entails subordination of all production, exchange and consumption decision to the behavioural norms of Islam' has been challenged by Kuran (1983). This paradigm shift follows the trajectory of evolution of the strategies of the Jordanian Muslim Brotherhood, in the sense of moving from charitable institutions to support the underprivileged, to profit-making private institutions aiming at the middle-class section of the population, such as the Islamic Hospital of Amman. This process may also be observed for what concerns the *Jami'yat al-Rakha* (Businessmen's Prosperity Association) founded in 1997 in the aftermath of a visit to Jordan of the MÜSIAD, the association of Turkey's Islamist businessmen (Malley, 2004: 204–205).

The same dynamics are observed in Islamic banks on the operational level. While Islamic economics *qua* moral economy of Islam aims at creating an economy based on sharing and co-operation, epitomised by contracts such as *mudarabah* and *musharakah*, Islamic banking and finance relates mainly to the prohibition of interest or *riba* in conducting the financial activity in compliance with the forms of *shari'a*, with contracts such as the *murabahah*, whose first mention in the modern literature, parenthetically, seems to be in the PhD dissertation of Sami Hamoud, the pioneer of Islamic banking in Jordan (Kahf, 2004: 33).

Overall, it can be argued that, while Islamic economics refers to the substance, contemporary Islamic finance relates to the form (Asutay, 2012). The transactions of Islamic banks are entirely constructed through the *fiqh* process. They have also essentialised the *shari'a* boards as an overseeing body in the Islamic banks consisting of Islamic scholars, and therefore have institutionalised their impact in relatively secular regimes and financial systems in the Muslim world, such as Jordan. Their emergence and development represent an interesting example of merging between the paradigms of globalisation and Islamisation and of cross-fertilisation between the anthropological models of *homo economicus* and *homo islamicus*. They are the products of processes of articulation of Islamism since, as it has been argued, identity politics played a crucial part in their establishment. Indeed, they need to be read within a broader process of articulation of Islam *qua* system, which took place in the socio-economic sphere since the 1970s, thanks to the opportunity spaces provided by the transformations of political economy. The social construction of an 'authentic' form of living Islam as a system is indeed profoundly related to both political economy factors and the conscious efforts of Islamist social movements to promote social change in the opportunity spaces available. Thus, since the 1970s, a transformation of Islamic consciousness has occurred simultaneously with processes of socioeconomic change. Moreover, the fact that Islamism was allowed to operate within the economic sector contributed to a paradigm shift in the theory and praxis of social movements such as the Muslim Brotherhood of Jordan. This process, which has been defined as a cross-fertilisation between the paradigms of *homo economicus* and *homo islamicus*, has produced hybrid identities; Islamic economics and banking have been at the same time a product and a producer of such a merging. The outcome is an original synthesis of Islamic and capitalistic practices that have developed into a nexus of discursive traditions, which are here conceptualised as 'Islamic modernities' within the broader framework of 'multiple modernities' (Eisenstadt, 2000).

Conclusion

Chapter 1 in this study argued that the rise of Islamism needs to be read in its dialectical links with political economy transformations, while Chapter 2 introduced through the lens of social science the crucial theme of the agency of social movements. The two processes can be observed at play in Jordanian society. Overall, a constructivist approach to the study of social movements helps to understand how Islamism, like all the social movements, is not a 'thing in itself'. In other words, it does not have a nature, in an abstract sense, but it is the product of the actual daily interactions between different social actors, such as, in this case, the Jordanian state and the Muslim Brotherhood.

In Jordan, different trends of Islamism still operate against the background of an official 'political Islam', produced, reproduced and diffused by the

Hashemite monarchy and a pillar of its legitimacy. What may look like two distinct narratives, the official discourse of the monarchy and the Muslim Brotherhood's worldview are actually intertwined, and both appear to attempt to unify heterogeneous ethnic groups and cultures through the frames provided by Islam. Indeed, Islamic symbols have been wisely used to cement Jordanian society, restraining centrifugal drives. Both of the two narratives, it must be noticed, notwithstanding their 'modernity', profoundly overlap with traditional tribal discourses, which are extremely influential in Jordanian society.

Despite the fact that the Hashemite monarchy and the Muslim Brotherhood may seem to articulate two different Islamic discourses, those are not necessarily at odds: the common point between the two narratives is the acknowledgement that Islam constituted the essence, the very fabric of Jordanian identity. At the same time, both these agents actively engage in producing and reproducing Islamic discourses in *fora* such as the schools and the universities. The ideology and the strategy of the Brotherhood coincided, in a first phase, with the imperatives of the Hashemite monarchy. In this phase, the articulation of Islamic frames conducted by the Islamist movement was therefore supportive of the official narrative. Such an endeavour was carried out through the establishment of Islamic social institutions, as well as with the infiltration of state apparatuses. In this period, the ideology and the strategies of the Islamists converged with the state also because the two were expressions of the same social groups. In a second phase, from the 1970s onward, the Brotherhood developed counter-hegemonic features, because it ended up as representing both a new middle class of professionals and growing segments of the Palestinian-Jordanians, who were ever more dissatisfied with state policies. Islamic identities were, therefore, outcomes of these negotiations between social actors, as well as reflecting wider transformations of the political economy. This also explains the emergence, but also transformation, of the idea of Islamic economics and the current reality of Islamic banking and finance, rooted in the interplay between globalisation and Islamisation, as well as between the paradigms of *homo economicus* and *homo islamicus*. Jordan offers, indeed, an interesting case study to observe the articulation of Islamism in the social realm through the establishment of Islamic social activities and businesses in the opportunity spaces provided by political economy. The next chapter will attempt to empirically substantiate the theses of this research.

4 Trajectories of political identity development in Jordan

Introduction

This chapter is concerned with the analysis of the semi-structured interviews and focus groups conducted for this research during the fieldwork in the Hashemite Kingdom of Jordan between June and December 2010. The aim of the fieldwork was to locate the trajectories of Islamic identities in Jordan in terms of identifying their changing patterns, by focusing in particular on the relationships between globalisation and Islamisation. In total, fifteen semi-structured elite interviews were conducted and recorded. The interviews were conducted both in Arabic and in English. The interviewees belong to three different main categories; for the purpose of the analysis they are here labelled as 'Islamists', 'analysts' and 'public figures'. None of the real names of the interviewees will be used here, in order to preserve the privacy of the respondents. The first category, the Islamists, comprises six people who belong to organisations which have, or used to have, close links with the Muslim Brotherhood. Four of them, who will be called here Mustafa, Tareq, Samer and Zaid, are or have been among the most prominent leaders of the Islamic Action Front Party, the political expression of the Muslim Brotherhood. Two of the interviewees, Taher and Amer, are prominent members of organisations established by the Muslim Brotherhood; they, therefore, represent the social activities of the Brotherhood. These six interviewees are all engaged, or at least have been engaged, in the Islamist movement in positions of responsibility. Regarding the second category, it is composed of seven people. They are social, economic and political analysts, whose research focus is on the transformations of contemporary Jordanian society. Two of them, Professor Tawfiq and Professor Khaled, are distinguished academics, economists whose research focuses on the socio-economic transformations of Jordan. Five of them are prominent journalists, researchers and scholars whose research deals with the socio-political situation of Jordan, and in particular with topics such as Islamism and Jordanian identity. The Catholic priest Father Matthew was added to this category. He is the only interviewee who is not Jordanian nor Muslim. However, he lived for a long period in Jordan and could provide an 'external' point of view on the dynamics of Jordanian society, in particular highlighting the extent to which Islamic identities have been changing in recent decades. The third category consists of two public figures of a different kind: Mahmoud is a pop singer, while Professor Hassan is a Muslim scholar and preacher. As for the focus groups, the participants were students or recent graduates of the University of Jordan, who are briefly introduced in the succeeding sections, when their interviews are analysed.

The primary data collected from the interviewees and the focus group are analysed through a narrative method with the objective of developing a narrative to identify the trajectories of identity construction in Jordan. This chapter is divided into four parts: the first section explores the aspirations of participants, focusing on their conceptualisation of Islam as a holistic way of life. This notion is seen as the outcome of processes of social construction of identity, and not as automatically deriving from an alleged essence of Islam. Thus, the second section explores through the perceptions and opinions of the participants the processes of social construction of Islamism in Jordanian society and their relevance in contributing to a transformation of consciousness. The institutions that have been set in place to achieve *homo islamicus* are therefore taken into consideration. *Homo islamicus* is here defined as an individual whose world view and behaviours are imbued with and shaped by Islamic principles; this model differs from the paradigm of *homo economicus* because, while the latter's goal is the maximisation of profit, the objective of the former is assumed to be the adherence to Islamic principles and, as far as socio-economic issues are concerned, the welfare of the community (Asutay, 2007b). In the present research, consistent with the theoretical framework developed in the foundational chapters, the social construction of *homo islamicus* is seen as the goal of Islamist movements. The third section highlights the tensions as well as the cross-fertilisation between the *homo islamicus* and *homo economicus* paradigms. The conclusion analyses the material generated through the interviews against the background developed in the previous chapters.

Islam as a system of life

This section explores the extent to which Islam is often conceptualised by social actors not 'merely' as a religion, in the Western sense, but as an organic system of life, an ideology that encompasses the political, social and economic domains, as theoretically discussed in the foundational chapters. Tareq, who is one of the founders and leaders of the Islamic Action Front Party, sums up this line of reasoning as follows: 'My philosophy of life is that we are created by one God, this God holds all the universe and he created mankind.' These are, in his view, the principles of Islam that should be the cornerstone of the basis on which to reform society, since, for Tareq, 'through Islam we can save our citizens and others'. In Islamism, Islam is seen as bringing salvation to a mankind which is facing tremendous challenges. It can be argued that, for Tareq, globalisation is triggering problems that can be solved exclusively through the adoption of a genuine Islamic framework. The holistic understanding of Islam within the epistemological axiom of *tawhid*, which is a cornerstone of the ideology of the Brotherhood, is clearly highlighted also by Mustafa, one of the most prominent leaders of the Islamic Action Front Party, in relation to politics:

> An Islamic state is a state inspired by the Qur'an and the Sunna and which takes from the other civilisations everything that is in accordance with Islam. Leaders rule on the basis of Islamic principles. Islam is different from Judaism and Christianity. We respect Christians and Jews, but we believe that Islam is the last and final revelation, which develops and improves the previous revelations. Christianity exclusively focuses on the spiritual side, while Islam does not merely deal with faith, but also with the relationships between people and the relationships between rulers and ruled. That is why we think that the principles of Islamic economics are also useful in contemporary society. Islam is a religion, [which has implications for] state, justice, law, culture, civilisation, solution of social and economic problems, in all aspects of life.

The first interesting point consists in Mustafa's selective approach to modernity. Other civilisations should not be rejected; inasmuch as they present features which are in accordance with Islam, these features can be adopted. Moreover, Mustafa stresses that Islam, as the final revelation, completes all previous ones and, while the former were merely focusing on the spiritual side, Islam proposes an all-encompassing world view, which can be described as an 'ideology'. By doing so, Mustafa rationalises the development of an Islamist ideology from Islam as a religion. Mustafa further expands on this and, in justifying his position, he offers the example of the Syrian Christian statesman Faris al-Khouri, who allegedly declared that he used to pray in the church, but that he preferred Islam in the public sphere: 'Christianity lacks a social and economic side, thus some Christians, such as this Syrian politician, were saying: yes, I am Christian, but I want an Islamic economic and social system.' Thus, the message and the position is that Islam is presented as an all encompassing system whose rules can be beneficial also for non-Muslim citizens. When asked how this idea of state should be implemented, Mustafa answered as follows: 'There is a golden principle which says that there is no compulsion in religion. Thus, the path is not compulsion, but *da'wa* [appeal or invitation]. We want each human being to choose his faith, his regime and his rulers.'

The Muslim Brotherhood implemented its *da'wa* through the establishment of Islamic social institutions, as it will be seen in the next section. It is crucial, here, to underline that the concept of *da'wa* in contemporary Islamism goes beyond the actions of the Muslim Brotherhood.

The Jordanian scholar and preacher Professor Hassan seems to epitomise the relevance of the concept of *da'wa* in the process of construction of contemporary Islamic identities in Jordan. Professor Hassan is an Islamic scholar, as well as a popular preacher. From the interview with him, one element clearly emerged: the persuasion that Islam is not 'merely' a religion in the Western sense, but a system, a holistic way of life. The fact that he produces and reproduces ideas that used to characterise the discourse of the Muslim Brotherhood shows to what extent these views are now hegemonic. To begin with, Professor Hassan poignantly reflects:

> How do I define Islam? What is Islam for me? Islam means submission, to submit yourself to the will of your Lord. Islam is for me the final testament revealed by God Almighty, whose proper name is Allah, to mankind. ... This final testament is a full and comprehensive system for life, for every single human being, group, nations, up to the day of Judgement. Islam is designed by God in the following way: Islam is a system that covers all aspects of life including politics, ethics, family money, finance, economics ...

When asked whether Islam can be defined as *din wa dunya* (literally, religious and worldly), Professor Hassan answered as follows:

> Yes, but we don't have a difference between *din* [religion] and *dunya* [world]: the *din* itself is a system of life. The idea of *rijal al-din* [men of religion] and *din wa dunya* came to us from the secular West: it does not exist in our system. The idea of *rijal al-din* came from the Catholic Church: the hierarchy, the clergy does not exist in Islam. The idea of the infallibility of the Pope, the idea of the priests, of the relationship between the Pope and the priests, the Bible in Latin language, who has the right to translate it? Who has the right to interpret it? The idea of secularism comes from XVII century in France: the cut between Church and State, Church and life: this package is completely Christianity, Western made. The whole nature of this issue does not exist in Islam. In Islam we do not have the concept of a church, or a *masjid* [mosque], which used to control some certain things in life, then people came at a certain point and they asked people of the church, or the *masjid*, to disconnect their relationship with the state, or life. Islam is a system of life: it has to say something in state issues and economic issues.

The idea that Islam is a system of life, which involves social, political and economic dimensions, is extremely common in Jordanian society and shared by several of the interviewees who participated in this research. It constitutes the core of the ideology of the Muslim Brotherhood, but it is widespread well beyond the membership of this organisation and extends to the belief system of ordinary practising Muslims. The discussion with the interviewees indicates that secularism is labelled as a 'package' that 'is completely related with Christianity', and thus extraneous to an Islamic world view.

Interestingly, the metaphors from the symbolic world of consumerism are extremely abundant in Professor Hassan's interview. This shows to what extent the imaginary world of global capitalism shapes even the production and reproduction of religious concepts. Professor Hassan offers in the following passage a metaphor, which illustrates to what extent the imaginary world of global capitalism is used to articulate even theological concepts, such as Islam being a way of life.

> Look at Adobe Photoshop: it has to do with Photo Editing. If someone asks: why aren't we able to do word processing with Photoshop? I answer: excuse me, but this program is for photos, by default! By default, Islam is a system of life. A common way of misunderstanding Islam is to read it through Western, secular glasses. ... Those who believe in this system of life believe in the literal divine revelation for mankind until the Day of Judgement. By default, Islam is a globalised and universal system. It is designed as such. From one angle, Islam has an amazing flexibility. From another angle, it has something really stable and solid.

In this passage, both form and content are extremely interesting. From a formal point of view, it is important to notice the extent to which theological concepts that express the 'nature' of Islam are explained through the language of commodities. This passage, therefore, reveals in practice what cross-fertilisation between *homo economicus* and *homo islamicus* means in the sense that, for example Professor Hassan, used the *homo economicus* form with the *homo islamicus* content or substance. From the point of view of the content, Professor Hassan further stresses the features of Islam as a philosophy of life, while secularism is seen as a foreign product, extraneous to the 'nature' of Islam.

The second point that deserves to be highlighted is Professor Hassan's belief that Jordan 'does not represent Islam'.

> Jordan does not represent Islam. I believe there is no Arab country that you can take as a model to represent Islam. It is unfair to accept the idea that there is a country as a whole that represents Islam. We have some good practising Muslims in Jordan, in Syria or elsewhere ... but there is no political state, system, country, where the concept of state represents Islam, not even Saudi Arabia. Most of our laws are secular. This system is applied for individuals and groups, but not at state level.

When pursuing the subsequent question that concerns what is missing in Jordan in order for it to be considered an Islamic country, Professor Hassan's response is as follows:

> The first reference in making laws should be the Islamic law (*shari'a*), which is not the case here. Our constitution states that Islam is the state religion in Jordan but practically speaking Islam is not the main source of

legislation. It is the main [source] just in personal status law, like marriage, divorce, inheritance. For what concerns international law or crime law, Islam is just a minor factor. We are still part of the French system and the British colonial system. ... Jordan is a Muslim country, because 97% of the population is Muslim, but not an Islamic country, because the state does not represent the Islamic system. For example, interest is strictly prohibited in Islam: we have 45 banks in Jordan and 42 of them are dealing with interest. Just three of them do not deal with interest: the Jordan Islamic Bank, Dubai Islamic Bank and the Arab Islamic Bank. This is proof of what I'm saying: the financial system, which is one of the most important systems in Islam, it is based on a non Islamic vision.

Professor Hassan, hence, introduces a crucial epistemic distinction between a 'Muslim' and 'Islamic' country. According to him, a Muslim country is a Muslim majority country, whereas an Islamic country is one where *shari'a* is enforced. Thus, no Muslim country can be defined as Islamic. Broadly speaking, the rift between 'traditional' Islam and Islamism may be established in this identity questioning, especially on issues concerning what a Muslim society is and what an Islamic society is. In this positioning, Islam should not be taken for granted, as part of the landscape of Muslim societies: it constitutes a way of life that should be consciously lived and applied by Muslims. Not only the arguments of the interviewees but also the available discourses identify that, by doing so, a Muslim society can become an Islamic society. This requires a transformation of consciousness. These concepts, which may have had 'radical' and 'revolutionary' implications for Qutb and his followers, are today shared by a preacher such as Professor Hassan, who may be considered as representing a mainstream, 'moderate' trend of Islam. The point is that these ideas and arguments have lost their revolutionary fervour and are today perceived as common sense.

It should also be noted that for the present study, the financial system is singled out by Professor Hassan as the most obvious example of the fact that Jordan is not a Muslim country. A tension between the economic practices of global capitalism and the worldview of Islam as a way of life is identified. Regarding the methods through which an Islamic society should be brought into existence, Professor Hassan's understanding seems to be very close to that of the Muslim Brotherhood, when his views were sought for whether an Islamic society should be built from the bottom-up or from the top-down:

> I am closer to an approach from below. Now most of the people are ignorant of their religion. They hate Islam because they do not understand it. ... It is not about having an Islamic caliph; you need to spread consciousness again, you need to modify the consciousness, you need people to re-understand their Islam, to modify concepts, to fill the gaps in the understanding, you need to be working a lot with the people to bring them back to a clear understanding of their religion.

As can be seen, Professor Hassan favours a bottom-up approach, which has been conceptualised in this study as the attempt to establish Islamic social institutions in order to achieve hegemony. While these aspects will be analysed in the next section, what is significant here is the crucial importance of raising or transforming consciousness. Professor Hassan's position is not political if we intend to define politics in a narrow sense, but it is political in the sense of the production and reproduction of identity politics focused on transformation of consciousness, aimed at reframing Islam as an all-encompassing ideology. In this passage, Professor Hassan seems to share the idea that contemporary Muslim societies live in a state of ignorance (*jahiliyya*), since they do not practise 'real' Islam as a system of life, which should include *shari'a*. This is a common discourse for the Muslim Brotherhood, especially for the trends influenced by the ideas of Qutb.

Professor Hassan further stresses the features of Islam as a philosophy of life:

> Islam is a system of life. A common way of misunderstanding Islam is to read it through Western, secular glasses. ... Those who believe in this system of life believe in the literal divine revelation for mankind until the Day of Judgement. By default, Islam is a globalised and universal system. It is designed as such. From one angle, Islam has an amazing flexibility. From another angle, it has something really stable and solid.

The issue of the transformation of consciousness has been crucial for Islamist thought.

Professor Omar, a political analyst and a former Islamist, identifies the emergence of Qutbism as signalling a watershed in Islamic identity, especially for what concerns the crucial theme of consciousness. Professor Hassan's emphasis on the 'transformation of consciousness' reveals the centrality of the process of re-Islamisation *qua* articulation, which has been suggested at the beginning of this book. Re-islamisation may therefore be conceptualised as a re-articulation of frames pertaining to the symbolic worlds of Islam with the goal of making them hegemonic through the transformation of consciousness. However, it is not anymore only the Brotherhood that have this goal. When asked specifically about his opinion on the Muslim Brotherhood, Professor Hassan asserts that no Islamic group has the right to declare itself the only true representatives of Islam. Interestingly for this research, Professor Hassan acknowledges that the most important difference between the Muslim Brotherhood and other Islamic groups is the fact that they are involved in the political and social aspects, while Sufi, for example, focus on the spiritual dimension, neglecting society and politics. In other words, they do not intend Islam as a system.

Another important aspect of the perceptions of social actors concerns the extent to which participants identify Islam with concepts such as rationality, while criticising the West for not being able to control its irrational, negative drives. It is argued here that the identification of Islam with rationality is an important trajectory of the social construction of Islamic modernity. The focus group discussion with students at the University of Jordan was useful in shedding light on this aspect. A member of the focus group, whom we will call here Mariam, was a student at the Faculty of Modern Languages at the University of Jordan. She is of Palestinian descent, has lived for a long period in the West and does not wear *hijab*. Mariam was interviewed with a student whom we will call here Dara, who is also a Jordanian of Palestinian descent, but who wears a *hijab*. What follows is an excerpt of our conversation concerning the meaning of 'freedom', where Mariam and Dara articulate the concept according to which Islam provides the foundations to establish a truly human society.

MARIAM: The point is freedom from what? Do you want to be free from your parents, from the boundaries of society? Would a person be happy after that in the end? Freedom in my opinion, freedom in Islam is the ability to be able to think responsibly in a way that would benefit yourself and those around you.

DARA: I am free and I can do everything that I want but I cannot get drunk because religion told me that it's not acceptable. There should be a balance between my needs, my religion and me.

MARIAM: What would happen to you as a human being if you get drunk? How would you start behaving? Would that behaviour dehumanise you? Would that make you less of a human being? That's the concept of Islam. When you look at people who get drunk or take drugs... they look embarrassing, they look disgusting. The beauty of Islam is in the concept that you as a human being have to keep that dignity that God gave you as a human being. That's why smoking dope is wrong. Is that freedom? We don't need that freedom.

When she was asked during the focus group discussion whether she witnessed what she described as 'dehumanising behaviour' while she was in the West, she responded as follows:

MARIAM: I did, you can see homeless in the streets, and there is a bottle next to them ...
DARA: And they sleep next to rubbish bags ...
MARIAM: Even among people you know, there are people you see and think: I don't want to be like them, falling over the table.
RESEARCHER: Did witnessing these things have an impact on you?
MARIAM: Yes, I witnessed the dehumanisation of the person. God gave me dignity and I am supposed to preserve that dignity.

In developing the conversation, she was asked whether she has seen such risks in Jordan as well, and her response was as follows.

MARIAM: In Jordan, I'm sure it does exist, we all have friends and we hear these things, but to see it first hand, just once or twice at a wedding ... but no, not like in the States.

DARA: It's not just about the religion, people are afraid of being seen and judged, being labelled as drunk men ... it's not just a matter of religion, but of social pressure.

As the excerpts from the discussion and conversation indicate, Mariam articulates a dichotomy between Arab-Islamic society, seen as 'human', and Western society, seen as potentially 'dehumanising'. In this discourse and articulation, hence, globalisation is considered a potential threat to Islamic and Arab values: it becomes potentially harmful since it introduces a conception of total freedom whose intrinsic individualism threatens family and society. 'Drunkenness' is clearly identified as a dehumanising behaviour that constitutes a threat for society; 'drunkenness', and the loss of control associated with it, also appears as a powerful metaphor of the negative side of a limitless freedom that is associated with the West. On the contrary, Islam is seen as providing limits that allow mankind to preserve its dignity. In psychological terms, in this articulation, the West is deemed incapable of controlling irrational, subconscious drives that threaten to destroy social harmony. Islam may be assimilated into a mature and rational Freudian *ego*, able to control the social fabric by preventing the unleashing of the dark side. Interestingly, the interviewees in this research reverse the Western Enlightenment epistemology, which tended to depict religion as the domain of the irrational, as opposed to a secular society built on rational principles. In fact, in the discourse of the participants, Islam is constantly associated with concepts such as control, maturity and rationality, while the Western concept of freedom is described as a limitless freedom, which easily becomes licence and excess, in very different fields, such as morality, politics and economy.

It would be unfair, however, to claim that the West as such is identified by Mariam with Freud's irrational *id*; rather, the problem of the West is that it does not know how to fully control these irrational 'subconscious' drives, while Islam can provide that knowledge by showing the 'right path' (*al-sirat al-mustaqeem*) and, as argued, provides a moral filter to help the individual to correct the action that may be beyond acceptable criteria or can be seen as 'dehumanising'. That is another reason to argue that the ideal embodied by the *homo islamicus*, as seen by the interviewees, is intrinsically 'modern' by Western standards, since it embodies the very ideals that the emancipatory project of the Enlightenment claimed to represent, although these ideals are expressed through the adoption of Islamic frames. Thus, multiple modernities should be considered to explain such hybrid identities through processes of convergence and re-negotiation. For example, Mariam's polarisation between the 'dignity' of human beings that is threatened by 'dehumanisation' recalls crucial themes of 'humanistic' and 'enlightened' thought: the path to emancipation coincides with reason, like in Western thought, but here reason is identified with Islam.

The essentialisation of distinctions is also important to highlight. For example, Mariam, who has spent long periods of time in the West, affirms that she 'does not want to be like them', clearly identifying Arabs and Muslims as 'us' and Westerners as 'them'. As Mariam explained, during her stay in the West, she 'witnessed the dehumanisation of the person'. Her awareness of the alleged de-humanising sides of Western civilisation has arguably been crucial in her process of identity construction as a 'modern Muslim'. In other words, Mariam claims that the social and moral problems that she witnessed in the USA prove that the risk is that globalisation may bring to Jordan a freedom that 'we don't need'. For her and her fellow Jordanians, that freedom is therefore not real freedom, but only the excess and licence associated with the unleashing of the dark, irrational side of human nature, which leads to moral, social and economic harm.

In conclusion, as the discussion from interviews and focus groups related to this section identifies, Islam is framed not only as an organic way of life, but as a rational and 'modern' one. Thus, the following observations may be gauged from a discourse analysis of the material examined. The answers of the respondents appear to suggest that Islam offers to contemporary Muslims a way to live in the modern world without experiencing the sense of exile and dehumanisation which, according to them, seem to afflict Westerners. True freedom appears to be a freedom exerted within the boundaries of Islam; when freedom trespasses these limits, it becomes a form of licence which debases human beings. But, in order for Islam to exert this influence on mankind, it should not be lived merely as a set of moral principles, but as an organic system, as Professor Hassan suggests. Islam appears, therefore, as a project which still needs to be implemented in contemporary society. The fact that this persuasion is so widespread, as is maintained here, in Jordanian society, arguably reveals the success of the project of the Muslim Brotherhood, the socio-political movement which largely contributed to the revival of this line of reasoning not only in Jordan, but in the whole Arab world and beyond. At the same time, it is noteworthy that this message, this 'substance', is expressed in forms that are largely pervaded by the language and the symbolic universe of contemporary globalisation, to the extent that processes of cross-fertilisation between the Islamic and the globalised can be observed. Islamism, here seen as a world view, therefore seems to adhere to the allegedly humanistic and enlightened agenda of Western modernity, while, at the same time, claiming that this project has been Islamic since its origin, being rooted in God's revelation to mankind. Thus, an important difference between Western modernity and Islamism is that, while the project of Western modernity is yet to be realised, though the progress of history is tending to its realisation, the project of Islamism claims to have been already achieved in the lifetime of the Prophet Muhammad and of the first generation of Muslims who followed his example. They are seen as having built a community that based on values and principles that allowed mankind to live in a rational and human way, while at the same time preventing them from falling prey to the base tendencies of the human soul. On the contrary, Western modernity, despite its huge achievements in terms of material and technological advancement, is not seen as providing the necessary moral filter to prevent the unleashing of moral and social harm. Thus, the only way of being truly human, rational and modern, according to the respondents, seems to be living the Islamic experience in its authenticity and in its fullness.

Developing this debate, the next section analyses the links between Islam *qua* philosophy of life and the need to establish institutions in order to put this ideology into practice. It is one of the arguments of this research that the conception of Islam as an ideology is the outcome of modern processes of social construction, which will be analysed at a later stage.

Processes of re-Islamisation: constructing the *homo islamicus*

After discussing the nature of Islam and Islamism, as well as how Islamism is perceived in Jordanian society through the articulation of the participants, this section investigates how Islamic movements have been engaged in producing *homo islamicus* and in creating institutions, which have attempted to establish an Islamic 'moral community' throughout recent Jordanian history. Consistent with the theoretical background that informs this study, this chapter also attempts to assess the validity of the concept of counter-hegemony, testing whether the notion of 'war of position' can be useful in conceptualising the efforts of the Islamic social movements to promote their values in Jordanian society. The establishment of the Islamic Action Front Party is seen by the Muslim Brotherhood as their attempt to pursue, in their words, 'reform' in the political domain. This concept of reform needs to be understood within the context of the holistic vision of Islam explored in the previous section.

The foundation of Jordan

It would obviously be misleading to state that the Islamic character of Jordanian society is a result of the actions of the Muslim Brotherhood. What this research claims is not that the Islamic identity of Jordan is a new phenomenon, rather that Jordanian Islamic identities underwent a remarkable process of transformation, of re-framing, in recent decades. As is known, identities are not considered constant, but rather alive and changing, parallel to the social actors' incessant production and reproduction of them through processes of negotiation and re-negotiation. One of the interviewees of this study, the political analyst Professor Omar, stresses that the founder of Jordan used Islamic frames as part of his discourse in legitimising the establishment of the Hashemite Kingdom of Jordan:

> King Abdullah,[1] as he wrote in his book about the history of the establishment of Jordan, saw Islam as a main part of his state, but his state was not a religious state. He defined his state as Islamic and moderate at

the same time. It was not a *khilafa* [caliphate], but Islam was a part of it. So, Jordan state has been established on Islamic identity, but it is different from Saudi Arabia or Iran, it is like Turkey, Malaysia or Pakistan. ... King Abdullah, the founder of Jordan, saw Islam as an important factor, but he did not see Jordan as a religious state. He didn't look at himself as a religious leader, even if he was from *Ahl al-Bayt* [the family of the Prophet].

King Abdullah's Jordan was a country where Islam was certainly one of the main ontological sources of identity, although it was not an 'Islamic state'. Here, the difference between a Muslim and an Islamic society as articulated by Professor Hassan appears meaningful. In line with this, the present study argues that Jordanian Islamic identities have been undergoing profound transformations also because of the re-framing of Islam conducted by the Brotherhood, a process which is here labelled, following Ismail (2006: 2), 're-Islamisation'. At the time of King Abdullah, the world view of the Muslim Brotherhood, namely Islamism, was, according to Professor Omar, compatible with the official narrative.

King Abdullah, the founder of the state, thought that his vision was compatible with the ideas of the Muslim Brotherhood, which was operating in Egypt. He received many of its leaders, who were coming from Egypt. Hasan al-Banna did not personally meet him, but they exchanged letters. When the Muslim Brotherhood visited Jordan, in the 1930s, King Abdallah received them here in Amman and felt that their ideologies and vision were compatible. Hasan al-Banna sent a letter to King Abdallah, thanking him for the warm receiving of the Muslim Brotherhood in Jordan and he wished them they could work together: the Brotherhood engaging in social activities, the King as ruler. There was an integration between the two projects. The Muslim Brotherhood had been established in Jordan in 1945. The King sent one of his advisors, Abd al-Munim al-Rifa'i [who later became Prime Minister], the brother of the grandfather of the current Prime Minister.

For Professor Omar, there were therefore two projects: the project of the Brotherhood and the project of the monarchy, which were different, but close enough to allow a co-operation between the regime and the Islamists. In particular, as Professor Omar underlines, both the monarchy and the Islamists had a common enemy: the leftist forces, and Nasser in particular.

Zaid is an influential leader of the Islamic Action Front Party, and he is often considered as a hard-liner. According to him, the Arab and Islamic identity is at the core of Jordan, since the very foundation of the Jordanian state in 1921. He thinks that the relationship between the Muslim Brotherhood and the regime was good from 1945 to 1985, mainly due to the fact that both of them were countering leftist forces. In the light of Professor Omar's understanding, it may therefore be inadequate to define as counter-hegemonic the praxis of the Brotherhood at that time. The novelty took place, according to Professor Omar, between the end of the 1960s and the beginning of the 1970s; in this phase, the narratives of the Brotherhood started to diverge, leading to an open rift in the 1980s and 1990s. In this respect, Professor Omar describes an event which he deems a 'revolution without guns'.

> This was a great revolution, a revolution without guns. I remember I was a child at that time. I remember when the mosques were empty, just old people were going to church. In the middle of the 1970s, just old people were going to mosque. There were not so many mosques like nowadays. In the 1970s, there were about 400 or 500 mosques [in Jordan], now they are about 6000. In 1991, there were 1000 mosques. From the middle of the 1970s till the end of the 1980s the most of the young people who were going to mosque were Muslim Brothers or *salafi*. Now, most of the people who go to mosque are not Muslim Brothers nor *salafi*, but ordinary people. They are not organised by Islamic parties or movements. … I remember, in this university [of Jordan], in the 1970s there were no *hijabs* not even one.

The 'great revolution' Professor Omar is talking about is the process of Islamisation, which has been conceptualised in this study as the Islamists' quest for hegemony over Jordanian society. The Jordan of his childhood, which Professor Omar describes, is rather similar to contemporary European society, where religious attendance is in decline. The Muslim Brotherhood managed to reverse this trend, promoting a process of 'Islamic awakening', which influenced several aspects of Jordanian society. Proliferation of mosques and increased religious attendance are considered among the most visible signs of this process of re-Islamisation of Jordanian society.

This process of re-Islamisation, however, has coincided with a radicalisation of Islamist ideology. Several factors have contributed, in Professor Omar's view, to this outcome. Firstly, the confrontation in Egypt between the Muslim Brotherhood and the Nasserite regime led to the emergence of a radical trend of Islamism such as Qutbism.

> Throughout the decades, the Muslim Brotherhood developed and changed. In the 1940s and 1950s, they were different from now. Their vision, at the time, was very similar with King Abdullah's, they mainly saw Islam as a heritage. There wasn't a gap between their vision and the political system, in Jordan or in the Arab countries. The difference began at the end of the 1960s, with Sayyid Qutb. Qutb changed Islamic movements worldwide. Before Sayyid Qutb, Islamic movements and Muslim Brotherhood were considering themselves as part of the political system and the social system.

Professor Omar described the transformation of the ideology of the Muslim Brotherhood from a 'conservative' understanding of Islam to a 'revolutionary' one; McAdam (1999) would have called it the development of 'insurgent consciousness'. In Jordan, the old guard of the Muslim Brotherhood was loyal to the regime and was feeling part of Jordanian society, while the new guard, influenced by Qutb, started thinking that Muslim societies were living in a state of ignorance (*jahiliyya*) and that it was necessary for authentic Muslims to react against this decadence. Professor Omar, therefore, highlights a crucial metamorphosis of the consciousness of significant segments of the Islamist movements. This break, which happened in the 1970s during the cold war period in the international system, has had lasting consequences both on Jordanian society and on the Muslim Brotherhood itself.

Regarding current divisions, the political analyst Marouf states:

> Most of the hawks are Palestinians and most of the moderates are Jordanians, and there is mixing among the two groups. But this is the majority here, and this is the majority here. And the discourse of the hawks focuses on Palestinian issues, while the discourse of the reformers focuses on Jordanian issues.

The radicalisation *qua* 'Palestinisation' of the Brotherhood is a process which has been particularly emphasised, in literature, by Bar (1998). In particular, as it will be seen later, the Brotherhood is still split between conservative and radical trends, although the Jordanian media discourse of a rift between 'hawks' and 'doves' does not always capture the complexity of the Brotherhood's topography.

According to Professor Omar, this metamorphosis in the Islamist representation of themselves coincided with 'a religious wave', that is to say a process that allegedly involved all major world religions. Another major factor was the defeat of Nasser by Israel and the interrelated intensification of the Palestinian question, which had a specifically remarkable impact on Jordanian society, following the relocation of hundreds of thousands of refugees from Palestine. In particular, the latter factor elicited an identity crisis in Jordanian society, which involved the Islamist movement. As Professor Omar affirms:

> The problem started since the end of the 1960s. The Muslim Brotherhood started to question themselves and their ideology and to change their view regarding the political system, considering it not Islamic. Before the end of the 1960s, the Muslim Brotherhood was not asking: 'Who are we? Who are they?', because it was considering itself as being the same with the political system. There was no difference in ideology or in religion. By then, they started to rename themselves and to see themselves as differently from other people, especially from the governments. Some movements, such as Takfir or al-Jihad, saw themselves as different form society. The Muslim Brotherhood was mainly seeing themselves as different from the political system. ... This [the defeat against Israel] triggered a series of questions, such as: 'Who are we? What do we need? What was the problem?'.

> The main answer was that we had lost Islam and we need to go back to Islam to have back our power. This defeat encouraged this feeling of going back to heritage and Islam to get back our power and unity against Israel.

This transformation of the Islamist consciousness therefore happened because of wider social and political phenomena. However, the alliance between the regime and the Muslim Brotherhood had not broken, since they both still had common enemies: leftist forces and Palestinian irredentism. When asked what the attitude of the Jordanian regime towards the Brotherhood was, while Professor Omar was a young Islamist activist, he answered:

> It was a complicated situation. There had been a civil war at the beginning of the 1970s between the state and Palestinian movements [Black September]. By the end of the 1960s, society and state were divided between the PLO and the political establishment. When the Palestinian organisations were defeated and kicked out of Jordan, the political system needed a new political partner to replace the PLO and Fatah, and found it in the Islamic movement. So, they encouraged the Islamic movements to be the new leader or the new umbrella of the Jordanian Palestinians. The Prime Minister Wasfi al-Tal at the time found in the Muslim Brotherhood the new suitable umbrella for the Palestinian people, also given the Islamic awakening. The alliance with the Islamists was seen as a support both inside and outside. This is a point: so there was an alliance between the political system and the Islamists. But at the same time the political system was careful regarding this new wave of extremism, new wave of Islamic behaviour, new wave of Islamic thinking. The political leadership felt that these Islamists were not the traditional Islamists of the 1950s and 1960s. But at the same time the political system needed the Islamists against Palestinian organisations, leftists and communists. So by the middle and the end of 1980s, the political system changed its partnership, felt that it didn't need the Islamists as before. They became a strong power, more than the political system wanted.

In the 1970s, on the one hand, the regime still needed the Muslim Brotherhood to counter their common enemies, but on the other hand, the state was aware of the deep on-going changes within the Brotherhood. Throughout the 1970s, the Islamists became more assertive, persuaded as they were that history was on their side.

> The *hijab* began from the 1970s, we started to control the student councils, the professional associations. We felt we were developing. Also the Islamic revolution gave us a boost. After the Iranian revolution, there have been many Islamic revolutions in other Islamic countries, but they

failed, such as in Algeria, in Saudi Arabia, in Egypt, in Afghanistan, in Pakistan. There were Islamic revolutions in many countries, and Islamic parties in Turkey, with Erbakan, and of course in Jordan. There was a strong feeling that the atmosphere was changing.

It is in the 1980s that, once leftism and Palestinian irredentism inside Jordan had been weakened, Islamism started being perceived as a threat by the regime. By then, the Muslim Brotherhood was already controlling vast sectors of civil society. However, according to Professor Omar, this very Islamisation, which was the goal of the Muslim Brotherhood, happened to such a degree that it left the Islamist movement displaced.

In reflecting on the performance of the Brotherhood, Professor Omar was asked, since the goal of the Muslim Brothers was to Islamise society, and this goal has been reached, what their projection of the future was. In this regard, Professor Omar's response was as follows:

> It's the end. In history, when you reach your goal, you are finished ... States and organisations need new goals. If they don't create new goals, they finish. This means the end of the MB, because they didn't create new goals. From the 1920s and 1930s, when they have been established, their goal was Islamisation. Now they reached a level of Islamisation which is bigger than what they could aim or imagine ...

Moreover, he states:

> I think Islamic movements are finished. Their goal was Islamisation, they reached their goal. It is happened now. What will they do next? There is no need for Islamic movements now.

According to Professor Omar, the Islamist movement continued talking about Islamisation without defining what Islamisation means, which resulted in Professor Omar rethinking his political stances. In the end, he left the Brotherhood and later on he abandoned Islamism as an ideology, because he had changed his world view. His scepticism towards Islamism is summed up in his question: 'They say that Islam is the answer, but what's the question?' However, Professor Omar recognises the important transformations of Jordanian Islamic identity, which have taken place since the 1970s, identifying in the Muslim Brotherhood an important player in the process. In one response, Professor Omar seemed to emphasise the role of political economy at the expense of the agency of the Islamists. It is therefore interesting to compare his analysis with that of Samer, one of the most influential politicians in the history of the Muslim Brotherhood. When interviewed, Samer stressed to the contrary the conscious role played by the Islamist movement in this transformation. He has arguably been one of the most important organisers of Islamist hegemony over Jordanian society. As both Gramsci and al-Banna, Samer identified in education a crucial field in order to transform the consciousness of Jordanians, to 'awaken' them to a deeper understanding of Islam.

Islamic social institutions: institutionalising counter-hegemony

A crucial aspect of the present research concerns the role played by the Islamic social institutions of the Muslim Brotherhood in the social construction of contemporary Islamic identities in Jordan. Interviewees such as Taher, who held at the time of the interview a position of responsibility at the Islamic Centre Charity, and Amer, who held a position of responsibility at the Islamic Hospital, strongly emphasised to what extent Islamic social institutions such as the Islamic Centre Charity and the Islamic Hospital, both established by the Muslim Brotherhood, have contributed to the social development of the country. While the goal of the Islamic Centre Charity was to provide a vast array of welfare services to the underprivileged, the Islamic Hospital was not a charitable institution; and while the representatives of both the institutions were proud of their Islamic inspiration, they affirmed the institutions would deliver services to Muslims and non-Muslims alike. It is also worth mentioning that both institutions, at the time of the interview, officially had no more formal ties with the Brotherhood.

Political analyst Marouf reconstructs the ties of the Islamist movement with these institutions, as well as the actions of the government to take over Islamic social institutions from the Muslim Brotherhood:

> The Brotherhood used to be very strong in social networks, such as the Islamic Charity Center, Zarqa Private University. What happened between 2006 and 2008 [the government takeover] and what has been the impact on the movement, which does not control anymore a social network. It is true, the Islamic Centre was the social and economic hand of the Brotherhood. It was very important to communicate with people, to do economic work. In 2006, the regime began to think: how should we decrease the power of the Brotherhood, given the results of Hamas in the 2006 elections? When the regime here saw the results of Hamas in 2006, their very big victory they were afraid of the desire of the Brotherhood to have the same results. They began to think how to decrease their power and how can we have a guarantee that they will not benefit from their money in the elections? It's like I cut your hand, cut your leg, cut your foot, but keep you alive to decrease your strength. This is what is behind the government's strategy. Many people, the enemies of the Brotherhood, advised the government about the fact that 60–70% of the power of the Brotherhood depended on the Islamic Centre and social welfare. ... Of course the Brotherhood has been affected by this situation. It is not just the Islamic Centre, it is also the Islamic private university at Zarqa. They [the government] took it in a soft way. Supporting persons against the Brotherhood and playing in the shadow to convince people to... (phone rings). They

took the private university in a soft way, supporting some people in the shadow to take this university...
Did they buy it?
They supported rich people to buy it, to take it away from the Brotherhood in a soft way. But my opinion is that the Brotherhood has been affected, but not in a strong way. Why? First, the strong body inside the Islamic Centre is still there. They are working and they are active. They [the government] changed the administration, but they did not change the body. That does not mean anything, maybe the only important issue is that the Brotherhood lost one billion.
So the Brotherhood used to control 1 billion Jordanian Dinars?
Yes. The Brotherhood lost this. But on the technical level their people are still strongly working in the Islamic Centre and they strongly benefit from their contact with people. For what concerns the Zarqa Private University, the new owners fired the people of the Brotherhood and hired new staff. So they don't have power there.

The role of the Muslim Brotherhood in establishing these institutions was not denied by the leaders of the Islamist political movement. Tareq, among the founders of the Islamic Action Front Party and influential Islamist politician, recognises the importance of establishing institutions in order to spread Islamic values in society, thus solving the problems of contemporary society. When discussing the institutionalisation of Islam in Jordan, the Islamic bank emerged as an important part of the institutionalisation. About the establishment of Islamic banks in Jordan, Tareq stated that:

The Muslim Brothers did not establish this Islamic bank [the Jordan Islamic Bank], some other people established it. Anyway, they supported that. We would like to start building institutions based on this religion which saves all people, according to our principles. Our principles state not to use *riba*, because God forbade it.

An example of other successful Islamic social institutions is, according to Tareq, the charity al-Afaf. Al-Afaf helps poor people to get married, lending money without using *riba*. According to Tareq, also the Islamic Centre Charity was established in 1963 to help poor people and orphans. Islamic social institutions, thus, appear as a concrete response towards the solution of contemporary social challenges. The reaction of the government against the Islamic social institutions, however, has been motivated by their desire 'to cut the roots of the Islamists in the society', as they considered these as an alternative system. According to Tareq, 'The government said: why are the Muslim Brothers strong in this country, what do they have? They have schools, universities, the Islamic Centre Charity; let's close them down to make them weak.'

Also Mustafa, one of the most prominent leaders of the Islamic Action Front Party, attributes a core importance to the Islamic social institutions, the network through which counter-hegemony is constructed. In discussing the role of Islamic social institutions established by the Muslim Brotherhood, such as the Islamic Centre Charity and the Islamic Hospital, Mustafa stated that:

> We established universities, schools, charities, as means of reform: educational reform, cultural reform, social reform, for co-operation among people, to have doctors with the right moral principles, nurses with right moral principles and the results have all been very positive. But the government was worried: instead of helping and supporting this experiment, the government took control of it, fired the old employees and hired new ones. Both this sides, the moral side and the support to people, have been lost.

The concept of reform seems to assume great relevance in the discourse of the Muslim Brotherhood; this reform may be conceptualised as the creation of a counter-hegemonic power through the establishment of institutions. Reform is also seen as being at the core of the establishment of the IAFP, as Tareq affirms:

> After the 1989 elections, for the 11th Parliament, ... we found that we were facing a lot of things, political, social, educational, and we found ourselves that we have to face all the new challenges in society, and that we have to work actively in this field to meet the needs of the people. We thought we had to share other citizens in our programme for reform, and we thought of forming a front, a wide front, to accept all kinds of people who would like to work for reform, Muslims and not Muslims. So we decided to create the Islamic Action Front Party. ... That means co-operation of all people, not just Muslim Brotherhood people, but all the people, to work for specific national objectives for reform.

The goal of the IAFP was to articulate the project of the Muslim Brotherhood in a specific setting, by overcoming its limits. Also the establishment of Islamic social institutions is identified as a crucial endeavour for the Brotherhood to carry out reform. Interesting also are Tareq's views about the rift that took place between the Brotherhood and the regime. Mustafa is persuaded that the relationships between the Muslim Brotherhood and the Jordanian regime worsened after the Iraqi war of 1991, when the USA opted for a stronger role in the Middle East, and after the 1991 Madrid Conference and the subsequent Wadi Araba peace agreement between Jordan and Israel of 1994. According to Mustafa, that peace cannot be accepted because it is unjust; moreover, that peace agreement compromised the democratic process in Jordan, since it strained the relationships between the Parliament, seen as the true representative of the Jordanian people, and the government. In fact, while the government signed the peace agreement of Wadi Araba, Parliament opposed it. The relationships, termed as 'symbiotic' by Boulby (1999: 1), between the Muslim Brotherhood and the regime ended, for Mustafa, because of the initiative of the government. The crackdown of the regime against Islamic social institutions, therefore, appears to be a consequence of this crisis.

This narrative is shared by Zaid, according to whom, since the failure of socialism on a global scale, the Islamists have started to become too powerful. The Islamist victory in the 1989 elections demonstrated the power of the Brotherhood in Jordanian society. Then, the 1994 Wadi Araba peace agreement further strained their relationships, which became even more complicated after the 11th September 2011. The biennium 2006–2007 was also difficult for the relationship between the regime and the Islamists, since the Muslim Brotherhood lost control of the Islamic Centre Charity. According to Zaid, the marginalisation of the Muslim Brotherhood, pursued by the Jordanian government in accordance with the USA, led to the radicalisation of some Islamist groups, leading to the emergence and strengthening of the Salafi and al-Qaeda types of groups. It is not a coincidence that several interviewees underlined the need to involve the IAFP, the political wing of the Brotherhood, in the political process.

The centrality of Islamic social institutions established by the Brotherhood, such as the Islamic Centre Charity and the Islamic Hospital, clearly appears also in Professor Hassan's view:

> I think they are one of the best attempts to present an Islamic model. They have a lot of shortcomings, but they are still an excellent attempt. For example, the Society for the Preservation of the Quran has 750 branches in Jordan. It teaches Islam, the Quran, Islamic teachings and morals. The state is not able to do this. In the Arab world, when you mention the state, people have no trust. Because there is no government that represents the people, because you do not have real elections.

Remarkably for the present research, Professor Hassan compared the positive model of the Islamic social institutions with the negative model of the Arab state. In particular, Professor Hassan underlined the fact that Islamic social institutions such as the 'Society for the Preservation of the Quran' provide religious and moral education, while the state fails to do that. Thus, the development of Islamic social institutions is rationalised and justified through the failure of the state. In other words, it emerges as the contraposition between the embryo of an Islamic society, represented by the attempts of the Islamic social institutions, and Arab states that are incapable of gaining the trust of their citizens as they fail to represent their citizens.

Professor Hassan, in his responses during the interview session, echoes many of the core issues of the Muslim Brotherhood. He uses the language and the themes of the Brotherhood; however, he cannot be considered as a Muslim Brother or as an opposition figure. Rather, his interview shows to what extent the discourse of the Muslim Brotherhood has become hegemonic to the point that a mainstream Islamic scholar and public figure adopts it. However, even if this discourse, counter-hegemonic with respect to the state has now become hegemonic among Islamic groups and in various segments of Jordanian society, the Muslim Brotherhood is not perceived any more as the collective subject, as the 'vanguard', which can bring into existence a truly Islamic society. Nevertheless, Professor Hassan shares the discourse of the Islamic alternative to the shortcomings of the Arab state, a narrative whose socio-economic grounding has been previously analysed in this study.

It should be noted that the process of re-Islamisation is interestingly often described as 'reform' (*islah*). Both the party and Islamic social institutions are seen as working together, in their different roles and responsibilities, towards *islah*. Zaid effectively summarises the division of the role, within the Islamist movement, between the party and Islamic social institutions when he argued that:

> The political side of the Muslim Brotherhood is the party, through which they participate to political life. For what concerns social work, there are associations such as the Islamic Centre Charity and the Islamic Hospital.

The term 'reform', which is commonly used by Islamist activists and leaders to describe their final goal, is a particularly dense concept in the discourse of Islamists. Asked about the establishment of the IAFP, the political wing of the Muslim Brotherhood, Tareq declared that: 'Our main political goal was, therefore, reform. ... Reform in all aspects of life: social, political, educational. Because change covers all kind of activities in society.'

In their discourse, reform is the word chosen to describe an all-encompassing transformation of present society: all aspects of life and all kind of activities need to be reformed through the creation of *homo islamicus*. That is why the project of the Muslim Brotherhood can truly be characterised as 'counter-hegemonic', since it aims at an organic, molecular transformation of present society by creating its Islamic alternative through laying the foundation of such a society, in other words by establishing its foundations through the establishment of social institutions. It may be argued that the declared goal of the Brotherhood is not merely to seize power or to make limited changes to Jordanian society, but to reform it in all of its aspects to move from the state of *jahilliyah* to the state of 'knowing' or *homo islamicus*.

The goal of the IAFP is indeed, according to them, an organic reform of society. For Zaid, an influential leader of the IAFP, the objective of the party is 'a complete economic, social and economic programme [whose] objective is a real democratic reform, a real democratic life, so that the voice of the people will be represented in the Parliament'. Zaid affirms that:

> We believe that the people, the *ummah*, the community is the real source of power, and that is not implemented in today's society [since] real power is in the hands of the government which does not represent the will of the people.

For Zaid, reform means both implementing the Jordanian constitution, and at the same time amending it according to the norms of the future society to be built. According to him, boycotting the elections, as happened in 2010, is intended to send a message: 'the boycott is a way to say: elections do not represent the will of the people'. In fact, in his opinion, in Jordan 'there is no political competition, but a tribal competition'. The way out is, for Zaid, to establish a great coalition with all the other oppositional forces to reform the electoral law. It should be noted that he is considered by many a 'hawk', a representative of the pro-Hamas, hard-line faction of the Brotherhood. Interestingly, his discourse stresses the need for democratic reforms, in order to overcome the tribal features of Jordanian society.

Also for Tareq, one of the main Islamist leaders, the main goal of the IAFP is reform, which should involve all aspects of society. The task of the IAFP, therefore, is to articulate the Islamist project of reform in the political domain, in order to implement its programme of all-inclusive reform of the society. In his words, 'our goal is to start from Islamic principles in order to raise people towards good things'. In line with this vision, education should raise children according to these principles, by spreading the idea that all humans have been created by one God, and hence referring to the *tawhidi* epistemology of Islamism. Hence, the goal of Islamist politics, according to Tareq, is to administrate according to the Islamic 'philosophy of life'. In his words:

> Politics in Arabic means administration, to administrate according to clear objectives, and reform should aim towards reaching these objectives. This is politics, and politics should not be separated from dealing with your lives according to these objectives. ... Some aspects are social, educational and so on, but politics means to administrate your daily life according to your philosophy of life, to your national or human objectives.

Islam is, therefore, as has been already seen in the articulation of the Jordanian Muslim Brotherhood, conceptualised as a holistic 'philosophy of life' that should not only direct and shape the daily life of the individuals but also the administration of society as a whole.

This section has analysed the historical process through which Islamists have been realising their hegemony over Jordanian society by initially developing it as counter-hegemony. The next part focuses on the question of the emergence of Islamic modernities, seen as the outcome of a dialectics between the paradigms of *homo islamicus*, which the Brotherhood contributed to construct through its institutions, and of *homo economicus*. 'Islamic modernities' suggests the emergence of multiple or hybrid modernities, as the modern is re-created through the ontological and epistemological sources of Islam.

The emergence of multiple modernities through the cross-fertilisation between the *homo economicus* and *homo islamicus* paradigms

According to Massad, Jordanian society, like many other post-colonial societies, is shaped by the colonial 'dyad of modernisation and tradition' (2001:

50). In other words, the construction of the Jordanian self is shaped by categories regarding what constitutes the 'other', both externally and internally. Even though Islamic frames are widely used to make sense of the social world, the epistemology that informs Jordanians' narratives is to a large extent informed by Western discourses about 'modernity', as the outcomes of everyday life according to Islam are interpreted as modern by definition. This implies, again by definition, the concept of 'multiple modernities'. The focus groups with Jordanian students helped to highlight to what extent these categories are still relevant in the everyday life of educated Jordanians. In fact, this 'dyad of modernisation and tradition' appears to be still shaping the symbolic universe of Jordanians. However, this dichotomy is reinterpreted in an original way, through the refusal to relegate 'Islam' to 'tradition'. It is, therefore, possible to witness a creative process of cross-fertilisation between Western epistemologies and Islamic frames, which may be termed multiple modernities (Eisenstadt, 2000; Göle, 2000).

The student whom we will call here Hamza is a young graduate, who defined himself as an Islamist. He claims to have been participating in the activities of the Muslim Brotherhood's group at the University, although he does not consider himself as a member of the movement. He claims to be very religious. Latif is a student with Western-Jordanian background, and he is a native speaker of both English and Arabic. Dara, as we already have seen, is a student of Foreign Languages at the Jordan University, who wears a *hijab* and adopts a conservative dress-code. The following excerpt of a conversation between three students (Dara, Latif and Hamza) and the researcher well illustrates the permanence of Massad's 'dyad of modernisation and tradition'.

DARA: I live in Eastern Amman, in a traditional [conservative] neighbourhood.
LATIF: If we talk about neighbourhoods in Western Amman, they are high class. They have different thinking, they don't go by the tradition. You can do whatever you want.
RESEARCHER: How would you define the differences between Eastern and Western Amman?
LATIF: There are huge differences.
RESEARCHER: Do you agree with the fact that a girl cannot go out alone at a certain time?
LATIF: Forget about this AM/PM thing ... in Amman you can go wherever you want. She might say this, but she's not going to do it. Right?
DARA: Of course.
RESEARCHER: Dara, do you agree that it's not good for a girl to go out alone?
DARA: Yes.
RESEARCHER: So it's not an imposition from outside, but something you agree with?
DARA: Yes.
LATIF: It's all about tradition, not about being afraid.
DARA: If I was afraid, I wouldn't talk with you.

LATIF: If you go to certain areas in the west and south of Jordan, it's so much different ... like Karak, Tafilah.
RESEARCHER: Why?
DARA: Because they are Bedouins.
LATIF: Not Bedouins ... They have strict traditions. If you do this, you get an X on you ... while Amman is modern.
RESEARCHER: What do you mean by modern?
LATIF: For me, Jordanian boys and girls are like Australian boys and girls.
RESEARCHER: So, Australia is not more modern than Jordan?
LATIF: No, maybe Jordan is more modern than Australia.
(General laughter)
RESEARCHER: What do you refer to?
LATIF: Maybe in the culture ... It [Jordan] is so close to European culture, Australian culture and American culture ... Because most of the Jordanians these days live in America, Canada and Europe and most of them are starting to move back to Jordan. That's why it's changing.

This debate shows to what extent Massad's 'dyad of modernity and tradition' shapes their imaginary. First, the dyad shapes their space: Eastern Amman belongs to 'tradition', while Western Amman belongs to 'modernity'. Dara comes from Eastern Amman, while Latif comes from Western Amman. Both of them seem to accept the symbolic order that collocates the first in the realm of tradition, and the second in the realm of modernity. Hamza portrays himself as 'modern'; Dara accepts her identification with tradition. Hamza says that Western Amman is characterised by 'different thinking' and that there 'you can do whatever you want'. The 'modern West', a West, which indicates both Western Amman and Western civilisation at large, is again primarily characterised by 'freedom'. However, Dara, who is of Palestinian origin, distances herself from the 'Bedouins' who live in the west and the south of Jordan. It should be noted that the Bedouins still inhabit a primordial space that is opposed to the 'modern' Amman. Following Massad's suggestion, we can here notice the extent to which the Western epistemology of modernity builds on a traditional Arab dichotomy between *hadari* and *badawi*, which is to say between urbanites and nomads. This epistemology draws a clear distinction also between men and women, who inhabit different times (modernity vs. tradition) and spaces (public vs. private life). As Dara states, she fully agrees with this value system. Interestingly, Latif provocatively affirms that Jordan is 'more modern' than Australia: and it is modern because 'it's so close to the European culture, the Australian culture and the American culture'. This cross-fertilisation happens, according to Latif, because Jordanian immigrants in the West are 'starting to come back', therefore bringing Western culture to Jordan. Paradoxically, as argued, Jordan may therefore be more modern than Australia, but it is so because it is influenced by Western culture. However, this does not go without criticism, and the following excerpt shows to what extent Hamza, Latif and Dara criticise those who blindly accept Western 'modernity':

HAMZA: My brother just came back from the US and told me: I'm not going back! There is something wrong there ... He didn't see a family. He went there and told me: I wish I saw there one normal family: wife, husband, boys and girls. Someone was living with his girlfriend for 25 years, but not married ... come on, get married! She said: why should I get married to him and share fifty-fifty with him?

LATIF: It's all about money!

RESEARCHER: Can we describe your approach as a selective attitude towards modernity?

HAMZA: Yes, you should select.

LATIF: You cannot say that we select ... sometimes we select, sometimes we don't. We do have clubs, we do have bars, we have all these things. But they are limited, *mahduda*.

HAMZA: For me, it's wrong to be there in the first place, but for the government it's ok, so we can't do so much.

LATIF: Yeah, the government allows it. It's up to you, if you want to go, you go.

HAMZA: Even if the bar isn't there, still people will make their way to drink alcohol, they won't stop. But why to promote it? Maybe a good guy gets invited by a friend, and then he becomes a bad guy, a drunkard, an alcoholic.

LATIF: In Jordan, you can do whatever you want. But it's up to you, to your conscience, because we are Muslims.

RESEARCHER: Are you practising Muslims?

LATIF: Yes, but even if you are not practising, it doesn't mean that you have the right to go there. Basically, it's up to you. Nobody is going to tell you: don't go, stop.

RESEARCHER: In your view, people who go there, are they giving up part of their identity, trying to be something that they are not?

LATIF, HAMZA: Yes.

LATIF: They don't understand everything around us. For example, especially when we talk about bars and clubs: they see them in the movies, they want to do like the movie stars. Go to the bar, drink some whisky, go dancing, disco, with some girls ...

RESEARCHER: Is there an influence of the media, trying to change Jordanian society?

HAMZA: They are trying to copy Western culture ...

LATIF: Copying without thinking ... Blind imitation!

HAMZA: Yes, it is a blind imitation because they don't know what they are doing. Latif and I are practising Muslim, but most of them are not practising. They are generally irreligious.

As Hamza points out, 'there is something wrong', in the West, as the West is seen as threatening Islamic societies with its influence. As argued, there is, therefore, a dark side of modernity, which emerges when freedom is not limited. 'Real' freedom needs to be *mahduda* (limited, bounded). The argument goes on in stating that Jordanians, hence, lose themselves when they try to 'blindly imitate' the other. For the participants of the focus group, Western modernity is fascinating but dangerous, while the Islamic way is seen as human, rational and reassuring. They see that some elements of Western modernity can be critically accepted, others need to be discarded. Those who go to bars and clubs are seen as Westernised, as colonised: such an assumption rests on an essentialised view of Arabs and Muslims, who are not supposed to adopt such a lifestyle, which is seen as intrinsically 'foreign'.

As the discussion indicates, all the participants in the interviews and the focus groups reject associating Islam with 'tradition'. On the contrary, they claim, in different forms, it is possible to live a life which is at the same time Islamic, modern, rational and truly human, therefore challenging the colonial assumption, which relegates religion to the spheres of tradition and irrationality. Islam is seen as the embodiment of tradition, but also as the way through which contemporary Islamic societies can gain access to modernity.

The discourse on Islamic modernity is often articulated in reference to a 'golden age' of Islam. Tareq affirms that the reactivation of the 'golden age' of Islam stands at the very core of the socio-political ideology of the Muslim Brotherhood. Asked about the goal of the IAFP, he significantly starts with a historical anecdote. He affirms that the private library of the caliph al-Hakim II, who reigned over al-Andalus (in Southern Spain) between 961 and 975, numbered 60,000 volumes, while the library of Paris, the largest in the West, had at the time merely 9,000 books. As Tareq affirms, 'we were the top of the whole world'. As Asutay (2009) affirms:

> Islamism, hence, introduces modern to the world of Islam, but with a different time orientation; as, unlike modernity, the ideal is not conceived in the future-oriented terms requiring validation by the progressive forces of history, but expressed in the past.

Such a discourse is extremely common in Jordanian society. The present, which is conceptualised as characterised by backwardness and subjection to the West, is compared to a glorious past in which Islamic society, identified with 'we', was 'the top of the whole world'. Thus, as expressed, the original sin of Muslim societies, which led to their exclusion from the garden of Eden of the golden age, has been their abandonment of 'authentic' Islam. Jordanians, therefore, seem to share the dichotomy according to which the West is 'modern' and Muslim societies are 'traditional', but they refuse the colonial narratives that attribute an alleged 'backwardness' to Islam. The Islamic 'awakening', hence, is seen as the key that can re-activate an authentic Islamic modernity. The West is envied and admired for its wealth and technical progress, but also associated with a sort of 'limitless freedom' that threatens its civilisation from the social, economic and moral points of view.

Tareq learned about the library of the caliph when he was in the USA. The re-discovery of the greatness of Islamic civilisation while being in the West is a very common experience among the participants in the interviewees of this research. In other words, acquiring awareness of the prominence of Islam is often connected with an experience of 'exile'. The word 'exile' is here employed both metaphorically and non-metaphorically. It is employed metaphorically because our interviewees come from privileged backgrounds, having lived in the West to study for their Masters or PhDs. However, it is probably not entirely coincidental that all of them are Jordanian citizens of Palestinian descent, and therefore have an experience of forced 'exile' in their family history.

In addition, several among the interviewees gained awareness of their roots, origins and spiritual heritage while living abroad in the West. Living abroad, they had to question their identity and they rediscovered the meaning of being Muslims. This topic is crucially relevant to the research question constructed in this study, since it highlights processes of construction of the 'Islamic self'. This process is very common among the interviewees of this study, but in each case it provoked a different answer. The story of the pop singer Mahmoud is a very interesting prism through which processes of social construction of identity can be gauged.

The interview with Mahmoud took place at the Muslim Brotherhood headquarters in an elegant street of Western Amman. He was wearing an elegant suite and spoke perfect English with an American accent. The interview took place in the attic of the building. Mahmoud lived in Saudi Arabia for ten years, he also lived and studied in the USA. At a certain point, he decided to go back to Jordan, to pursue a musical career there. However, he affirms that his main reason for returning to Jordan was the fact that he was missing his family, after several years abroad. He, thus, decided to re-prioritise his life, after having understood that the most important thing in his life was his family, i.e. his parents and his two brothers. To try to pursue his musical career in Jordan was his secondary priority, and he viewed it as a 'gamble'. He rediscovered the importance of family while he was in the USA. What is interesting about Mahmoud is his successful attempt to portray himself as both 'cool', in a Western sense, and 'pious'. Indeed, during the interview he defines himself as 'a Western pop singer with the values of Islam inside' and a practising Muslim.

As he admits, the inspiration, which triggered his musical quest came from his religious education in Saudi Arabia.

> We were praying every day, as part of school. There were five different classes of Islam, such as the teachings of Muhammad, the reading of the Quran, the actual memorising of the Quran. So, the principles and fundamentals of Islam were really engrained from an early age for me. ... One of the first songs I ever wrote was my own melody while reading the Quran ... I was reading the Quran in my own melody, in my own special way ... that is one of the first melodies I came up with. This very much influenced my song-writing.

Mahmoud explains the extent to which, by living in the USA, he discovered the importance of his 'roots', a term which he uses to speak about his family, his country, his religion and his values.

> My roots ... these are things you can't forget. When you are raised in a country like this, families are always very much involved in your life. At times it can get really frustrating, and you really want your privacy; but if you look at the other end of the spectrum you are completely independent and let alone. This world can be really a lonely planet. ... You can get lost, you can forget your values and who you are and what you stand for and what your principles are. Everything you do during the day relates to your principles and if you make one bad move it can really get you in serious troubles. It's good to have that sense of fear, or like that sense of someone watching over you so you know to correct yourself or you know not to get yourself into any troubles and to continue striving to gain their acceptance and to be sure they are always proud of you ... it's as plain as day that I come from an Arab country, so it is not that I can hide and pretend that I am completely American. Part of it, it is accepting who you are, but also being proud of it and telling people what you stand for, even though the popular opinion might be against you. It is very important that you stand your ground.

On the one hand, he clearly highlights the risk of 'getting lost... total independence indeed leads you to discover that this world can be really a lonely planet'. While Mariam, a student participant in this study, emphasised the dimensions of Western freedom as excess, licence and 'drunkenness', Mahmoud stressed the fact that complete independence ends up coinciding with loneliness and being uprooted. Arab-Islamic societies, with the importance they give to families, provide the individual with a web of relations, which prevent the individual from experiencing loneliness. Interestingly, Mahmoud and Mariam, who are both educated, belong to a high social background and spent years in the West, articulate the same dichotomy, while stressing different aspects of the question. Mahmoud consciously formulates his idea of 'Islamic modernity', while affirming:

> I want people to know that we are not a bunch of terrorists. We are just like everyone else, we love to go to school, we love to get educated, we love our families, we love to work, to build our careers. This is what the new world is about: independence but not forgetting your roots, always striving to improve your life, so that you can pass it down to your generations.

Mahmoud's depiction of 'what the new world is about' presents several reasons of interest. First, the fact that this world is defined as 'new' suggests that Mahmoud is talking about the contemporary, globalised world. It is difficult not to notice, in his words, the formulation of a sort of 'Calvinistic' ethic, which is consistent with Islamic values. Even his 'striving to improve your life' may simultaneously allude to the necessity of improving one's morals and of pursuing one's career. On the basis of what the singer had said before, it is clear that he identifies in globalisation the risk of making people forget their roots: it is therefore essential to find a balance between independence and rootedness.

It is common for the interviewees to conceptualise globalisation as, at the same time, an opportunity and a threat. Among the Muslim Brotherhood, both Mustafa and Zaid articulated the relationships between globalisation and Islam in an interesting manner. On globalisation, Mustafa states:

> Islamic *da'wa* [appeal, invitation] is a global appeal. Men and women of different languages have been created in order for them to know each other. However, contemporary globalisation has colonial goals. In particular, we think that globalisation has two goals: to impose American culture on the world and to impose American economy in the world. Small enterprises have to submit to the big enterprises, and get expelled. We do not share these American goals; that is why this globalisation is problematic. We have no problems with foreign enterprises, as long as they do not endanger our workers and industries.

For Mustafa, who seems to share the universalistic claim of modernity, globalisation is not intrinsically bad; Islam itself is a global faith. What is criticisable is the specific historical development of contemporary globalisation, which is seen as having colonial objectives. There is no prejudicial hostility towards capitalism, as long as competition is fair. Concerning globalisation, Zaid affirms:

> There is no society in the world which is not influenced by globalisation. You are influenced by it, but you influence it at the same time. It has negative impacts, but positive too, and it presents opportunities as well. It shortened distances and made communication easier.

Zaid, thus, stresses what has been here conceptualised as a dialectical approach to globalisation: it is not that globalisation unilaterally determines society, since social actors can influence it at the same time. It is in this sense that the relationships between globalisation and Islamisation have here been defined as 'dialectical'. Zaid also affirms that the adoption of the capitalistic model widened the gap between rich and poor, in stating that 'the Islamic economic system is a complete system which provides solutions in all aspects, while socialism failed, capitalism is failing; the Islamic model is the successful one'. The Islamic system, hence, is seen as the best one, able to overcome the shortcomings of the secular economic systems, because of its holistic approach.

The clash between the paradigms of homo economicus and *homo islamicus* is also highlighted by Professor Khaled, who affirms:

Jordan is certainly becoming more integrated with other economies in the world, its is becoming more open, more globalised and more liberalised and that sometimes is happening at the expense of the traditional Islamic values and practises, which are becoming less strict. Globalisation and economic development means different consumption habits, business environment habits, values ... this is also reflected in people's behaviour and way of thinking. I can see that clearly in Ramadan. Ramadan traditionally used to be strictly for religious duties, spiritual things and people were strictly obeying their spiritual duties. Now, with globalisation, people are emphasising more materialistic things, such as consumption, they are focusing a lot on meals after fasting ... Meat consumption during Ramadan trebles, and the price of most of food commodities increases during Ramadan. People are less committed to their religious duties and their lifestyle becomes more materialistic and Westernised. They go to restaurants, they go together men and women and these phenomena increase as we become more globalised. Some people call it modernisation. ... Sometimes they accept things that may not be 100% consistent with Islamic rules. ... They mix modern values and traditions, and this is sometimes causing confusion. For example, a girl is wearing *hijab* and very tight jeans... and this is not permitted, but this is very common. ... People pray and fast but, outside the mosque, they forget it and go back to their modern life. Religious things are there but they are not guiding and affecting people very strongly.

Thus, Professor Khaled underlines the threat posed by globalisation, and by its world view, on Islamic societies, whose moral fabric is endangered. So, the holy month of fasting, Ramadan, risks becoming a period of conspicuous consumption; in the same way, wearing *hijab* may cease to be a sign of modesty and piety, and become an object of fashion, since *hijab* can also be worn together with tight jeans, which are considered to be immodest. Thus, Professor Khaled envisages the risk of Islam remaining as a mere façade, the 'form', where the 'substance' is un-Islamic. Professor Khaled renews in his argument worries about globalisation that seem to be shared by many interviewees, and by the respondents to the survey questionnaire, as we will see in the next chapter.

This point has been further expanded by Professor Tawfiq, an economist, who, when interviewed, stated that the real clash is not between *homo economicus* and *homo islamicus*, but within Western civilisation itself. In his view, *homo islamicus* is not a social construction, but the anthropological model that describes mankind as it was created by God; on the contrary, it is the *homo economicus* model which is unnatural, and socially constructed by Western civilisation. Thus, elaborating on that, it can be argued that it is this clash between human nature (i.e. *homo islamicus*) and a false anthropological model imposed on mankind which causes social harm and imbalances, within the West and, because of the pervasiveness of globalisation, also in Muslim societies. The conclusions of Professor Tawfiq are interesting inasmuch as they challenge the assumption that *homo islamicus* is a model socially constructed by Islamic movements, by affirming that this paradigm defines authentic human nature.

However, political analyst Marouf seems to imply that this clash between the two paradigms is now deeply affecting the Muslim Brotherhood itself, when he states:

> People already began to search for new kind of Islamisation. The institutions, the schools, the universities of the Brotherhood became boring to many people inside the Brotherhood and to customers. For example, Dar al-Arqam [a private school controlled by the Brotherhood] it's a school inside the Brotherhood. Dar al-Arqam is going down, so they search for a new kind of Islamic school. Also the Brotherhood people looked that they didn't personally benefit from the Islamic school, because it is owned by the Brotherhood. They want their personal interest. So they began to go in the economic activity outside the Islamic Centre, to establish new institutions, private. They have the same project, Islamic project, but without the direct control by the Brotherhood. They are independent, but owned by the members of the Brotherhood ... Many small trade offices, many Hajj organisers, many businesses. ... So now the Brotherhood has other activities ... with other mentality in control ... because it's now private, so they are now searching to have wealth, to have money, but with people from the Brotherhood, with Islamic spirit. This is why the Brotherhood has not been affected so much by this strategy [he is referring to the Islamic Centre takeover by the government]. The Brotherhood already went from the social ground to the political ground. In the 1970s, 1980s and 1990s the Brotherhood depended so much on the Islamic Centre, hospitals, voluntary work, red Crescent, schools, mosques, they depended on these social networks to recruit people, to preach and have their discourse in the society.

In other words, it could be argued, the Muslim Brotherhood abandoned the project of establishing Islamic social institutions which provided welfare services in order to generate the *homo islamicus*. Instead, wealthy members of the Brotherhood establish for-profit Islamic institutions, by wielding Islamic inspiration with profits. Thus, it seems that the 'overpowering of *homo islamicus* by *homo economicus*' (Asutay, 2007b) is taking place within the very organisation that acted for decades as the Islamist vanguard. Marouf explicitly acknowledges that this shift took place because of the impact of globalisation on Jordanian society and on the Islamist movement itself.

As this research suggests, the articulation of Islamic modernities needs to be viewed against the background of social and economic transformation. In particular, the construction of the paradigm of the *homo islamicus* has provided an answer to the perceived shortcomings of the paradigm of the *homo economicus*. The notion of *homo islamicus* is deeply related to the social construction of an authentic Islamic modernity. The concept of 'Islamic modernity' is nurtured by the idea of Islam as a 'middle way'. If the students Hamza, Dara and Latif mainly underline the social and moral risks derived from the unleashing of the dark side of the modernisation process, Professor Tawfiq applies these concepts to the economic sphere. Following the thought of the founding fathers of Islamic economics, such as Umer Chapra, Professor Tawfiq affirms, with regard to economic freedom, that 'complete freedom is like chaos ... Islam calls always for a middle position'.

It is, therefore, argued that, in a true Islamic society, the financial system should be Islamic. When asked whether Islamic banks should be considered 'really' Islamic considering that there is an observed scepticism over their Islamicity, Professor Hassan introduces a crucial distinction.

> To the best of my knowledge, I consider them Islamic, with some restrictions. The term 'Islamic' has more than one aspect: Islamic in terms of the practical teachings and applications of the financial transactions and Islamic in terms of the full package of applications. It is true that they are not dealing with the interest system and they are doing their best to apply the shari'a law. ... In Islam, the goal of money is to be a means of transaction to help people to solve their problems, not to make multi-millionaires from the people who keep on accumulating money without risk, just putting their money in 100% guaranteed projects. In Islam we have the *mudarabah*, a partnership between bank and people. Some Islamic banks do not apply these parts of the whole Islamic vision. ... They do it because we live in non Islamic states, people are cheating and lying, the banks are afraid, they think that none will protect them, so they take precautions and they stay in the corner. On the one hand, their reaction is justified because they have no backing, no support, because we are in a non Islamic society, so they want to protect themselves. On one angle, they are Islamic; but if you mean the general spirit of Islam, they are not.

Existing Islamic banks based their Islamic credentials on their alleged avoidance of *riba*, identified as interest. In other words, their 'form', or *shari'a* compliancy, fulfils the narrow definition of Islamic banks. On the other hand, if we embrace a wider perspective, or substance, taking into consideration the *maqasid al-shari'a* (objectives of *shari'a*), the Islamicness of Islamic banks may be challenged. Thus, 'form' versus 'substance' constitutes the nature of the debate (Asutay, 2012).

Beyond this internal debate on the Islamicness of Islamic finance, Islamic finance interestingly represents one of the terrains where the paradigms of *homo islamicus* and of *homo economicus* meet and cross-fertilise with each other generating Islamic modernity, for Islam, and multiple modernities in general. Moreover, the contending definitions of 'Islamicness' confront each other, allowing contemporary Jordanian Muslims to exert their individual *micro-ijtihad*, namely re-interpretation of Quranic injunctions in everyday life according to the realities rather than entirely relying on the injunctions of *shari'a* scholars. In relation to this, the following is a discussion between Mariam and Dara regarding Islamic banking upon the question directed to them asking for their opinions and whether they have accounts with Islamic banks.

RESEARCHER: What do you think of Islamic banks? Do you have an account with them?
MARIAM: Yes, I do have an account with an Islamic bank. Even if I could get a significant interest with a conventional bank, I would rather not get that money. I do not want to get involved in *riba*. Moreover, they may put my money in things I don't want to be involved with.
DARA: What can make you sure?
MARIAM: At least I can wash my hands clean from the fact that my money is not involved in something I wouldn't accept. At least, my hands are clean.
DARA: I can put my money in any bank, but I don't want to get any interest out my savings. *Riba* is a big problem. I think conventional and Islamic banks are the same. They just use different names, such as *murabaha*.
MARIAM: No, there is a difference.
DARA: My friend wanted to buy a house which costs 26.000. The Islamic bank bought it for him for 40.000 ...
MARIAM: And how much would he have paid paying interest to a conventional bank?
DARA: I don't know. Anyway, you can't trust them 100%.
MARIAM: At least, you are sure that they are not funding ... I don't know what.

For both Mariam and Dara, the avoidance of dealing with *riba* is of crucial importance. Islamic frames inform their views on how to engage with the banking system. However, their *micro-ijtihad* leads them to act in very different ways. Mariam is convinced that, since she has an account with an Islamic bank, her 'hands are clean'. On the contrary, Dara is convinced that there is no real difference between Islamic and conventional banks. The lack of a universally agreed norm of what constitutes the 'right way' to deal with the banking system leads Mariam and Dara to elaborate different answers, which both claim to be authentically Islamic. If by 'modernity' we imply an emancipatory project that empowers the individual, then contemporary Jordanian Muslims are engaged in processes of construction of 'Islamic modernities', since their quest for Islamicness is shaped by individual choices through *micro-ijtihad*. It is precisely in this individualisation of religion that an important feature of the social construction of Islamic modernities can be identified.

On the whole, in contemporary Jordan, the symbolic universe of Islam provides frames through which social actors express their aspirations and frustrations. Such an adoption of Islamic frames is common throughout different social strata and ethnic groups. Jordanian society appears to be profoundly permeated by Islamic world views, although Islamic frames are articulated in different ways. 'Islamism' and its institutional forms, therefore, appear not merely as a political phenomenon, but as a language in which social actors articulate their desires and structure their existences, producing and reproducing their social lives.

Conclusion

This chapter has analysed the interviews and the focus group discussions conducted during the fieldwork in Jordan, with the aim of assessing the research questions of this study. At this stage, a few points need to be highlighted. First the belief according to which Islam is not a religion, in the Western meaning, but a whole system of life appears rather widespread. This process is here conceptualised as the social construction of Islam as an ideology. The Muslim Brotherhood can be considered a collective social actor that greatly contributed to this process of social construction. This endeavour has been mainly carried out through the establishment by the Brotherhood of a network of Islamic social institutions that played a major role in transforming Islamic identities in Jordan. This process of social construction has been greatly influenced by the relationships of the Muslim Brotherhood with the regime, as well as by the political economy.

Regarding the first point, the Muslim Brotherhood may be described as a movement that aimed at hegemony over Jordanian society by creating a counter-hegemony. The attitude of the Brotherhood has been at times supportive of the government, at times confrontational. The social construction of Islamic identities in Jordan has been greatly influenced by the relationships between these two, sometimes overlapping, networks of institutions. As far as the second point is concerned, the movement seems to have been greatly influenced by the globalisation process, which also had an impact on Islamic identities. A model which combines the paradigms of *homo economicus* and *homo islamicus* seems to be the construction of the contemporary Muslim individual in Jordan, suggesting a bi-directional causality between Islam and modernity and Islam and globalisation. On the whole, Islamic modernities appear to be the outcome of interdependences between economic forces and cultural practices. The notion of Islamic modernities can be used to conceptualise an ongoing cross-fertilisation between different and often contrasting approaches to modernity.

Massad (2001: 80) illustrated, following Jürgen Habermas' conceptualisation, the extent to which the categories of 'modernity', which is associated with 'civil society', and 'tradition', which is related to the 'private sphere', shape Middle Eastern symbolic universes. According to Massad (2001: 80), while the dichotomy between *hadar* and *badiyah*, which divides settled and nomadic populations, has characterised Arab symbolic universes for centuries, 'their new significations of modern versus traditional resulted from their integration into the nation-state's modern epistemology of space'. This dichotomy is, for example, significant with reference as to how men are located in the modern public sphere, while women are still seen as primarily belonging to the private sphere; similarly, the urban population embodies the modern, while the Bedouins embody traditions. Along similar lines, Palestinians see themselves as the most dynamic and modern part of society, while Transjordanians are associated by them with tradition. In line with this, in Jordan, Amman is seen as the modern space par excellence, while the rural areas belong to tradition. Furthermore, within Amman, the poor slums of Eastern Amman are associated with tradition, while Western Amman, with its shopping malls and skyscrapers, is connected with modernity. Thus, this dichotomy between modernity and tradition still shapes the imagination of Jordanians.

It should be noted that this Westernised epistemology of modernity was introduced in the Middle East, according to Massad (2001), at the time of the Ottoman *Tanzimat* or reform. This dichotomy still shapes the life worlds of contemporary Jordanians. Interestingly the spatial dyad dimension also concerns the dichotomy between 'Islam' and the 'West'. The 'modern' West is in fact constructed as the 'significant other': it is seen, at the same time, as an object of attraction but also repulsion. From the point of view of time, the dichotomy is between the contemporary, Westernised, age and the 'golden age' of Islam. It is interesting to observe to what extent the language of Islam merges with the epistemology of modernity to structure space and time. Several of the interviewees who participated in this research, as discussed so far, had developed an identification between Western modernity and unlimited freedom, where the latter is associated with chaos and it seems to be closely linked with the Islamic concept of *fitna*. Thus, Western influences are seen, on the one hand, as potentially modernising and emancipatory, but on the other hand as threatening and potentially destructive. What is interesting is that this perception of the West as 'chaos', as the place where traditional values and categories are subverted, is very common among people, and also scholars, who have lived and studied in the West. In their reflections, the West is essentialised and criticised, but also dialectically overcome through the articulation of a distinctive 'Islamic alternative', seen as a truly rational and human model. Such an Islamic alternative is not seen in opposition with the Western model, but as its sublimation, and hence it may be conceptualised in a multiple-modernities understanding. The Islamic alternative, by addressing the shortcomings of the Western model, allows contemporary Muslims to formulate their own dynamic and polymorphic projects of Islamic modernities.

Social actors are critical inasmuch as they denounce with equal vigour 'blind imitation' of tradition and of the West. They visualise a society where the emancipatory project of Islam and the emancipatory project of modernity find a harmonic synthesis. According to the debate, it is not that Islam needs to be modernised or that modernity needs to be Islamised: Islam is already modern. Modernity is seen as something that can potentially free Arab societies from un-Islamic 'traditions', allowing them to re-discover the kernel of the emancipatory project of Islam. That is why the dichotomy between modernity and Islam, which permeates Western colonialist discourses, but also Arab (and Turkish) nationalistic discourses, seems to be utterly extraneous to the symbolic universe of contemporary Jordanians. In this understanding, Islam is not merely regarded as a tradition or heritage that needs to be preserved, but rather as the authentic path to modernity that needs to be realised through the use of reason within the historical experience.

This new version of the articulated modernity is a modernity that is perceived as human and it is opposed to the dehumanising features intrinsic to Western modernity, according to which, Western modernity is not rejected, but critically scrutinised, out of the persuasion that modernity, when not limited by Islam, risks to unleash its negative aspects, threatening the very foundations Arab societies are based upon. Therefore, Islam is not seen as opposed to modernity: on the contrary, Islam, in contemporary Islamism, allows modernity to be sustainable, through the correction of its imbalances by providing a moral filter.

In this process of construction of Islamic modernity leading to multiple modernities, processes of identity construction take place through the articulation of dichotomies that are permeated by Western ideas of modernity and are expressed through Islamic frames.

In this context, hence, it is argued here that the dialectics between *homo economicus* and *homo islamicus* can be singled out as one of the major features of the emergence of Islamic modernities.

Note

1 Abdullah the First, Amir of Transjordan (1921–1949) and then King of Jordan (1949–1951). Followed by Talal (1951–1952), Hussein (1952–1999) and Abdullah II.

5 The social construction of contemporary Islamic identities
The case of Jordan

Introduction

Following the exploration of the interviews and focus groups, the objective of the present chapter is to offer a theoretically informed interpretative discussion of the results of this study, on the basis of the arguments put forth in the first part of this book. This is expected to further contextualise the findings in the larger body of literature.

This discussion chapter attempts to answer the research question of this study, which consists of assessing to what extent contemporary Islamic identities in Jordan have been influenced by processes of Islamisation and globalisation, seen in their dialectical relationships. The hypothesis of this research is that an interpretive connection can be proposed between these two processes, and that the interaction between them played a major role in shaping contemporary Islamic identities. Firstly, answering this question means to gauge whether the crisis of the development model of the Arab state has been a factor in the social construction of Islamism as an alternative. Moreover, this very development of Islamism has been related to wider transformations in the modes of global capitalistic production. It is in this sense that the rise of Islamism has been linked with processes of globalisation and emergence of new social classes.

Global capitalism and Islamism seem to be inspired by two antithetical conceptions of human anthropology, which may be termed as *homo economicus* and *homo islamicus*. However, the present analysis shows to what extent these two paradigms are intermingled, converging through re-negotiation processes sustained by social agents. It is this very process of hybridisation through the social practices of the agents that may offer the analytical categories useful to conceptualise the emergence of 'Islamic modernities' in relation to Islam and Muslim societies, but also the emergence of multiple or hybrid modernities as opposed to the universalist, hierarchical and unitarian claims of 'modernity'. In particular, three themes are developed in this chapter.

Firstly, the conceptualisation of Islamism as an originally counter-hegemonic discursive articulation that is now largely hegemonic in Jordanian society. From a theoretical point of view, this point also implies a critical discussion on whether the theoretical framework proposed in the foundational chapters of this study has proved adequate to conceptualise the subject matter. Secondly, the extent to which Islamist worldviews merged and cross-fertilised with globalised worldviews is examined. Such an argument is explored as a consequence of the persuasion that it can contribute to the theoretical debate on the relationship between economy and culture. Thirdly, the degree to which the findings of this study can contribute to the debate on the concept of multiple modernities and in particular on distinct forms of Islamic modernities is questioned.

The articulation of Islamism in Jordanian society

This study suggests that the development of the identity politics of Islamist movements has been shaped by socio-economic transformations, such as the crisis of the Arab state and globalisation. In this respect, this study challenges essentialistic readings of Islam. As Talal Asad (1986: 10–11) has argued:

> We shall then write not about an essential Islamic social structure, but about historical formations in the Middle East whose elements are never fully integrated, and never bounded by the geographical limits of 'the Middle East.' It is too often forgotten that 'the world of Islam' is a concept for organizing historical narratives, not the name for a self-contained collective agent.

Thus, in the present work, the study of the historical formations has been located in a precise context, out of the theoretically informed persuasion that processes of re-discovery and re-invention of identity, aimed at constructing 'authentic' forms of these identities, express a dialectical reaction to the crisis of the Arab state and the challenges of globalisation. This hypothesis is not meant to undermine the agency of Islamists *qua* social actors, but to locate their actions in their context. As Marx famously argued: 'Men make their own history, but they do not make it just as they please: they do not make it under circumstances chosen by themselves, but under circumstances directly encountered, given and transmitted from the past' (Marx, 1994: 188). In particular, this study has argued that, in the context of the crisis of the Arab state, the Muslim Brotherhood of Jordan consciously pursued the goal of becoming hegemonic. However, it is important to take into account Antoun's (2006: 370) consideration regarding 'relations between state and civil society in Jordan, and … in the Middle East generally: these are not separate formations, but rather, part of a web of social relations that cut across different institutional and legal settings'. Thus, to a certain extent, different social formations are already profoundly intertwined, as it is demonstrated by the public educational sector, at the same time controlled by the state as well as by the Brotherhood, to the point that even classrooms become loci of negotiation between different and competing Islamic discourses (Atia, 2012).

In particular, the Muslim Brotherhood constructed Islamist hegemony in Jordanian society, especially for what concerns the educational sector: hegemony has been pursued through the control of the public educational system and the construction of a private network of schools. It appears clear that the Muslim Brotherhood clearly identified educational and charitable networks for welfare services as apparatuses where social practices are established. The centrality of these institutions in the social construction of collective identities has always been a keystone of sociological thought. State institutions have been conceptualised by Althusser (1971) as ideological state apparatuses, a concept that seems to anticipate Foucault's analysis of disciplinary institutions such as schools, hospitals and prisons.

The Muslim Brotherhood recognised since its inception, in Egypt, the importance of educational institutions as the loci where, to use the Althusserian metaphor, subjects are produced and, in Bourdieu's terms, their *habitus* are constructed. The mission of Islamic social institutions may therefore be conceptualised as the transformation of the individual into the *homo islamicus*, or, from the point of view of the Islamists, the process through which an individual living in a state of *jahiliyya* may rediscover his true 'self'. It is precisely in these institutions that the processes of construction of Islamist hegemony over society may be observed.

The findings of this study seem to suggest that this strategy has played a major role in shaping the imaginary of contemporary Jordanians, thus influencing their self-perceptions and representations. In other words, the Muslim Brotherhood seems to have played a major role in the process of re-Islamisation of Jordan. The Islamist leader Samer, interviewed here, seems convinced that his movement has played a major role in this respect. His informed views, thus, seem to confirm that it is possible to describe Islamisation as a 'deliberate process of mobilization initiated and sustained by Islamic counter-elites' (Wickham, 2002: 8). Such a process can be described as bottom-up; even if it is promoted by elites, it is a process that starts from grass-roots level, not envisaging a top-down Islamisation enforced by the state. As Professor Hassan's affirmed in his interview:

> It is not about having an Islamic caliph; you need to spread consciousness again, you need to modify the consciousness, you need people to re-understand their Islam, to modify concepts, to fill the gaps in the understanding, you need to be working a lot with the people to bring them back to a clear understanding of their religion.

What Professor Hassan defines as 'modify[ing] the consciousness' has been conceptualised here as articulation within a social constructivist framework. Together with his 'clear understanding' this closely recalls Lukács' (1971) invitation to a transition from the 'false consciousness' of capitalism to the 'true consciousness' provided by Marxism.

However, it is interesting to note that Professor Omar, who is a former Islamist as well as a political analyst, undermines the role played by the

Muslim Brotherhood in this process of modification of consciousness. In his view, the re-Islamisation of Jordan, which has occurred since the 1970s, has not been solely caused by the mobilisation to which Wickham refers, but by wider transformations of the political economy, which occurred at a global level in that decade. However, Professor Omar does not deny the role played by the Brotherhood in the process of re-Islamisation, which he terms 'a great revolution, a revolution without gun'.

The effort of this research, hence, has been to combine these two lines of reasoning: one, which stresses the agency of social movements, which is shared by Samer, and the other that focuses on the role of global political economy, which is suggested by Professor Omar. The approach of this research, hence, is termed as 'dialectical', because it highlights the interdependence of these two ranges of factors. However, it is interesting to notice that these two perspectives exist not only in social sciences, but also within the leadership itself of the Muslim Brotherhood of Jordan. The present research attempts to merge these two approaches through the utilisation of Gramscian and post-Gramscian perspectives, social constructivism and social movement theory, analysed in relation with the conditions of political economy. The Gramscian perspective has been crucial in identifying this 'deliberate process of mobilisation' as an articulation of Islamic frames with the objective of establishing their hegemony over Jordanian society. However, such a Gramscian framework presents several flaws, which limit its application to the Jordanian experience. In fact, as Boulby (1999: 1) argued, the relationship between the Hashemite Regime and the Muslim Brotherhood has been 'symbiotic' in several phases of Jordanian history. This also appears clear when taking into account turning points of Jordanian history, such as the civil war of 1970 and the bread riots of 1989. In these critical moments, the Muslim Brotherhood sided with the regime against the threats to its legitimacy. Moreover, the Islamist movement has been allowed to build its network of social institutions for decades, contributing through their educational and charitable activities to strengthening its hegemony.

In line with this argument, thus, can the Muslim Brotherhood be truly defined as counter-hegemonic? Arguably, the answer cannot simply be affirmative or negative. In specific historical phases, the Muslim Brotherhood has exhibited counter-hegemonic features, while in others it has supported the hegemonic narrative of the regime. For example, Professor Omar underlines that, at the inception of the Muslim Brotherhood, 'King Abdullah, the founder of the state, thought that his vision was compatible with the ideas of the Muslim Brotherhood, which was operating in Egypt'. This passage stresses to what extent the foundation of the Jordanian state and the establishment of the Muslim Brotherhood were interrelated. Although the vision of King Abdullah and that of the Muslim Brotherhood were different, since they were based on different interpretations of Islam, they were 'compatible'. Further on, Professor Omar speaks of 'an integration between the two projects'; thus, he acknowledges the existence of two different projects, but he is persuaded that they cross-fertilised each other. In those years, the Muslim Brotherhood was an ally of the regime, and together they were involved in the struggle against the leftist and Nasserite forces. Thus, as has already been stressed, the strategy of the Brotherhood was mainly focused, in this phase, on the creation of an historical bloc, by engaging the state and at the same by conquering it from within, for example by taking over the public education system. In this period, as it seems, the Muslim Brotherhood's positions were not confrontational towards the state (Boulby, 1999). For Professor Omar, the watershed should be located in the 1960s and coincides with the ideological paradigm shift brought about by the Islamist intellectual Sayyid Qutb. Thus, for Professor Omar, it is only when Qutbism develops out of the official ideology of the Muslim Brotherhood that it is indeed possible to define the Muslim Brotherhood as a counter-hegemonic movement. For Professor Omar, Qutbism reflects a crisis of the Muslim Brotherhood, since its members started to question their identity. While before Qutbism, the Muslim Brotherhood was more similar to a religiously inspired conservative movement, after that, a new radical trend developed. Qutbism was, thus, the answer to the identity crisis suffered by Islamists after the Arab defeat against Israel, as it provided a 'modern answer' to the identity crisis, in the form of the project to establish an Islamic state. On the contrary, previous Islamist theoreticians, such as Hasan al-Banna, the founder of the Muslim Brotherhood of Egypt, seemed more inclined towards reviving the concept of Muslim community. For sure, further research is needed in this respect.

What is certain is that the defeat of Nasser in 1967 implied the crisis of his ideology, Pan-Arabism. But, Professor Omar argues, this defeat meant also an identity crisis for Islamism that, before 1967, did not have an organic ideology. This ideology developed during Nasser's persecution of Islamism and, in the aftermath of Nasser's defeat, it succeeded in presenting itself as the answer to the crisis of Pan-Arabism. Thus, during the following decade, these new trends of Islamism spread throughout Arab and Muslim societies also thanks to the financial support from the Gulf monarchies fed by oil revenues (Warde, 2004).

Interestingly, as discussed in Chapter 4, Professor Omar adds that, even if the Muslim Brotherhood was developing its counter-hegemonic identity, it continued to help the regime against its enemies. Indeed, as we have already seen, in the civil war of 1970 the Muslim Brotherhood sided with the regime against the Palestinian militias. Moreover, Professor Omar suggests that, after the expulsion of the PLO from Jordan, the regime attempted to set up the Brotherhood as the representative of the Jordanians of Palestinian origins. However, the regime was aware of the fact that the Islamist movement was not any more what it had been at its inception, in the 1940s. Indeed, as reported in Chapter 4, according to Professor Omar: 'The political leadership felt that these Islamists were not the traditional Islamists of the 1950s and 1960s. But at the same time the political system needed the Islamists against Palestinian organisations, leftists and communists'. By the 1980s, the Brotherhood was not needed any more; but it was now, in Professor Omar's words, 'a strong power, more than the political system wanted'. Professor Omar's analysis demonstrates that assuming a fixed nature, such as a counter-hegemonic one, of the Muslim Brotherhood, is inadequate to account for a much more nuanced reality, while the theoretical contributions of social movement theory can amend the flaws of a rigid adherence to Gramscian categories. Concepts such as 'hegemony' and 'historical bloc' are still valid hermeneutical categories, when understood through the lenses of a social constructivist framework.

This study, however, argues that the concept of hegemony still provides a considerable epistemic value. Farhan's account of the tactical phases through which the Brotherhood operated in Jordanian society (Wiktorowicz, 2001: 97), by focusing firstly on the mosques, secondly on the educational institutions, then on charitable and professional associations and lastly on direct participation in the electoral process, well highlights to what extent the goal of the movement was hegemony over Jordanian society. In the same vein, it can be read as the movement's attempt at establishing a historical bloc, as part of its counter-hegemonic project, sometimes even infiltrating into state apparatuses. In other words, the Islamist movement was extremely able to exploit the opportunity spaces available. They have been, in this respect, conscious organiser of Islamist hegemony, since they clearly identified the loci where the social construction of the *homo islamicus* could be conducted. Professor Omar's thesis is that this very process of re-Islamisation was successful beyond the expectations of the Muslim Brotherhood; for him, the Muslim Brotherhood ignited the process of re-Islamisation, but did not manage to control it. In Gramscian terms, the Muslim Brotherhood did not manage to operate as a Machiavellian 'modern prince'.

The difficulty of the Brotherhood in governing this process may be attributed to different factors, such as the firm opposition of the regime to excessive power of the Brotherhood and the lack of a common strategy within the movement because of its perpetual inner strife. The result of the process seems to be a re-Islamised society where the power of the Islamist movement, although remarkable, appears to be fragile. While the vision of Islam of the Brotherhood is apparently hegemonic, the direct consensus of the movement, however strong, does not seem as high. Professor Omar argues, in this respect, that the goal of the Muslim Brotherhood, since its inception in the 1920s, has been the Islamisation of society. The problem is that, since this has been achieved, the movement is in crisis, because Islamists did not set new goals: the Muslim Brotherhood has therefore lost its *raison d'être*. It is this line of reasoning that made Professor Omar question his own belief and abandon not only the Muslim Brotherhood, but Islamist ideology all together. However, it is worth repeating that while the project of Hassan al-Banna, the founder of the Muslim Brotherhood of Egypt, was the Islamisation of society, the goal of Sayyid Qutb was rather the creation of an Islamic society. This nuance is not irrelevant, since the apparent failure of the former may even be interpreted by some as a vindication of the latter.

Therefore, the concepts of hegemony and counter-hegemony may still be valid to produce a topography of the social. It is important, however, not to use them in a deterministic fashion. In other words, notions such as 'hegemony' and 'counter-hegemony' should not be used to gauge an alleged, meta-historical nature of social movements, but merely to describe their historically situated actions. Thus, for example, the Brotherhood was supporting the regime against nationalist and leftist forces in the 1960s. At that time, it was indeed engaged in the establishment of its counter-hegemonic power, which required the elimination of other existing counter-hegemonic forces, such as the leftists. In that phase, the regime supported the Muslim Brotherhood and the Muslim Brotherhood supported the state. On the other hand, the Brotherhood adopted strategies that may be conceptualised as counter-hegemonic in relation to the regime in the last decades, especially following the 1994 Wadi Araba peace agreement between Jordan and Israel. Thus, from a theoretical point of view, hegemony and counter-hegemony need to be located in their historical situatedness, considering both the relationship with the living social forces and the opportunity spaces available (Asad, 1986: 7). Within this framework, opportunity spaces not only shape the strategies of social movements, but also contribute to the mind-set of the social actors engaged in the transformation of social reality. For example, the establishment of Islamic social institutions and businesses arguably contributed to the cross-fertilisation of the paradigms of *homo islamicus* and *homo economicus*, whose outcome was 'the Islamization of neoliberalism as it is the neoliberalisation of Islam' (Rudnyckyj, 2009: 131).

It is also important to note that different factions of the Muslim Brotherhood adopted different strategies. While openly pro-Palestinian factions may be seen as counter-hegemonic, when they criticise the very social pact Jordan is founded upon, Transjordanian groups within the Brotherhood have often been showing loyalty to the official narrative of the regime. However, even this scheme can be challenged: as Professor Omar pointed out, pro-Hamas factions may at times find compromise with the regime, focusing their efforts on supporting Hamas outside Jordan, without interfering with domestic policies of the regime.

The discussion, hence, suggests that the concepts of hegemony and counter-hegemony need to be interpreted in a non essentialistic fashion, stressing instead the historical situatedness of Islamic movements, which incessantly develop within the opportunity spaces available to them and, at the same time, contribute to shape them, as a social constructivist framework contributes to explain (Yavuz, 2003). Despite the aforementioned criticism, the concept of hegemony may still retain considerable analytical potential, when revised by social constructivism and social theory. Indeed, the concept of hegemony may shed light on the process through which collective forces spread in their societies in conformity to their ideology.

While consistent with the non-deterministic approach followed by this study, it cannot be unquestionably affirmed that the strategy pursued by the Muslim Brotherhood has been the cause of the re-Islamisation of Jordan. The findings of this research merely suggest that the Brotherhood has arguably played a major role in the process of 'Islamic awakening' or re-Islamisation of Jordanian society. More research is certainly needed in order to further substantiate these claims. It would certainly be helpful to have reliable statistics documenting, from a quantitative point of view, variables such as mosque attendance and wearing of the *hijab* since the post-independence period up to the present day. However, since these data seem to be lacking, researchers need to rely on the almost universal perception that, since 1967 and throughout the 1970s, Jordanian society, as well as other Arab societies, did experience a process of re-Islamisation. Professor Omar argues, for example, that the Muslim Brotherhood has been extremely able to take advantage of a general trend of rediscovery of religion on a global scale, but he denies that the Muslim Brotherhood has been the cause of re-Islamisation of Jordanian society. However, it is worth asking whether the goal of the Muslim Brotherhood was the Islamisation of society as such or, instead, the creation of an Islamic society. The two objectives, indeed, should not be conflated, since the second implies a thorough, molecular transformation of the present society into a new one. It may be argued that the Muslim Brotherhood played a crucial role in the Islamisation of society, but that it failed to implement the Islamist utopia, as mentioned above. Islamists, however, have been successful in spreading the belief that Islam is not simply a religion, but a holistic system that has solutions for the social and economic spheres.

A remarkable proportion of the 229 students of the Business School of the University of Jordan interviewed during this study share opinions, which can be described, albeit inadequately, with the term 'moderate Islamism'. In other words, a significant proportion of the students is of the opinion that Islamic principles should play a major role in society, including economics. For example, 56.7% of the respondents 'strongly agree' and 24.1% 'agree' with the statement 'Islam has answers to all the problems of the modern world, including economics'. These answers seem to imply that Islam is not seen, by the students who participated in this survey, merely as a religion that according to Western conceptions of modernity, merely regards the private sphere. On the contrary, it is seen as a holistic system; as the leading Islamist thinker Mawdudi (1997: 1) has argued that the 'Islamic concept of life':

> does not confine itself merely in purifying the spiritual and the moral life of man in the limited sense of the word. Its domain extends to the entire gamut of life. It wants to mould individual life as well as the social order in healthy patterns, so that the Kingdom of God may really be established on the earth

Such an understanding of Islam, which is 'modern' in the sense that it corresponds to a re-interpretation of Islam which took place in the twentieth century to answer modern questions, seems to be widespread in contemporary Jordanian society. The respondents of the questionnaire were not, say, students at the Faculty of Shari'a, where a high degree of religious observance can be assumed, but at the Business School. They are, in all likelihood, future businesspersons, managers and technocrats. At the same time, they recognise the alleged 'systemic nature' of Islam. While it is not the purpose of this study to discuss whether such an interpretation of Islam has been constructed by Islamic thinkers such as Mawdudi, or whether he merely re-constructed, re-discovered or re-vived the holistic nature of Islam, this research argues that what Mawdudi (1997: 1) terms 'the Islamic concept of life' is a set of modern answers to modern questions (the term 'modern' is not used here with positive or favourable connotations, as nowhere else in this book, but only to differentiate Islamist ideology from 'traditional' Islam). Such an understanding arguably permeates the world view of vast segments of contemporary Islamic societies, and certainly inspires the attitudes and perceptions of the respondents to this research questionnaire, who may have never heard of Mawdudi, let alone read his works.

Such an attitude, which may be termed the re-construction of Islam as an ideology, was clearly expressed, as reported in Chapter 4, by Mustafa, one of the most prominent leaders of the Islamic Action Front Party, who stated: 'we think that the principles of Islamic economics are also useful in contemporary society. Islam is religion, [which has implications for] state, justice, law, culture, civilisation, solution of social and economic problems, in all aspects of life'. This persuasion is also echoed by Professor Hassan's own views ('Islam is a globalised and universal system') on the holistic nature of Islam. In a similar vein, regarding the question 'What is your idea of the "good society"?', 5% of the respondents answered 'A society ruled by Islamic principles' and 45.2% 'A society inspired by both Western and Islamic principles', while only 4.8% answered 'A society which follows Western principles'. When asked 'Should a society be ruled by Islamic principles?', 88% of the respondents answered 'yes'. The majority of the respondents, amounting to 78.7%, also answered 'no' to the question 'Should alcohol be legal in Muslim countries?' Alcohol is at present legal, even if its sale is strictly regulated, in Jordan. Thus, it could be inferred that, according to the respondents, 'Jordan does not represent Islam', as Professor Hassan affirmed, since 'The first reference in making laws should be the Islamic law (*shari'a*), which is not the case here'. In Chapter 4, Mariam provided a rationale for this prohibition, when she was linking the consumption of alcohol with 'dehumanisation'. Similar discourses have been observed by Adely (2012: 303) who, during an ethnographic study conducted at al-Khatwa Secondary School for Girls in Bawadi al-Naseem, Jordan, observed the extent to which 'the fear that moral chaos is threatening a way of life' was widespread among the girls.

In other words, the Islamic prohibition of *riba* is not seen as a rule that limits human freedom: it is instead seen as a profoundly rational advice aimed at preserving human dignity. Islam is indeed seen as providing the moral filter through which mankind can live a truly free and human existence. Slavery is not the consequence of blindly following the 'superstition' of religion but, on the contrary, is the outcome of submitting mankind to false 'idols' that ultimately enslave human freedom and determine harm for society. Within this framework Islam, by freeing mankind from 'idolatry', allows human dignity and freedom to thrive: thus, traditional Islamic principles are interpreted in a wholly 'modern' framework, further substantiating the concept of 'Islamic modernities' adopted by this study.

To sum up, these findings seem to confirm that Islamist movements such as the Muslim Brotherhood have been successful in their efforts of spreading their 'modern' readings of Islam as a holistic system throughout Jordanian society. Of course, this argument may be challenged by affirming that those views were common in Jordanian society also before the wave of Islamisation, the 'revolution without guns' of the 1970s Professor Omar referred to. In order to unequivocally demonstrate that these perceptions are the outcome of a process of Islamisation, in which the Muslim Brotherhood played a significant role, it should be necessary to compare the findings of this survey with a similar survey realised, say, in the 1950s. Unfortunately, these results are not available; and Jordan University was established only in 1962. However, the existing body of literature on Islamism seems to agree that a process of re-Islamisation, or of Islamic revivalism, actually did take place in the Arab world after 1967. Thus, it may be safely inferred that a paradigm shift did take place in those years: the process which has been conceptualised here as the articulation of Islamism by an Islamist social movement, such as the Muslim Brotherhood, with the goal of hegemonising Jordanian society. It is beyond the goal of social sciences' qualitative research to 'prove' something; instead, it is possible for researchers to explore social phenomena and to propose theories that can help to better understand them. Thus, what clearly emerges from this study is the extent to which the articulation of Islamism as a holistic system of life is widespread in Jordanian society.

However, we have seen that Professor Omar observes that this profound Islamisation of Jordanian society, which was the primary goal of the Muslim Brotherhood, has contributed to provoking an identity crisis of the Islamist movement. In fact, re-Islamisation took place to such a degree that it was probably beyond the expectations of the Islamists. The visible increase of mosque attendance and women using head-covering testifies an intensification of religious practice. Another important area is education: the establishment of Islamic schools by Islamist groups such as the Muslim Brotherhood through the Islamic Centre Charity, and the power that the Muslim Brotherhood obtained through the control of the Ministry of Education, when Ishaq Farhan was in charge of it, had a profound impact on Jordanian society. For example, as Adely affirms, in Jordan 'all the textbooks make religious references' (2012: 299). Besides that, she affirms (2012: 300): 'I observed myriad ways and spaces – in the classroom, prayer room, school-yard, and teachers' room – within which actors attempted to teach others about religion, religious practices, and pious living.'

However, the pervasive cultural hegemony of Islamism over Jordanian society did not end up in an increased grip of the Muslim Brotherhood over

Jordanian society. The Muslim Brotherhood appears today as being weak and highly affected by factionalism. Since the Muslim Brotherhood boycotted the 2011 elections, it is difficult to quantify its weight in Jordan: however, in the last two decades, it has constantly been losing votes. What are the causes of what can be labelled a paradoxical 'hegemony without a vanguard'?

An important cause has probably been the response of the Jordanian regime, which devised a complex system of incentives and disincentives in order to control Islamic activism (Wiktorowicz, 2001). The response of the regime may be conceptualised as a 'passive revolution', to use a Gramscian expression that has also been used by Bayat (2007: 12) in relation to the Egyptian case; a process which Esposito (1996: 96) called 'institutionalization of Islamic Revivalism'. In other words, the regime, instead of directly challenging Islamism in the name of a staunch defence of secular values, as Ben Ali did in Tunisia, has not opposed the re-Islamisation of Jordanian society. Re-Islamisation of Jordanian society, therefore, has taken place in a way that did not ultimately represent a threat to the legitimacy of the regime. In other words, unlike Tunisia and even Egypt, the Jordanian regime has managed the emergence of Islamism by providing controllable opportunity spaces through a selective internalisation of Islamist symbols and practices (Wiktorowicz, 2001). Such a conduct of the regime is epitomised by its behaviour towards the Islamic social institutions established by the Muslim Brotherhood. The Islamic Centre Charity, the Islamic Hospital and the University of Zarqa were conceived as the possible establishment of an alternative, authentically Islamic society within present Jordanian society. The regime, when it felt threatened by their power, did not forbid or shut down Islamic social institutions, but, partially buying their assets and partially playing the different factions of the Islamist movement against each other, ended up controlling these Islamic social institutions. These institutions seem to be largely pursuing their old goal, that is the spread of Islamic values throughout Islamic society, but this is happening not against the regime, but with its active support. The consequence of this 'passive revolution' is that the Muslim Brotherhood cannot any more claim to be an alternative, since the regime has been strengthening its Islamic credentials. That can explain why the Islamist counter-hegemonic project failed exactly when it became hegemonic, under the wings of, and through the opportunity spaces created by, the state. The concept of opportunity space, defined by Yavuz (2003: 24) as 'a forum of social interaction that creates new possibilities for augmenting networks of shared meaning and associational life', possesses considerable epistemological value, since it allows conceptualisation of the loci where conflicting processes of articulation, hegemonic and counter-hegemonic, take place. In the Jordanian case, since the opportunity spaces available to the Islamist movement have always been 'managed' by the state, the regime carefully avoided them to develop their counter-hegemonic potential, thus preventing them to challenge the state's legitimacy (Wiktorowicz, 2001). The counter-hegemonic project of the Muslim Brotherhood could not, in other words, trespass certain boundaries fixed by the state, as the regime determined the size and substance of the opportunity space in which the Muslim Brotherhood could expand. Therefore, the regime, when it felt threatened, subsumed these spaces, as had happened in the case of its take-over of the Islamic Centre Charity from the Brotherhood after 2006. Thus, expansion and contraction of opportunity spaces by the regime has determined the nature of activism by Muslim Brotherhood.

Moreover, the Muslim Brotherhood failed in the construction of a historical bloc on which to build its counter-hegemonic power. While the Brotherhood was keen on utilising the opportunity spaces provided by the regime, such as education and welfare spheres, it opted not to use its counter-hegemonic potential to directly challenge the state with the goal of realising a truly alternative project. Thus, the hegemonic power managed to succeed, for the time being, in defusing the Islamist challenge. The Jordanian regime strategy of managing Islamism through a complex strategy of incentives and disincentives therefore appears successful in the neutralisation of the counter-hegemonic potential of the Islamist project (Wiktorowicz, 2001). Thus, the process of Islamisation of Jordanian society may be interpreted as a complex process of negotiation among different social actors. As Adely (2012: 298) affirms:

> Competing projects to define religious orthodoxy characterize religious discourse and practice in Jordan today. A religious revival in the region has spanned nearly three decades, and the power to define and monitor religious knowledge has been at the center of struggles between the state, various Islamic groups, and citizens who seek to live as good Muslims.

Among the competing actors mentioned above, this research has especially focused on the two main agents, that is the Muslim Brotherhood, the largest and oldest Islamist group in Jordan, and the regime, whose struggle 'to define and monitor religious knowledge' (Adely, 2012: 298) has been here conceptualised as a struggle over hegemony.

The argument of this section, thus, could be briefly summarised as follows. The Muslim Brotherhood has always enjoyed a complex relationship with the regime. At times, the Islamists supported the regime, at times they challenged it, depending on the shifting opportunity spaces and the size of the opportunity spaces available to them. Moreover, the Muslim Brotherhood has never had one single and monolithic strategy; its theories and practices have always been influenced by a complex range of factors, such as the relationships with the regime and the wider political economy. While the approach of the Muslim Brotherhood has relentlessly focused on reaching hegemony over Jordanian civil society, also thanks to the efforts of some its leaders, it is questionable whether its attempt to establish a counter-hegemonic power in relation to the state and a hegemonic position in relation to other Islamic groups was really successful. In fact, while, on the one hand, its ideology is pervasive in Jordanian society, the movement no longer seems to exert any Gramscian 'intellectual and moral leadership'. As Öncü (2003: 310) explained, using Gramscian categories in relation to the Turkish experience: 'All counter-hegemonic social movements and organizations are forced to find a moral force guiding their members in their collective activities.' The Muslim Brotherhood's failure to exert this role of 'moral force' may explain this crisis.

There is, however, another element, crucial for this research that needs to be taken into account in order to explain the recent transformation of the Brotherhood, and the way the latter reflects wider transformations of contemporary Islamic identities. This issue is important, since it opens up a new range of problems. The political analyst Marouf, as previously reported, stressed to what extent Islamic social institutions, which historically have been the lungs of the Islamist movement, are less important in comparison with business activities owned by important members of the Brotherhood. For Marouf, the members of the Muslim Brotherhood are now establishing institutions, such as Islamic hospitals, as private institutions. However, according to Marouf, the goal of the new Islamic private sector is not so much the spread of Islamic values, but individual profit. These institutions still promote conformity to Islamic values, but they are mainly seen as for-profit enterprises. They may be conceptualised within the framework of what defines, with regard to Indonesia, as Rudnyckyj (2009: 131) calls them, 'articulations of religious resurgence and economic globalization'. In the past, the Islamic social institutions operating under the umbrella of the Islamic Charity Centre Society, established by the Muslim Brotherhood, were non-profit organisations, primarily focusing on community development. It would be easy to dismiss, as it is often heard among ordinary Jordanians, that the new Islamists are hypocritical and money-driven. In the fieldwork of the present research, these accusations have been repeatedly made against the Islamic banking sector. Certainly, further studies are needed to substantiate this claim. However, this tendency, if demonstrated, could indicate a significant paradigm shift in the practices of the Islamist movement, thus further grounding the hypothesis of the present research.

As the discussion indicates it can be argued that an interesting phenomenon is at play. This shift may be indeed explained as a result of the cross-fertilisation between the paradigms of the *homo economicus* and *homo islamicus*. The new Islamic private sector, not unlike the global industry of Islamic finance, seems to have amalgamated these two anthropologies, which are not perceived as conflicting. It is precisely this merging process that has contributed to the emergence and success of 'Islamic capitalism'. The next section discusses this crucial aspect of the present research.

Cross-fertilisation between the paradigms of *homo islamicus* and *homo economicus*

If the theoreticians of Islamic economy were proposing an Islamic system inspired by Islam as an alternative to the alleged shortcomings of socialism and capitalism (Chapra, 1992), current practices of the Islamic private sector suggest a merging between Islamism and capitalism. In *Das Kapital*, Marx aptly describes capitalism using the metaphor of 'social metabolism' (*Stoffwechsel*), which illustrates the ability of the capitalistic mode of production to interact with and transform the environment. The success of capitalism was indeed due, according to Marx, to its endless power of renovating itself. Thus, Islamic capitalism, that is to say an evolution of the capitalistic mode of production reframed and renewed through the adoption of Islamic metaphors, may well be an example of the aforementioned power of capitalism. The belief that Islam provides an alternative system to the alleged shortcomings of Western systems such as socialism and capitalism is widespread in Jordanian society. From a theoretical point of view, the vast literature of Islamic economics has offered interesting solutions to overcome the supposed limitations of Western economic systems. However, it is argued that the operations of Islamic banks and financial institutions do not show this systemic understanding; rather, they tend to locate themselves within a neo-classical model of capitalism (Asutay, 2007a, 2012).

In line with this argument, the attitudes and practices of the students of the Business School of the University of Jordan can be conceptualised as outcomes of the interactions between the two paradigms of *homo economicus* and *homo islamicus*. The extent to which the paradigm of *homo islamicus* permeates the world view of the respondents has been illustrated in the preceding section. The cross-fertilisation between the two paradigms is well summed up by the opinions and attitudes of the respondents regarding the issue of Islamic economics and banking.

Zaid, who was at the time among the leaders of the Islamic Action Front Party, seems to suggest an awareness of these dialectical relationships between Islamisation and globalisation, when affirming in the interview: 'There is no society in the world which is not influenced by globalisation. You are influenced by it, but you influence it at the same time.' Indeed, on the one hand he is aware of the influence that globalisation is having on Muslim societies but, on the other hand, he appears to imply that Islam can impact globalisation as well. He further states: 'It has negative impacts, but positive too, and it presents opportunities as well.' Globalisation, hence, presents unique challenges to the project of Islamisation, but also huge opportunities. It is precisely in this nexus that the complexity of dialectics between globalisation and Islamisation lies. Among the 'negative' effects that Zaid alludes to, it is indeed possible to include the 'commodification' of Islam, exemplified by what Professor Khaled was criticising, when he addressed the fact that, for example, meat consumption grows during Ramadan, with the risk of transforming the holy month of fasting into a period of conspicuous consumption. Thus, he was affirming that: 'Lifestyle becomes more materialistic and Westernised. They go to restaurants, they go together men and women and these phenomena increase as we become more globalised. Some people call it modernisation.'

Globalisation and modernisation are seen as inextricably linked with, in this case, intermingling of sexes, which is identified as moral laxity. Also Mariam was stressing the risk of globalisation bringing to Jordan a sort of freedom 'we don't need'. On the other hand, interviewees such as Professor Hassan emphasised, in words and in deeds, the opportunities provided by globalisation, for example in terms of allowing *da'wa* (appeal, invitation to Islam) to be diffused through new media. Professor Hassan himself represents the epitome of a new breed of Islamic scholar, what Atia (2012: 816) defines as 'the cool preacher, the Islamist in jeans who knows how to talk to young people in a language they understand'. Thus, globalisation can challenge Islamic values but, at the same time, it offers extraordinary opportunity spaces for their diffusion, as Professor Hassan's *da'wa* on social media shows. Thus, globalisation has provided marketing opportunities for religious activism to reach out to larger segments of societies in various countries instead of leading to a diminished role of religion. The ambivalence of globalisation is well highlighted by Mustafa, one of the most prominent leaders of the Islamic Action Front Party, who stated: 'Islamic *da'wa* [appeal, invitation] is a global appeal. Men and women of different languages have been created in order for them to know each other. However, contemporary globalisation has colonial goals'. Thus, the contradiction between Islam and globalisation is not ontological, since Islam is a global religion in itself; the problem is rather represented by the historical developments of this process, which is, in the current phase, seen as hegemonised by a colonial project. Indeed, Mustafa further explains that: 'we think that globalisation has two goals: to impose American culture to the world and to impose American economy in the world ... We do not share these American goals, that is why this globalisation is problematic.' To put it simply, the problem is not with globalisation, but with *this* globalisation. This observation is further confirmed by the findings of the survey questionnaire; as we have already repeated in this chapter, a stark majority of the Muslim respondents agreed with the statement 'Islam is a global religion in essence'.

This research, however, shows that, even if the paradigms of *homo islamicus* and *homo economicus* are often conceived as a dichotomy, in practice they undergo complex processes of cross-fertilisation. The interplay between the two has been observed in the respondents' opinions regarding Islamic banking, for example highlighting the extent to which rational factors, or *homo economicus* factors, are considered more significant than religious obligations in their banking relationships. Here, the most important factor was service quality, followed by convenience, availability of branches and convenience of location. The factor 'the account is free from any interest', which is the main *raison d'être* of Islamic banking, as well as 'religious obligation/requirement', were not as important as non-religious factors. If these particular findings are read outside the context of this research, it could be easy to assume that religion does not play a big role in the attitudes and choices of the respondents. However, since the findings of this study demonstrate the opposite, the explanation must lie elsewhere; the process of globalisation seems to be intermingled with globalisation to such an extent that Atia (2012: 816) affirmed that 'the rise of Islamism is in some ways both a response to and a product of neoliberalism'.

The 'Islamic modernities' emerging from this dialectics are revealed also by the fact that, despite the respondents' worldview being shaped by Islam, they do not seem to show any particular enthusiasm towards Islamic religious scholars. For example, 49.3% of the respondents of this survey were 'neutral' with regard to the statement 'religious scholars are the moral pillars of Jordanian society', while 20.5% declared they 'agree' and merely 3.5% 'strongly agree'. In a similar vein, concerning the statement 'religious scholars work for the development of Jordanian society', 37.6% were 'neutral', while only 5.7% stated they 'strongly agree'. Furthermore, 42.8% of the respondents were 'neutral' towards the statement 'religious scholars pursue their own interests rather than those of Jordanian people'. Also the following statement reveals the same attitude, since 38.9% of the respondents were 'neutral' with regard to the statement 'religious scholars create conflict in Jordanian society'. Arguably, this shows a certain degree of scepticism in relation to the religious establishment; this may lend support to the emergence of a process of individualisation of Islam (Roy, 2004). It needs to be stressed that just for one question the degree of scepticism was considerably higher among the Christian respondents: this was the statement 'religious scholars work for the development of Jordanian society'. In all the other questions related to this issue, no significant difference emerged between Muslims and Christians.

On the whole, it can be affirmed that a strong penetration of Islamic values co-exist with an amount of doubt in relation to the religious establishment, which is, parenthetically, a common feature of Islamism. Unfortunately, no sound empirical evidence can be offered to document this penetration of the paradigm of *homo economicus* in Jordanian society; this process may just be inferred. However, what this study empirically verifies is to what extent the *homo economicus* value system influences the opinions and behaviours of respondents of the survey questionnaire.

Indeed, this research shows to what extent the respondents live in the symbolic world of global capitalism. For example, when asked about their feelings towards globalisation, 46.3% of the respondents opted for 'globalisation contributes to creating a free world', 32.8% for 'globalisation brings jobs and wealth to developing countries', while merely 10.5% opted for 'globalisation works against the interests of developing countries' and 6.6% for 'globalisation is an instrument of imperialism/colonialism'. Thus, it is very clear that the majority of the respondents have a favourable view of globalisation, which is seen as bringing opportunities. However, regarding the statement 'globalisation is not in contradiction with Islam', the opinions are much more fragmented, since those who 'strongly agree' are 7.0%, 'agree' 26.6%, 'neutral' 26.6%, 'disagree' 26.2% and 'strongly disagree' 11.4%. Similarly, divided opinions emerged in relation to the statement 'globalisation undermines Islamic values', since 7.0% opted for 'strongly disagree', 24.0% for 'disagree', 36.7% for 'neutral', 25.3 for 'agree', 4.4% 'strongly agree'. The following statements shed light on these findings. Indeed, 41.9% of the respondents declared that they 'agree' with the statement 'globalisation has brought new Islamic ideas and practices to

Jordan', thus lending support to the main argument of this research, namely the cross-fertilisation between Islamisation and globalisation. Indeed, a surprising 43.2% of the respondents chose 'agree' with regard to the statement 'globalisation opens up new opportunities for the propagation of Islam', while merely 10.5% opted for 'disagree' and 2.2% for 'strongly disagree'. The possibility of merging the discursive traditions of globalisation and Islam is further confirmed by the last statement, 'Islam is a global religion in essence', since 24.0% chose 'strongly agree', 32.8% 'agree', while only 5.7% 'disagree' and merely 3.1% 'strongly disagree'. Thus, as it has been observed by Zaid, it is not the alleged 'nature' of globalisation that is perceived as being against Islam, but only some of its features; in other words, it may be argued that globalisation is seen as needing the moral filter provided by Islam in order not to show its exploitative and dehumanising features. Regarding the Jordanian context, this study showed that only a small minority of the respondents chose 'strongly agree' (3.5%) or 'agree' (7.9%) with regard to the statement 'globalisation has not produced any positive change in Jordanian society and business'. Similarly, an extremely high percentage of the respondents 'agree', totalling 49.8%, and 'strongly agree', totalling 12.7%, with the statement 'globalisation helps Jordanian entrepreneurs to connect with the rest of the global economy'. The same attitudes are evident in the statement 'globalisation provides new business opportunities for Jordanians', where 14.8% opted for 'strongly agree' and 51.1% for 'agree', while only 7.9% for 'disagree' and 0.9% for 'strongly disagree'. The majority of the respondents also agreed with the statement 'globalisation provides new ideas and innovations in business', as well as with 'globalisation provides an opportunity for cultural understanding', where in total 61.6% opted for 'agree' and 'strongly agree'. On the contrary, concerning the statement 'globalisation undermines traditional values in Jordan', the majority opted for 'agree' (32.8%) and 'strongly agree' (24.0%). Also in this respect, the respondents acknowledge a positive side of globalisation, in terms of innovation and development, and a negative side, in terms of a threat to the moral fabric of the society.

Indeed, different and contrasting views towards the relationships between globalisation and Islam emerged also among the interviewees, since globalisation is seen as providing opportunities for *da'wa* (invitation to Islam), for example by Professor Hassan, but also as a challenge to traditional values, for example by Professor Khaled. A staggering majority of the respondents, totalling 62.9%, considers that 'the West has negative attitudes towards the Muslim world'. Thus, the problem of the respondents is not with globalisation as such, but with the Western approach towards Muslims.

The patterns of consumption of the respondents are another field where the pervasiveness of globalisation is revealed: 88.2% of the respondents prefer shopping in the 'modern' shopping malls of Amman, such as Mecca Mall, while only 13.1% in the more traditional city centre. Also regarding the kind of restaurants where they prefer to dine out, 40.2% prefer fast food such as McDonald's, while only 15.7% chose 'traditional Arab restaurants'. Similarly,

64.6% of the respondents declared that branded clothes are important for them to have. The integration of the respondents in the globalised world is further confirmed: 63.3% of the sample declared that they use Internet 'several times a days' and 24.9% 'at least once a day'. Also for what concerns Facebook, 49.8% use it 'several times a day' and 20.5% 'at least once a day'. In a similar vein, the penetration of two symbols of global capitalism, such as the FIFA World Cup 2010 and McDonald's, was extremely high: 70.7% of the respondents followed the World Cup and the views towards McDonald's are generally positive, with only 8.7% who opted for 'agree' or 'strongly agree' with the statement 'McDonald's should not be allowed in Muslim countries, including Jordan' and only 14.4% who opted for 'disagree' or 'strongly disagree' with the statement 'McDonald's is a pleasant environment for socialising'.

This penetration of the *homo economicus* paradigm did not occur at the expense of Islamic values though. To put it differently, the penetration of individualistic and consumerist life styles has not determined secularisation. On the contrary, as the analysis of the fieldwork material has shown, the two paradigms cross-fertilise each other. These cross-fertilisations seem to have produced not only Islamic forms of capitalism, epitomised by the Islamic financial system, but also capitalistic forms of Islam. Instead of a clash between the two paradigms, the emergence of a mixed paradigm is on the agenda, a sort of *homo economicus et islamicus*, whose symbolic universe is profoundly influenced by both value systems.

It is a working hypothesis of this research that the Muslim Brotherhood constitutes an interesting prism through which to explore this complex phenomenon. As Wickham (2002: 1) underlines, one of the apparent paradoxes of contemporary Islamism is that:

> The prototypical Islamic activist is not an illiterate peasant or laborer but a young, upwardly mobile university student or professional, often with a scientific or technical degree. Far from embodying the defensive protest of traditional social classes on the decline, the Islamic movement is strongly associated with the most 'modern' citizens in Arab societies.

It is this striking modernity of the Islamists who legitimise their relevance in the present study. The Muslim Brotherhood is, indeed, at the same time the subject that articulates Islamist ideologies, and the object that has been affected by the transformations of the political economy. Indeed, also the Muslim Brotherhood has been affected by this cross-fertilisation. As has been said in the previous section, when interviewed, the journalist and researcher Marouf noticed that the emphasis of the Brotherhood had been shifting away from the engagement in Islamic social institutions to the establishment of private enterprises directly owned by leaders of the Brotherhood. Apparently, both the Islamic social institutions and this new Islamic private sector are engaged in the spread of Islamic values. However, in the case of Islamic social institutions, social reform was their primary goal; for what concerns the new

Islamic private sector, the main objective is profit. This process may document remarkable transformations of the landscape of Jordanian society and of other Arab and Muslim societies. Islamist movements may have contributed in the creation, through their mobilisations, not only of a political constituency, but also of a market segment that is now targeted by Islamist and non-Islamist businessmen. In other words, the counter-hegemonic project may have not ended in the desired reform of society; however, it has contributed to generating a demand for Islamic commodities, such as Islamic health services, Islamic educational services, Islamic financial services or Islamic tourist agencies that organise the *hajj*. Utvik (2006: 24) affirms, following François Burgat, that:

> The Islamist movement could be seen as an attempt to regain the identity and viability of contemporary Muslim societies by reconnecting with an indigenous system of references for producing meaning, thus creating a separate symbolic universe within which to debate the proper understanding of the modern world and how to tackle the problems with which it confronts Muslim societies.

Utvik (2006) points out the attempt of contemporary Muslims to create new 'separate symbolic universes'. Undoubtedly, Mawdudi's original attempt was marked by a desire for separation of the 'Islamic' from the 'non-Islamic' with the objective of developing an authentic Islamic identity, but whether this phenomenon still characterises Islamic movements is open to question, as in the case of Islamic banking and finance; while it was considered as part of the Islamic political identity, it is arguably no longer possible to make this claim due to the nature of the operations of these institutions.

This idea of separation characterises the theorisations of influential Islamist thinkers, such as Mawdudi and Qutb, but the empirical findings of the present study challenge the idea that the creation of 'separate symbolic universes' still characterises Islamic movements such as the Muslim Brotherhood of Jordan. For what concerns Jordan, this may have been true for the 'Qutbist' Muslim Brothers who were pursuing a counter-hegemonic project. It may certainly be still true for segments of the movements or for the Salafis.

However, as the empirical evidence generated by this study demonstrates, the worldview of Islamist and non-Islamist Jordanians who took part in this study seem to be characterised by a patchwork of Islamist and globalised worldviews. Although more accurate and detailed studies are needed, contemporary Islamic identities in Jordan seem to be characterised by an original synthesis of these understandings. In fact, Islamic movements seem to be actually promoting the merging between apparently different systems. This process is evident where patterns of consumption are concerned: 'Islamic' patterns of consumption' are distinguished from 'non Islamic' patterns of consumption. The paradox is that, exactly through this process of selection, Western patterns of consumption are thoroughly legitimised through a '*halalisation*' process.

This study indeed evidences through empirical findings an on-going cross-fertilisation between symbolic systems. The web of attitudes and practices analysed document to what extent Islamic symbols and practices, which are claimed to be, from a theoretical point of view, alternative to the Western capitalist one, are actually merged with the symbolic universe of global capitalism. This argument has important theoretical consequences. One consequence is that it shows how untenable is the clash of civilisations argument. The problem of this paradigm consists in postulating cultures as essences that are not subject to historical transformations. Adopting such a framework, it is therefore natural to interpret Islamism not as a historically situated phenomenon, but as an eternal attribute of Islam, which periodically re-emerges. On the contrary, Islamism should be understood as a historically situated discursive formation, therefore as a modern phenomenon, as the evidence generated by this study suggests.

This approach is not only vitiated by a neo-colonial will of domination expressed through the apparently neutral desire to know the other, but it is also inadequate to describe social reality. The idea according to which the 'essence' or 'nature' of a culture, be it Islam or Confucianism, determines the behaviours of the individuals which were born 'inside' it is highly questionable, since it fails to take into account historicity, but rather expresses itself in the universality and hierarchical notion of modernity as defined by Hegelian understandings. However, the recognition of the importance of historicity should not lead to the other extreme, namely historicism, when the term historicism refers to a form of relativism that, while affirming that everything changes and is contingent, ultimately denies the possibility of comprehending, or acting upon, social reality (Meszaros, 1972: 48).

Can we, thus, really imagine the existence of a contemporary Western civilisation essentially different from contemporary Islamic civilisation? The findings of this study suggest that it would be more appropriate to talk of a global civilisation based on capitalistic values that, in different contexts, is cross-fertilised with pre-existent value systems in developing multiple modernities. Another problem of Utvik's (2006: 24) statement quoted above is that he sees the Islamic movement as engaged in coping with 'the problems with which it [the modern world] confronts Muslim societies' (Utvik, 2006: 24). This assertion is problematic, since it still relies on an epistemology that postulates a dichotomy between the 'modern world' and 'Muslim societies', and it sees the 'Islamic movement' as engaged in filling the gap between them. This issue raises crucial questions about the definition of modernity itself, which is examined in the following section.

The emergence of Islamic modernities

The main argument of the previous section may have led to the emergence of a misunderstanding. Affirming that a global society based on capitalistic values, in different contexts, merges with different symbolic universes does not imply that these symbolic universes are necessarily 'traditional'. The process described above should not, in our understanding, be necessarily conceptualised as a clash between the modernity of global capitalism and indigenous, traditional mindsets. In particular, Islamism should not be understood as a traditional ideology. Rather, it represents a modern attempt of re-inventing tradition, as evidenced with the empirical analyses presented. Talal Asad (1986) suggested considering Islam a discursive tradition:

> If one wants to write an anthropology of Islam one should begin, as Muslims do, from the concept of a discursive tradition that includes and relates itself to the founding texts of the Qur'an and the Hadith. Islam is neither a distinctive social structure nor a heterogeneous collection of beliefs, artifacts, customs, and morals. It is a tradition. ... These discourses relate conceptually to a past (when the practice was instituted, and from which the knowledge of its point and proper performance has been transmitted) and a future (how the point of that practice can best be secured in the short or long term, or why it should be modified or abandoned), through a present (how it is linked to other practices, institutions, and social conditions). An Islamic discursive tradition is simply a tradition of Muslim discourse that addresses itself to conceptions of the Islamic past and future, with reference to a particular Islamic practice in the present.

Within this framework, Islamism can be conceptualised as a modern discursive tradition or, better, a nexus of discursive traditions, within the broader discursive tradition represented by Islam. In other words, Islamism embodies a process of modernisation that has been originally articulated as alternative to the Western one, for example by Mawdudi. As Utvik (2006: 24) suggests in the statement quoted above, it is characterised by an attempt to 'create a separate symbolic universe'.

This research argues that some of the contemporary forms of Islamism, such as those which have been the object of this study, share to such an extent the mindset of global capitalism that they cannot any more claim to be alternative. However, what Islamism certainly does challenge is the modernisation paradigm, which Spohn (2010: 51) summarises as follows:

> In a nutshell, the classical modernization paradigm assumed a cluster of basic evolutionary processes that in the end would lead to a common form of modern society and polity. These basic evolutionary processes, though with different emphasis in the many strands of modernization theory, encompass social and functional differentiation, individualization, capitalist development, rising standards of living, state formation, nation-building, democratization, cultural development, value generalization and secularization.

The coincidence of Europeanisation and modernisation can be criticised on two grounds. One argument is that such an assumption is intrinsically ethnocentric, since it assumes that the alleged social evolution that occurred in European societies is not specific to its historical context, but presents a general validity (McDaniel, 2005: 37). The evolutionary and teleological thrust of modernisation as a paradigm has been criticised on the ground that it conceals an imperialistic project of domination through the establishment of hierarchical relations with the 'others'. Binder (1988: 83) has conducted a thorough critique of development ideologies, both of liberal and Marxist origins, which postulate the need for the West to intrude on other cultures, and in particular Muslim societies, in order to 'modernise' them. Development ideologies assume diverse forms and criticise Muslim societies on different grounds, but they are all characterised by the persuasion that these societies should follow the Western path to modernisation, which is conceived as universal. In Salvatore's (2009: 4) words, Orientalist discourse postulates an 'allegedly deficient capacity' of Islamic societies to find a place in the space of modernity. This deficiency of Muslim societies justifies the continuous interference of the West in order to constantly 'correct' the trajectory of Muslim societies. It is in this respect, therefore, that the Western concepts of modernity, modernisation and development are used to justify social, political, economic and military interventions in the Muslim world. It is evident that the concept of modernity, and hence developmentalism, is not politically neutral, but is entrenched in historically situated understandings of Muslim societies. As Spohn (2010: 50) sums up: 'The modernization paradigm grounded political sociology in a macro-sociological Western-centric evolutionist framework. It served not only as a value-free analytical frame of reference but also as a self-legitimizing ideology of the Western and particularly US-American developmental models.'

Mehmet (1990, 1999) argues in the same vein that even the theory-making in developmentalist studies has been entirely based on a Eurocentric world view. Therefore, he suggests that theories and models produced through the experience of Europe have not and cannot produce any success in the rest of the world. Mehmet (1990, 1999) therefore suggests the adoption of culturally correct forms of strategies and policies for development.

Another argument is that the emergence of Islamism itself represents a blatant refutation of the modernisation paradigm. As Esposito (1984: 310–311) has concisely expressed:

> The resurgence of Islam has challenged many of the presuppositions and expectations of development theory. Modernization for the Muslim world did not necessarily follow the general wisdom of Western political theories by resulting in the progressive secularization of state and society.

The main difference between 'Western modernisation' and what has been observed in the field is, clearly, the relevance attributed to religion. The present research suggests that Islam constitutes the framework through which large segments of Jordanian society attribute meaning to life, and notably to social life. However, the symbolic frames of Islam are re-articulated by social actors to answer contemporary issues.

Eickelman and Piscatori (1996: 23–28) conducted a thorough critique of the paradigms of modernization theory, according to which the entrance of Muslim societies into the global division of labour would have led to political reforms and the fading away of religion; they have convincingly argued that Muslim society embarked upon a process that led to the invention of tradition. The dichotomy between modernity and tradition is untenable, since what is identified as 'tradition' is in reality the use of symbolic frames borrowed from the past to make sense of the contemporary world. Integral to this process of re-articulation of tradition is, accordingly to Eickelman and Piscatori (1996: 37) what they define as 'objectification of Muslim consciousness'. The contact with Western societies and the secularisation of various aspects of life even in Muslim societies had as a consequence that religion is not anymore taken for granted, but has been put into question, it has become an 'object'. In Eickelman and Piscatori's (1996: 38) words:

> Objectification is the process by which basic questions come to the fore in the consciousness of large numbers of believers: 'What is my religion?' 'Why is it important to my life?' and 'How do my beliefs guide my conduct?' ... These explicit, widely shared, and 'objective' questions are modern queries that increasingly shape the discourse and practice of Muslims in all social classes, even as some legitimize their actions and beliefs by asserting that they advocate a return to purportedly authentic traditions. Objectification is thus transclass, and religion has become a self-contained system that its believers can describe, characterize, and distinguish from other religious beliefs.

However, the objectification of Muslim consciousness needs to be accompanied by an objectification of modern consciousness. Horkheimer and Adorno (2002) have deconstructed the rationalist claims of Enlightenment as a mythology. Arguing that the propositions of Enlightenment were not universal, but historical, rooted in the context of eighteenth-century France, explicitly challenges their applicability to, say, twenty-first-century Jordanian society. Postulating that the struggle between 'reactionary' religion and 'emancipatory' secularism constitutes the key to explain the tensions that pervade contemporary Muslim societies, including Arab societies, may in itself be questioned.

The crusade against 'modernity' has long been identified, in Europe, with the political right. Joseph de Maistre (1994), one of the most outspoken opponents of modernity, criticised the Enlightenment project in the name of Catholic tradition. Throughout the nineteenth century, French political discourse was shaped by the opposition between the political left, which claimed to embody modernity, and the political right, which defended tradition. Both sides shared a common understanding of modernity, which was seen as positive and emancipatory by the left and as negative and threatening for society by the others. The opposition between left and right also reflected a polarisation between those who wanted to radically transform the political and socio-economic system and those who wanted to conserve it. However, in the twentieth century, in the discourse of 'anti-modern' theorists such as Réné Guénon (2004) and Julius Evola (1998), there is a remarkable shift. Both Guénon and Evola fully acknowledge the apparent victory of 'modernity' over 'tradition', and consequently their opposition to modernity is not anymore equated with social conservation, but becomes almost equated with revolution. Their conception of tradition vehemently opposes not only the political left, but also the bourgeois right, in the name of re-invented and vaguely Nietzschean aristocratic values.

The discourse of 'tradition' overlapped with the conservation of the socio-economic order, while the discourse of 'modernity' did so with socio-economic change. However, the notion of post-modernity has challenged the definition of modernity, implicitly paving the way for the emergence of other forms of modernity. The Jordanian case, with the generated empirical evidence and the discussion presented here, challenges the validity of adopting the concept of modernity *qua* secularism to other contexts.

The concept of secularism stems from a historical legacy that includes Christianity, the presence of the Catholic Church, the Reformation, the Enlightenment and the French Revolution. However, the ideology of modernity *qua* secularism conceals its historicity and it claims universality through the imposition of this paradigm to the 'other'. The originality of the Jordanian case analysed in this study consists of the fact that social actors thoroughly and consciously reject the unilateral notion of modernity imposed by the West, explicitly claiming the compatibility of Islam and modernity, and in fact affirming that it is through Islam that they can be truly modern. The idea that religion and modernity are incompatible appears absurd to them. Thus, even the apparent opposition between 'modernisation of Islam' and 'Islamisation of modernity' becomes obsolete, since 'modernity' and 'Islam' are simply not perceived as two different poles. This study, hence, criticises the essentialisation and absolutisation of concepts such as 'modernity' and 'Islam', inviting the reader instead to consider social practices in their historical and geographical situatedness.

Coherent with this approach, the notion of modernity needs not to be simply discarded, but to become itself an object of study. It is not among the goals of this study to argue for a thorough rejection of the concept of modernity itself. Instead, this concept needs to be re-articulated and re-interpreted, not out of a need of political correctness, but in order to account for observable social phenomena. Thus, a historically situated analysis of modernity needs to consider the complex webs of relationships between the concept of modernity and the development of the capitalistic mode of production. Identifying this nexus allows the establishment of the notion of 'individual' as one of the core principles of modernity. In other words, it may be argued that the universality of modernity could not be achieved through the convergence of the 'others' to the 'European modernity' project. Rather, 'the others', and this seems particularly true with regard to Islamic societies, have refused to be incorporated within this project. However, they have produced their own 'modernity' through their ontologies and epistemologies, such as what has been called here Islamic modernities, implying autonomous and indigenous versions of modernity, which cannot be read as a mere surrender of Islam to Western modernity. In this respect, Islamic banking and finance epitomise this cross-fertilisation between different paradigms. Indeed, the fact that Islamic banking and finance are developing within a neo-classical framework, yet complying with *shari'a*, seems to confirm this hypothesis, as the shift from Islamic institutions prioritising social development into Islamic business for profit purposes.

The emergence of the concept of the individual is rooted in Hellenistic and Roman culture, in Christianity, in the Renaissance and in the Reformation, and it has played a pivotal role in the rise of capitalism. At the same time, capitalism is not only the product of the individuals, but has, in turn, contributed to produce the 'modern' concept of individuals. The development of forces of production and relations of production radically transforms traditional structures.

Affirming that the development of relations of production that culminated in globalisation triggered re-articulations of identity does not mean to deny the agency of social actors and social movements, but merely to read them in a historical context (Etienne, 1987: 135). This research, hence, does not share the assumption that Islamism is a reaction against modernity. However, in our understanding, a causal link can be identified between the crisis of the old traditional structures and the emergence of Islamism. In other words, Islamism can be seen, instead of a reaction against modernity, as an attempt of answering the question: what does being modern mean for a contemporary Muslim? As Piscatori (1986: 31) affirms:

> Religion, precisely because in the past it answered questions of life and death and provides its followers with moral links to each other, becomes the means by which individuals hope to answer the new question of what it is to be modern.

The articulation of what can defined as Islamic modernities seems to be based on this possibility of religion being able to respond to the problem of being modern. Through the concept of multiple modernities it becomes possible to conceptualise the phenomena observed on the ground as Islamic modernities. The word 'modernities' is plural inasmuch as the outcomes of the processes of *micro-ijtihad* are plural and polymorphous, while the word 'Islamic' needs to be understood in an anti-essentialist fashion: it is not Islam that determines the different 'modernities', but social actors legitimise their paths to modernity through the adoption of Islamic frameworks. As Asad (1986: 15) argues: 'A practice is Islamic because it is authorized by the discursive traditions of

Islam, and is so taught to Muslims-whether by an 'alim, a khatib, a Sufi shaykh, or an untutored parent'. The religious identities of the Jordanian youth seem to be shaped by the same trends that Roy (2004: 35) described in relation with Islam and Christianity in the West, that is to say the reconstruction of religion as, more than a faith, an identity. The tendency of showing pride in belonging to Islam can indeed be observed, the process that Roy (2004: 36) effectively described as 'the shift from self-evident universal religions embedded in given cultures, to religious communities surrounded by secularised societies'. Such a process is read by Roy (2004: 38) as being in relationship with globalisation and with the concomitant individualisation and 'deterritorialisation' of religion. Moreover, in Jordan it is possible to observe the phenomenon that Roy (2004: 40) calls 'secularisation through religion', as he affirms:

> Islamisation of society led to the Islamisation of secular activities and motivations, which remain secular in essence: business, strategies of social advancement, and entertainment (like the five-star Islamic resorts in Turkey, where the real issue is fun and entertainment, not Islam). When everything has to be Islamic, nothing is.

The point raised by Roy (2004) sheds a new light on the findings of the present research, raising a set of new questions. Are the readings of Islam, influenced by Islamism and by globalisation, symptomatic of a paradoxical secularisation of religion? Roy (2004) indeed implies that religious frames are justified to legitimise business activities to such an extent that their religious status becomes problematic. Obviously, the same issues concern politics. However, Islamists could answer by questioning the Western definition of religion. Should religion be described, as by Rudolf Otto (1958), as a relationship between mankind and the numinous, the sacred? Or is it a way of life that also involves social, economic and political issues? The first approach could lead to describing one of the outcomes of the processes outlined in this essay as an interplay between Islamisation of commodities and commoditisation of Islam, resulting in a Weberian 'disenchantment of the world' that takes place not through the fading of religion, but through its transformation into a socio-political ideology.

Conclusion

The aim of this study is not to provide definite answers, but to propose a new set of questions. However, the present study concludes that dichotomies such as globalisation versus Islamisation or Islamism versus modernity are untenable: it cannot be affirmed that Islamic societies are trying to 'catch up' with Western modernity through their reconnection with Islamic tradition. The body of literature on Muslim societies indeed is often inspired by teleological ideas: this determinism is common to very different approaches, which all share the presumption that Muslim societies are on their way to reach various goals, such as democracy or modernisation. An objective of this essay has been to criticise these positivistic claims. The very concept of Western modernity has been challenged in this study, and the existence of Islamic modernities not only supports the adoption of a more pluralistic definition of modernity, but it ends up challenging the concept of 'modern' itself.

This study argues that Islam is a discursive tradition through which 'modern' problems, such as the aspirations and frustrations of social classes, are articulated. Hence, social actors contributed to the emergence of Islamic business, such as Islamic banks or Islamic schools and hospitals, which belong at the same time to the discursive tradition of Islam and to that of modernity. The overlapping of the two makes possible the emergence of the discursive traditions here defined as Islamic modernities, to be read within the broader concept of multiple modernities (Eisenstadt, 2009).

Hence, the paradigms of *homo islamicus* and *homo economicus* need not to be conceived as meta-historical essences, but as nexuses of social practices, constantly subjected to change. What seems, in appearance, to be contradictory, is actually the result of profound dialectical interactions between beliefs and social practices. Similarly, it would be to easy to dismiss the members of the Muslim Brotherhood who are establishing Islamic business firms as hypocrites who are simply varnishing business enterprises with Islam; what is at play is actually a vast social process of contamination, which Atia (2012: 809) calls 'pious neoliberalism' and defines as follows:

> I offer the term pious neoliberalism to explain the melding of religiosity and neoliberalism, a pattern that departs from prevailing readings of both phenomena as being in competition with one another or as having contradictory values in the contemporary era.

The present study shares Atia's (2012: 823) understanding that 'this neoliberal Islam emphasizes self-optimization and the cultivation of productive and entrepreneurial subjects' and that such a framework can help to shed light on 'the compatibility between religious and economic logics' (Atia, 2012: 823) through the study of historically situated phenomena. The concept of 'pious neoliberalism' allows us to conceptualise the cross-fertilisation this research focuses upon, since, as Atia (2012: 811) further argues, 'There is a dialectic relationship between religion and neoliberal development'. The present study underlines, indeed, the importance of a dialectical perspective, which allows appreciation of 'the melding of religiosity and neoliberalism' (Atia, 2012: 809) in its density.

Indeed, notions such as 'religiosity' and 'neoliberalism', such as *homo economicus* and *homo islamicus* should not be studied as pure and abstract essences, but, according to a social constructivist framework, as articulations and representations that social actors project upon themselves and upon other social actors. Their use in this research is justified not because they have an intrinsic epistemic value, but because they are expressions of representations of the self.

The paradigm of *homo economicus*, which constructs an image of mankind as primarily driven by individual profit (Smelser and Swedberg, 2005: 83), hence, may have spread through Jordanian society at the time of British colonialism, but it is probably becoming widespread because of the globalisation of Jordanian society and economy. It is remarkable to notice that the success of the *homo economicus* model in the Muslim world is profoundly related to the articulation of Islam as rational, which has been discussed earlier; a process which often took place against traditional religion, which in several Muslim societies, but to a much lesser extent in Jordan, was represented by Sufism. As Weismann (2011: 160) argues:

> Islamic fundamentalism's 'othering' of Sufism, and traditional religion in general, was instrumental in the constitution of its own Self as a modern subject. Presenting 'Sufism' as irrational, apolitical and submissive allowed the fundamentalists to introduce in its stead a rationalist form of *ijtihad*, the ideal of an Islamic state, and the principles of social justice and participation.

This is further illustrated by the scepticism of the respondents towards religious scholars, embodiments of the religious establishment, and concurrent processes of 'individualisation' of religion (Roy, 2006). The quest for a more personal relationship with religion is part of the dynamics of modernity.

Conclusion

Throughout this work, Islamism has been seen as a crucial, yet certainly not exclusive, prism to analyse the ongoing developments of contemporary Islamic identities. Hence, this research argues that economic practices and cultural representations cross-fertilise each other, contributing to the transformation of the symbolic universes social actors operate in. In this context, the collective construction of new frames, which in various forms draw from traditional cultures, reflects new ways of interpreting and transforming social reality. These frames are the outcome of the hybridisation between economic practices and cultural forms, but they are also the language through which individuals actively react to social and economic phenomena, in their attempt to attribute meanings to human existence and to transform the social world. In this respect, the developments of Islamism have been examined in their dialectical relationships with broader changes in the political economy landscapes of Arab societies. What is more, Islamic movements, such as the Muslim Brotherhood in the context of Jordan, are conceptualised as the totality of collective social actors who have contributed to the re-articulation of Islamic frames through a process, which here is defined as a quest for hegemony, adopting a post-Gramscian framework nurtured by social constructivism and social movement theory.

Besides, it has been argued that a process of cross-fertilisation has been taking place between the paradigms of *homo economicus* and *homo islamicus*, where the former indicates the anthropology of capitalism and the second the anthropology of Islam as articulated by contemporary Islamic movements. Such contamination between frames originally stemming from diverse world views has been contributing to the social construction of what can be defined as 'Islamic ways to capitalism'.

Overall, the aforementioned, profoundly inter-related, processes are challenging the claims of modernisation theory, according to which the advent of capitalism would have led to a secularisation of society. On the contrary, the growing integration of contemporary Arab societies into the global economy has not resulted in a fading of religion, but in processes of re-articulation of religious frames. It is on these bases that this research has suggested that the category of 'Islamic modernities' could be helpful in conceptualising the theoretical challenges, brought about by the processes highlighted in this study, to the mono-civilisational claims of Western modernity.

This study questions the extent to which the Muslim Brotherhood of Jordan could be conceptualised as a 'counter-hegemonic' movement. The findings seem to suggest that, at times, the Islamist movement has indeed played the role of a counter-hegemonic movement, while in other historical phases it has been, on the contrary, showing what has been defined as a 'symbiotic' relationship with the regime (Boulby, 1999: 1). In fact, in their quest for hegemony over Jordanian society, the Muslim Brotherhood contributed to the production and reproduction of Islamic frames through renegotiation, involving processes of hegemony and counter-hegemony construction, but also accepting the hegemony of the state depending on the politics of the period and the opportunity spaces available. In doing so, the Muslim Brotherhood has expressed the aspirations and frustrations of emerging but heterogeneous, social groups. This conclusion shows the limits of a strict adherence to a Gramscian perspective, highlighting the need for the latter to be integrated with a social constructivist approach, in order to produce a more accurate, and less ideologically biased, topography of the social.

Gramscian analytical categories, however, can still provide valid analytical tools when utilised to gauge the Islamist hegemony quest *qua* articulation of frames. In such a way, a post-Gramscian social constructivist framework, nurtured by social movement theory, seems to offer valuable theoretical tools to interpret the developments of Islamism within the broader history of the processes of social construction of contemporary Islamic identities. To put it simply, Islamism has been interpreted here as a historically situated grid of practices developed within an Islamic symbolic world by the agents, instead of a fixed ensemble of principles. This approach stems from the philosophically informed persuasion that social phenomena need always to be analysed in the specific historical, social and economic contexts in which they are situated, and that social facts should be conceptualised as dialectically related to the aforementioned contexts. Consistent with this approach, this study therefore challenges essentialism, that is to say the grand narratives that claim to infer the behaviours of Muslim or Islamist activists (whose boundaries are often conflated) from assumptions of what Islam, or Islamism, supposedly is. In other words, this study rejects the notions of imposing defined categories on the examination of Islam and Islamism. At the same time, this research criticises approaches, such as orthodox Marxism, which postulate deterministic relationships between economy and culture. On the one hand, this study argues that a sociologically and philosophically informed approach is fundamental to informed and substantial research; on the other hand, a theoretically cognisant attitude should not end up imposing a structure upon social reality. These positions stem from the conviction that social theory is always merely an approximation to the 'truth' of social reality: a truth that is ultimately constantly elusive rather than a defined and stagnant reality. It is out of these theoretically informed persuasions that contemporary Islamic identities have been interpreted in this study as the outcome of processes of interactions between socio-economic transformations and ideology reproduction.

The contemporary Jordan in which the Muslim Brotherhood operates has, in fact, already been remarkably shaped by the Islamists themselves throughout the decades. Neglecting this relationship, which has been conceptualised in this work as dialectical, presents the risk of leading to deterministic positions regarding the relationships between economic practices and cultural representations. It is as if, when talking about the relationship between mankind and nature, we neglect that not only mankind is part of nature, but that mankind has shaped nature and vice versa. This relational approach, called here dialectical, serves to remind us that when we analyse the role of Islamists in Arab or Muslim societies, it is essential to consider the fact that, being Islamists part of their societies, they contribute to shape them, and are at the same time shaped by them. That is why contemporary Islamic identities in Jordan have been read as outcomes of these processes. Such an approach is informed by the persuasion that classical sociological approaches such as the Marxian, Durkheimian and Weberian need not be opposed, but that they can cross-fertilise each other.

It is on the bases of these premises that the research question of this study can be answered by saying that contemporary Islamic identities seem to have been strongly influenced by both the so-called Islamic awakening of the 1970s and the socio-economic transformations of globalisation. Far from being static, Islamic identities, like all identities, are constantly undergoing processes of renegotiation and reinterpretation, and these processes are interrelated with socio-economic transformations. It is in the light of these relationships that Islamism can truly be considered part of a broader process of collective social construction of 'Islamic modernities', where the term 'modernity' is not used to imply a value judgement but to denote a connection with the complex changes brought about by capitalism. Hence, as it has already been stressed, this study argues that Islamist movements, such as the Muslim Brotherhood, have played a significant role in the process of the reframing of Islam. It appears that movements that emerged to criticise 'modernity' have paradoxically been vehicles of 'modernisation' themselves through their interpretation, but also submission, to the hegemonic nature of the political and philosophical frame of that modernity. However, the expression 'vehicles' is inadequate, since it does not capture the profoundly dialectical characteristics of this process. As has been shown, Islamist movements are, at the same time, a product of 'modernity' and an element of 'modernisation' itself, being both a subject and an object of modernisation. Indeed, on the one hand Islamist frames emerged because of the influence of processes of modernisation, which are profoundly inter-related with the socio-economic consequences of the penetration in Muslim societies of the capitalistic mode of production and of the ideology of Western modernity. On the other hand, as this study has shown, Islamism cannot merely be interpreted as a reaction, or as an Islamic answer to modernisation, since Islamism is the multi-faceted product of an indigenisation of the project of Western modernity. In other words, Islamism is also a subject of modernisation, representing the nexus through which multiple versions of modernity are expressed through the adoption of Islamic symbols. In other words, Islamism is not a 'thing', but a complex and changing web of ideologies and social practices. It is comprehensible to view 'Islamic modernities' as the outcomes of processes of hybridisation, as expressed with the notion of multiple modernities in the larger universe of knowledge, between the paradigms of *homo economicus* and *homo islamicus*. These two should not be seen as a dichotomy, but as being in a complex dialectical relationship. Thus, the multiple modernity framework conceptualises identities as dialectical products, outcomes of processes of convergence, merging and bi-causation carried out by social actors. Islamic banking, through the social practices of various categories of agents, such as individuals and organisations, is a very good example of a hybrid identity developed from the cross-fertilisation between *homo economicus* and *homo islamicus*.

The aftermath of the Arab uprisings and the wide success of Islamist movements and parties in a number of Arab states have made the understanding of contemporary Islamic identities, and of Islamism, of the utmost importance for the comprehension of the societies of the Middle East and North Africa. The findings of this study suggest, for example, that nothing concerning the relationships of Islamic movements with democracy can be said a priori: stating that Islamist movements are either *per se* democratic or anti-democratic implies postulating an unchanging nature of Islamist movements that determines future political outcomes. This research argues for the importance of always locating these experiences in their historically situated contexts through their particular political economies, thus avoiding submitting to the fascination of meta-historical narratives.

As far as any policy implications, which can be drawn from this research are concerned, for example about the potential role of the Islamic Action Front Party (IAFP) in the Jordanian democratic process, one issue should be highlighted. The IAFP, popularly known as the political wing of the Muslim Brotherhood, has been undergoing a profound identity crisis, which mirrors the identity crisis of Jordanian society as a whole. Islamism, as literature has consistently shown, responds to the social, economic and political context in which it operates through *micro-ijtihads* on individual and organisational levels; a context, which, as this study argues, it also significantly contributes to shaping. The processes of *micro-ijtihads* of social agents, rather than universally defined Islamic or Islamist essences, shape the articulation and practice of Islam and Islamism in Jordan and beyond.

Societies, organisations and individuals go through different phases in their development trajectories, and hence the contents of their identities dynamically follow such changes, being shaped by their changing contexts, and in turn shaping these contexts. Therefore, attempting to explain development trajectories of a society by insisting on rigid categories external to the society itself may not be necessarily the most appropriate approach. Hence, the dynamics of each period may require the application of a particular theoretical framework, which can also be gauged through empirical exploration rather than through the imposition of pre-determined categories. The empirical explorations will help to understand general patterns, and on these bases theoretical frameworks may be proposed. Thus, multi-theoretical approaches are more effective, as proven in this study, in explaining a social phenomenon as large and multi-faceted as Islamism.

Overall, the significance of this research lies in suggesting the adoption of a theoretically sound paradigm to explain the development of Islamic identities in their relationship with socio-economic transformations and with the agency of social movements. Thus, its findings are arguably useful in challenging the illusion of 'Islamic exceptionalism', which implies that Muslim societies should be studied with different analytical categories from those employed to study non-Muslim societies. In this respect, social constructivism and social movement theory can provide extremely valuable insights for the understanding of contemporary Muslim identities and of Islamism, revealing their dialectical relationships with political economy and social forces. Specifically, this study makes a significant contribution to the understanding of Jordanian society, by evaluating the role exerted by the Muslim Brotherhood in producing contemporary Islamic identities, as well as by studying perceptions, social attitudes and economic behaviour of the segments of this society. The results of this research can be helpful in studying the development of Islamic identities also in other contexts. What is more, the paradigm of 'Islamic modernities' adopted here may be enriched and developed, as well as challenged, by further enquiries. It is precisely in this sense that the concept of hegemony *qua* articulation has been employed to conceptualise the role played by the Muslim Brotherhood of Jordan. Its contribution could be useful in the development of more sophisticated theoretical paradigms to account for the complexity of social phenomena, especially for what concerns the development of social movements and the social construction of identities.

To sum up, the most important achievement of this study conceivably lies in suggesting refraining from limiting the analysis of Islamism to politics, intended in a narrow sense. Hence, this research stresses the importance of studying social movements, such as Islamist movements, in connection with political economy since, on the one hand, the economy provides these movements with opportunity spaces and, on the other hand, economic practices are one of the main loci where the impact of social movements can be observed. What is more, the understandings suggested by this research may provide an input for new explorations into the relationships between processes of social construction of ideologies and socio-economic transformations. Indeed, a main implication of these findings consists in advocating a closer link between the study of political economy and of culture, where the latter term is intended in its wide anthropological sense. Further research could benefit considerably from interdisciplinary approaches, able to combine theoretical frameworks and methodologies from social sciences such as sociology and anthropology. The study of contemporary Islamic identities could greatly benefit from analyses compared with other contexts.

Moreover, systematic scholarly attention should be concentrated on the articulation of Islamic frames by social actors, who may or not be Islamic activists, in their everyday lives. In particular, these processes of *micro-ijtihad* may reveal on-going processes of cross-fertilisation between the paradigms of contemporary global capitalism and Islamism. What have been termed here the 'dialectics between the paradigms of *homo economicus* and *homo islamicus*' offer interesting insights for conceptualising the Islamic way to capitalism, on both theoretical and practical levels, which could be developed in different directions. More research, both qualitative and quantitative, is needed to understand the relationships between ideology formation and the development of social classes, stemming from the theoretically informed persuasion that ideas do not float in a vacuum but are linked with socio-economic hegemonies and power structures. Hence, an interdisciplinary approach, combining anthropological, philosophical and sociological perspectives, could highlight different, yet inter-related, facets of processes of social construction of contemporary Islamic identities.

In particular, comprehensive study should focus on the emergence of different models of Islamic capitalism and on the potential tensions and contradictions that could arise within Islamic societies. To put it simply, both the 'winners' and the 'losers' of the on-going processes of globalisation seem to be likely to adopt Islamic frames, either to legitimise or to criticise the status quo. An interesting area of research is the articulation of Islamic frames outside Muslim majority countries: in this respect, the process of production and reproduction of Islamic identities in the Muslim diaspora in Western societies presents several areas of interest, as Roy (2004) has shown. Another interesting area of research is constituted by the social construction of Islamic identities in online spaces. The exploration into the relationships between the social construction of contemporary identities and political economy is indeed an important subject, rich in theoretical and practical consequences.

Bibliography

Abu Rumman, M. (2007). *The Muslim Brotherhood in the 2007 Jordanian Parliamentary Elections: A Passing 'Political Setback' or Diminished Popularity?* Amman: Friedrich-Ebert-Stiftung.

Adely, F. (2012). '"God made beautiful things": Proper Faith and Religious Authority in a Jordanian High School'. *American Ethnologist*, 39(2): 297–312.

Ahmad, K. (1980). *Studies in Islamic Economics*. Leicester: The Islamic Foundation.

Al-Azmeh, A. (2009). *Islams and Modernities*. 3rd edition. London: Verso.

Al-Faruqi, I. R. (1992). *Al Tawhid: Its Implications for Thought and Life*. Herndon, VA: The International Institute of Islamic Thought.

Al-Ghazali, Z. (1994). *Return of the Pharaoh: Memoir in Nasir's Prison*. Leicester: Islamic Foundation.

Althusser, L. (1971). 'Ideology and Ideological State Apparatuses', in *Lenin and Philosophy, and Other Essays*. London: New Left Books.

Anderson, B. ([1983] 1991). *Imagined Communities: Reflections on the Origin and Spread of Nationalism*. London: Verso.

Antoun, R. T. (2006). 'Fundamentalism, Bureaucratization, and the State's Co-optation of Religion: A Jordanian Case Study'. *The International Journal of Middle East Study*, 38(3): 369–393.

Arrighi, G. (2005). 'Globalization in World-Systems Perspective', in R. P. Appelbaum and W. I. Robinson (eds), *Critical Globalization Studies* (pp. 33–44). London: Routledge.

Asad, T. (1986). *The Idea of an Anthropology of Islam*. Washington, DC: Center for Contemporary Arab Studies, Georgetown University.

Asutay, M. (2007a). 'A Political Economy Approach to Islamic Economics: Systemic Understanding for an Alternative Economic System'. *Kyoto Bulletin of Islamic Area Studies*, 1–2: 3–18.

Asutay, M. (2007b). 'Conceptualisation of the Second Best Solution in Overcoming the Social Failure of Islamic Finance: Examining the Overpowering of Homo Islamicus by Homo Economicus'. *IIUM Journal of Economics and Management*, 15(2): 167–195.

Asutay, M. (2009). 'Co-existence of Modernity and Shari'ah Ruling: Considering the Developments in Islamic Banking and Finance in Multiple Modernities Framework'. Paper presented at the International Conference on 'Re-imaging the Shari'ah: Theory, Practice and Muslim Pluralism at Play', organised by Warwick Law School, 13–16 September, Venice.

Asutay, M. (2010). 'Islamic Banking and Finance and its Role in the GCC-EU Relationship: Principles, Developments and the Bridge Role of Islamic Finance', in C. Koch and L. Stenberg (eds), *The EU and the GCC: Challenges and Prospects under the Swedish EU Presidency*. Dubai: Gulf Research Center.

Asutay, M. (2012). 'Conceptualising and Locating the Social Failure of Islamic Finance: Aspirations of Islamic Moral Economy vs. the Realities of Islamic Finance'. *Journal of Asian and African Studies*, 11(2)(Special Issue): 93–113.

Asutay, M. (2013). 'Developments in Islamic Banking in Turkey: Emergence, Regulation and Performance', in V. Cattelan (ed.), *Islamic Finance in Europe: Towards a Plural Financial System*. Cheltenham: Edward Elgar.

Atia, M. (2012). '"A Way to Paradise": Pious Neoliberalism, Islam, and Faith-Based Development'. *Annals of the Association of American Geographers*, 102(4): 808–827.

Awad, T. (1997). 'The Organizational Structure of the Muslim Brotherhood', in H. Hourani (ed.), *Islamic Movements in Jordan* (pp. 81–92). Amman: Al-Urdun Al-Jadid.

Ayubi, N. (1991). *Political Islam: Religion and Politics in the Arab World*. London: Routledge.

Ayubi, N. ([1995] 2006). *Over-Stating the Arab State: Politics and Society in the Middle East*. New York: I. B. Tauris.

Bar, S. (1998). *The Muslim Brotherhood in Jordan*. Tel Aviv: The Moshe Dayan Center for Middle Eastern and African Studies.

Bayat, A. (2007). *Making Islam Democratic: Social Movements and the Post-Islamist Turn*. Stanford, CA: Stanford University Press.

Beinin, J. (2005). 'Political Islam and the New Global Economy: The Political Economy of an Egyptian Social Movement'. *The New Centennial Review*, 5(Spring): 111–139.

Berger, P. L. and T. Luckmann (1967). *The Social Construction of Reality: A Treatise in the Sociology of Knowledge*. New York: Anchor Books.

Binder, L. (1988). *Islamic Liberalism: A Critique of Development Ideologies*. Chicago, IL: University of Chicago Press.

Blumer, H. (1969). *Symbolic Interactionism: Perspective and Method*. Berkeley, CA: University of California Press.

Bobbio, N. (1979). 'Gramsci and the Conception of Civil Society', in C. Mouffe (ed.), *Gramsci and Marxist Theory* (pp. 21–47). London: Routledge and Kegan Paul.

Boulby, M. (1996). *The Ideology and Social Base of the Jordanian Muslim Brotherhood: 1945–1993*. PhD diss., University of Toronto.

Boulby, M. (1999). *The Muslim Brotherhood and the Kings of Jordan 1945–1993*. Atlanta, GA: Scholars Press.

Browers, M. L. (2009). *Political Ideology in the Arab World: Accommodation and Transformation*. Cambridge: Cambridge University Press.

Buci-Glucksmann, C. (1980). *Gramsci and the State*. London: Lawrence and Wishart.

Burke, E. III and I. M. Lapidus (1988). *Islam, Politics and Social Movements*. Berkeley, CA: University of California Press.

Burr, V. (1995). *An Introduction to Social Constructionism*. London: Routledge.

Chapra, M. (1985). *Towards a Just Monetary System*. Leicester: The Islamic Foundation.

Chapra, M. (1992). *Islam and the Economic Challenge*. Leicester: The Islamic Foundation.

Chase-Dunn, C. and B. Gills (2005). 'Waves of Globalization and Resistance in the Capitalist World System: Social Movements and Critical Globalization Studies', in R. Appelbaum and W. Robinson (eds), *Critical Globalization Studies* (pp. 45–54). London: Routledge.

Bibliography

Choueiri, Y. M. (2010). *Islamic Fundamentalism: The Story of Islamist Movements.* 3rd edition. London: Continuum International.

Clark, J. (2004). *Islam, Charity and Activism: Middle-Class Networks and Social Welfare in Egypt, Jordan and Yemen.* Bloomington, IN: Indiana University Press.

Dabbas, H. (1997). 'Islamic Organizations and Societies in Jordan', in H. Hourani (ed.), *Islamic Movements in Jordan.* Amman: Al-Urdun Al-Jadid.

De Maistre, J. (1994). *Considerations on France.* Cambridge: Cambridge University Press.

Dekmejian, R. H. (1985). *Islam in Revolution: Fundamentalism in the Arab World.* Syracuse, NY: Syracuse University Press.

Eickelman, D. F. and J. Piscatori (1996). *Muslim Politics.* Princeton, NJ: Princeton University Press.

Eisenstadt, S. N. (2000). 'Multiple Modernities'. *Daedalus*, 129(1): 1–29.

ESI (European Security Initiative) (2005). *Islamic Calvinists: Change and Conservatism in Central Anatolia.* Berlin and Istanbul: ESI.

Esposito, J. (1984). *Islam and Politics.* Syracuse, NY: Syracuse University Press.

Esposito, J. (1997). 'Introduction', in J. Esposito (ed.), *Political Islam: Revolution, Radicalism or Reform?* London and Boulder, CO: Lynne Rienner.

Esposito, J. (1999). *The Islamic Threat: Myth or Reality?* Oxford: Oxford University Press.

Esposito, J. and J. Voll (1996). *Islam and Democracy.* Oxford: Oxford University Press.

Etienne, B. (1987). *L'islamisme radical.* Paris: Hachette.

Evola, J. (1998). *Rivolta contro il mondo moderno.* Roma: Edizioni Mediterranee.

Eyerman, R. and A. Jamison (1991). *Social Movements: A Cognitive Approach.* University Park, PA: Pennsylvania State University Press.

Femia, J. V. (1981). *Gramsci's Political Thought: Hegemony, Consciousness and the Revolutionary Process.* Oxford: Clarendon Press.

Foucault, M. (1969). *L'Archéologie du savoir.* Paris: Gallimard.

Gamson, W. A. (1992). *Talking Politics.* Cambridge: Cambridge University Press.

Gellner, E. (1981). *Muslim Society.* Cambridge: Cambridge University Press.

Goffman, E. (1974). *Frame Analysis: An Essay on the Organization of Experience.* Boston, MA: Northeastern University Press.

Göle, N. (1997). 'Secularism and Islamism in Turkey: The Making of Elites and Counter-Elites'. *The Middle East Journal*, 51(1): 46–58.

Göle, N. (2000). 'Snapshots of Islamic Modernities'. *Daedalus*, 129(1): 91–117.

Guénon, R. (2004). *The Crisis of the Modern World.* Hillsdale, NY: Sophia Perennis.

Gülalp, H. (2001). 'Globalization and Political Islam: The Social Bases of Turkey's Welfare Party'. *International Journal of Middle East Studies*, 33(3): 433–448.

Hammad, W. (1997). 'Islamists and Charitable Work', in H. Hourani (ed.), *Islamic Movements in Jordan* (pp. 169–192). Amman: Al-Urdun Al-Jadid.

Harmsen, E. (2008). *Islam, Civil Society and Social Work: Muslim Voluntary Welfare Associations in Jordan between Patronage and Empowerment.* Leiden: Amsterdam University Press.

Henry, C. M. and R. Springborg (2001). *Globalization and the Politics of Development in the Middle East.* Cambridge: Cambridge University Press.

Henry, M. and R. Wilson (2004). *The Politics of Islamic Finance.* Edinburgh: Edinburgh University Press.

Horkheimer, M. and T. W. Adorno (2002). *Dialectic of Enlightenment*, Palo Alto, CA: Stanford University Press.

Bibliography 155

Hourani, H. (ed.) (1997). *Islamic Movements in Jordan*. Amman: Al Urdun Al Jadid.
Ismail, S. (2006). *Rethinking Islamist Politics: Culture, the State and Islamism*. London: I. B. Tauris.
Joll, J. (1977). *Gramsci*. Glasgow: Fontana.
Kahf, M. (2004). 'Islamic Banks: The Rise of a New Power Alliance of Wealth and Shari'a Scholarship', in C. Henry and R. Wilson (eds), *The Politics of Islamic Finance* (pp. 17–36). Edinburgh: Edinburgh University Press.
Kazem, A. A. (1997). 'The Historic Background of the Muslim Brotherhood and its Ideological Origins', in H. Hourani and J. Schwedler (eds), *Islamic Movements in Jordan* (pp. 13–43). Amman: Al Urdun Al Jadid.
Kepel, G. (1985). *Muslim Extremism in Egypt: The Prophet and the Pharaoh*. London: Al-Saqi Books.
Kepel, G. (1994). *The Revenge of God. The Resurgence of Islam, Christianity, and Judaism in the Modern World*. Cambridge: Polity Press.
Khan, I. (2006). 'Islamic Banking and Finance Experience around the Globe'. Paper presented at the Durham Islamic Finance Summer School 2006, Durham Islamic Finance Programme, Durham University, UK.
Khoury, P. S. (1983). 'Islamic Revival and the Crisis of the Secular State in the Arab World', in I. Ibrahim (ed.), *Arab Resources: The Transformation of a Society* (pp. 213–236). Washington, DC: Center for Contemporary Arab Studies, Georgetown University.
Kilani, S. (ed.) (1993). *Islamic Action Front Party*. Amman: Al-Urdun Al-Jadid.
Kuran, T. (1983). 'Behavioral Norms in the Islamic Doctrine of Economics: A Critique'. *Journal of Economic Behavior and Organization*, 4: 353–379.
Kurzman, C. (2004). 'Social Movement Theory and Islamic Studies', in Q. Wiktorowicz (ed.), *Islamic Activism: A Social Movement Theory Approach* (pp. 289–303). Bloomington, IN: Indiana University Press.
Laclau, E. and C. Mouffe (2001). *Hegemony and Socialist Strategy: Towards a Radical Democratic Politics*. 2nd edition. London: Verso.
Lewis, B. (2010). *Faith and Power: Religion and Politics in the Middle East*. Oxford: Oxford University Press.
Lukács, G. (1971). *History and Class Consciousness: Studies in Marxist Dialectics*. Pontypool: The Merlin Press.
Malley, M. (2004). 'Jordan: A Case Study of the Relationship between Islamic Finance and Islamist Politics', in C. Henry and R. Wilson (eds), *The Politics of Islamic Finance* (pp. 191–215). Edinburgh: Edinburgh University Press.
Mandaville, P. (2007). *Global Political Islam*. London: Routledge.
Marger, M. N. (2012). *Race and Ethnic Relations: American and Global Perspectives*. Belmont: Wadsworth Cengage Learning.
Marranci, G. (2009). *Understanding Muslim Identity: Rethinking Fundamentalism*. New York: Palgrave Macmillan.
Marx, K. (1971). *A Contribution to the Critique of Political Economy*. London: Lawrence and Wishart.
Marx, K. (1994). *Selected Writings*. Indianapolis, IN: Hackett.
Massad, J. A. (2001). *Colonial Effects: The Making of National Identity in Jordan*. New York: Columbia University Press.
Mawdudi, A. (1955). *The Process of Islamic Revolution*. Lahore, Dacca: Islamic Publications.
Mawdudi, A. (1997). *Islamic Way of Life*. Riyadh: International Islamic Publishing House.

Mayer, A. E. (1985). 'Islamic Banking and Credit Policies in the Sadat Era: The Social Origins of Islamic Banking in Egypt'. *Arab Law Quarterly*, 1(1): 32–50.

McAdam, D. (1999). *Political Process and the Development of Black Insurgency: 1930–1970*. 2nd edition. Chicago, IL: University of Chicago Press.

McAdam, D. et al. (2001). *Dynamics of Contention*. Cambridge: Cambridge University Press.

McDaniel, T. (2005). 'Responses to Modernization: Muslim Experience in a Comparative Perspective', in S. T. Hunter and H. Malik (ed.), *Modernization, Democracy and Islam*. Washington, DC: Center for Strategic and International Studies.

Mehmet, O. (1990). *Islamic Identity and Development: Studies of the Islamic Periphery*. London: Routledge.

Mehmet, O. (1999). *Westernizing the Third World: The Eurocentricity of Economic Development Theories*. London: Routledge.

Meszaros, I. (1972). *Marx's Theory of Alienation*. London: Merlin Press.

Milton-Edwards, B. (2004). *Islam and Politics in the Contemporary World*. Cambridge: Polity Press.

Milton-Edwards, B. (2005). *Islamic Fundamentalism since 1945*. London: Routledge.

Milton-Edwards, B. and P. Hinchcliffe (2009). *Jordan: A Hashemite Legacy*. 2nd edition. London: Routledge.

Mittelman, J. H. (2005). 'What is Critical Globalization Studies?', in R. P. Appelbaum and W. I. Robinson (eds), *Critical Globalization Studies* (pp. 33–44). London: Routledge.

Moaddel, M. (2002). *Jordanian Exceptionalism: A Comparative Analysis of State-Religion Relationships in Egypt, Iran, Jordan, and Syria*. New York: Palgrave Macmillan.

Moaddel, M. (2005). *Islamic Modernism, Nationalism and Fundamentalism: Episode and Discourse*. Chicago, IL: The University of Chicago Press.

Nasr, V. R. (2009). *Forces of Fortune. The Rise of the New Muslim Middle Class and What it Will Mean for Our World*. New York: Free Press.

Noland, M. and H. Pack (2007). *The Arab Economies in a Changing World*. Washington, DC: The Peterson Institute for International Economics.

Öncü, A. (2003). 'Dictatorship plus Hegemony: a Gramscian Analysis of the Turkish State'. *Science & Society*, 67(2): 303–328.

Öniş, Z. (1997). 'The Political Economy of Islamic Resurgence in Turkey: The Rise of the Welfare Party in Perspective'. *Third World Quarterly*, 18(4): 743–766.

Otto, R. (1958). *The Idea of the Holy: An Inquiry into the Non-rational Factor in the Idea of the Divine and its Relation to the Rational*. Oxford: Oxford University Press.

Piscatori, J. P. (1986). *Islam in a World of Nation-States*. Cambridge University Press: Cambridge.

Postone, M. (2003). 'Lukács and the Dialectical Critique of Capitalism', in R. Albritton and J. Simoulidis (eds), *New Dialectics and Political Economy*. Basingstoke and New York: Palgrave Macmillan.

Postone, M. (2004). *The Cambridge Companion to Critical Theory*. Cambridge: Cambridge University Press.

Richards A. and J. Waterbury (2008). *A Political Economy of the Middle East*. 3rd edition. Boulder, CO: Westview Press.

Robins, P. (2004). *A History of Jordan*. Cambridge: Cambridge University Press.

Robinson, W. (2005). 'What is a Critical Globalization Studies? Intellectual Labor and Global Society', in R. P. Appelbaum and W. I. Robinson (eds), *Critical Globalization Studies* (pp. 33–44). London: Routledge.

Roy, O. (1994). *The Failure of Political Islam*. Cambridge, MA: Harvard University Press.
Roy, O. (2004). *Globalized Islam: The Search for a New Ummah*. New York: Columbia University Press.
Rudnyckyj, D. (2009). 'Spiritual Economies: Islam and Neoliberalism in Contemporary Indonesia'. *Cultural Anthropology*, 24(1): 104–141.
Said, E. W. (1979). *Orientalism*. New York: Vintage.
Saleh, A. S. and R. Zeitun (2007). 'Islamic Banks in Jordan: Performance and Efficiency Analysis'. *Review of Islamic Economics*, 11(1): 41–62.
Salibi, K. (1998). *The Modern History of Jordan*. London and New York: I. B. Tauris.
Salvatore, A. (2009). 'Tradition and Modernity within Islamic Civilisation and the West', in M. K. Masud, A. Salvatore and M. van Bruinessen (eds), *Islam and Modernity: Key Issues and Debates*. Edinburgh: Edinburgh University Press.
Sassoon, A. S. (1980). *Gramsci's Politics*. London: Croom Helm.
Schwedler, J. (2006). *Faith in Moderation: Islamist Parties in Jordan and Yemen*. Cambridge: Cambridge University Press.
Sfeir, A. (ed.) (2007). *The Columbia World Dictionary of Islamism*. New York: Columbia University Press.
Shimada, K. (1993). *State, Power and Legitimacy: A Case Study of Jordan*. Niigata: IMES International University of Japan.
Sidahmed, A. S. and A. Ehteshami (eds) (1996). *Islamic Fundamentalism*. Boulder, CO: Westview Press.
Siddiqi, M. N. (2004). *What Went Wrong?* Keynote Address at the Roundtable on Islamic Economics: Current State of Knowledge and Development of Discipline, held at Jeddah, Saudi Arabia on 26–27 May. Jeddah: Islamic Research and Training Institute; Kuwait: Arab Planning Institute.
Simms, R. (2002). '"Islam is our Politics": A Gramscian Analysis of the Muslim Brotherhood (1928–1953)'. *Social Compass*, 49(4): 563–582.
Smelser, N. J. and R. Swedberg (2005). *The Handbook of Economic Sociology*. 2nd edition. Princeton, NJ: Princeton University Press.
Smith, C. (1991). *The Emergence of Liberation Theology: Radical Religion and Social Movement Theory*. Chicago, IL: Chicago University Press.
Smith, K. (2004). 'The Kuwait Finance House and the Islamization of Public Life in Kuwait', in M. Henry and R. Wilson (eds), *The Politics of Islamic Finance* (pp. 168–190). Edinburgh: Edinburgh University Press.
Snow, D. A. (2004). 'Framing Processes, Ideology, and Discursive Fields', in D. A. Snow, S. A. Soule and H. Kriesi (eds), *The Blackwell Companion to Social Movements* (pp. 380–412). Oxford: Blackwell.
Spohn, W. (2010). 'Political Sociology: Between Civilizations and Modernities. A Multiple Modernities Perspective'. *European Journal of Social Theory*, 13(1): 49–66.
Springer D. R., J. L. Regens and D. N. Edger (2009). *Islamic Radicalism and Global Jihad*. Washington, DC: Georgetown University Press.
Tibi, B. (2005). *Islam between Culture and Politics*. 2nd edition. New York: Palgrave Macmillan.
Tripp, C. (1996). 'Islam and the Secular Logic of the State in the Middle East', in A. S. Sidahmed and A. Ehteshami (eds), *Islamic Fundamentalism* (pp. 51–69). Boulder, CO: Westview Press.
Turner, R. H. (1969). 'The Theme of Contemporary Social Movements'. *British Journal of Sociology*, 20: 390–405.

Tylor, E. B. (1994). *Primitive Culture: Researches into the Development of Mythology, Philosophy, Religion, Art, and Custom*. London: Routledge.

Utvik, B. O. (2006). *The Pious Road to Development: Islamist Economics in Egypt*. London: Hurst & Company.

Vatikiotis, P. J. (1987). *Islam and the State*. London: Croom Helm.

Warde, I. (2000). *Islamic Finance in the Global Economy*. Edinburgh: Edinburgh University Press.

Warde, I. (2004). 'Global Politics, Islamic Finance and Islamist Politics Before and After 11 September 2011', in C. M. Henry and R. Wilson (eds), *The Politics of Islamic Finance* (pp. 37–62). Edinburgh: Edinburgh University Press.

Weber, M. (1978). *Economy and Society*. Berkeley and Los Angeles, CA: University of California Press.

Weismann, I. (2011). 'Modernity from Within: Islamic Fundamentalism and Sufism'. *Islam – Zeitschrift für Geschichte und Kultur des Islamischen Orients*, 86(1): 142–170.

Wickham, C. (2002). *Mobilizing Islam: Religion, Activism and Political Change in Egypt*. New York: Columbia University Press.

Wiktorowicz, Q. (2001). *The Management of Islamic Activism: Salafis, the Muslim Brotherhood, and State Power in Jordan*. New York: State University of New York.

Wiktorowicz, Q. (2004). *Islamic Activism: A Social Movement Theory Approach*. Bloomington, IN: Indiana University Press.

Yavuz, M. H. (2003). *Islamic Political Identity in Turkey*. Oxford: Oxford University Press.

Yavuz, M. H. (2004). 'Is there a Turkish Islam? The Emergence of Convergence and Consensus'. *Journal of Muslim Minority Affairs*, 24(2): 1–22.

Yilmaz, I. (2003). 'Muslim Alternative Dispute Resolution and Neo-Ijtihad in England'. *Alternatives: Turkish Journal of International Relations*, 1(5), December.

Zubaida, S. (2009). *Islam, the People and the State: Political Ideas and Movements in the Middle East*. London: I. B. Tauris.

Zubaida, S. (2011). *Beyond Islam: A New Understanding of the Middle East*. London: I.B. Tauris.

Index

Abdullah I, King 57, 59–60, 62–3, 92–4
Abu Mahfudh, Saud 78
Abu Qurah 59, 61
Afghanistan 65, 97
AKP (Justice and Development Party) 26
Algeria 97
Al-Andalus 107
Al-Banna, Hassan 72, 93, 97, 123
Al-Faisal, Muhammad (Prince) 30–1, 77
Al-Kilani, Ibrahim Zaid 77
Al-Khouri, Faris 84
Al-Nabulsi, Suleiman 62
Al-Qaeda 14, 101
Al-Sharif, Kamil Ismail 60
Althusser, Louis 51, 120
Arab Revolt (1916–1918) 57
Arab Socialism 8, 14, 18, 29, 79
Arab State, Crisis 12–13, 17
Arab Uprisings (2011) 1, 6, 35
Atatürk, Mustafa Kemal 15–16
Azzam, Abdullah 65

Ba'athism 33, 62–3
Bahrain 33
Berlusconi, Silvio 46
Black September (1970) 56, 72, 96
Bush Jr, George 46

Cairo Conference (1921) 58
Catholicism 46, 85, 140–1
Churchill, Winston 58
Civil Rights Movement 43
Cold War 69
Communism 60–2
Confucianism 137

Da'wa 50, 66–8, 70, 72, 84, 110, 132–3

Egypt 5, 23, 26, 18–20, 37, 43, 46, 50–2, 62, 70, 74, 76, 97, 128
Egypt, Muslim Brotherhood 28, 30, 70
Erbakan, Necmettin 97

Farhan, Ishaq 60, 68, 72, 77, 127
First World War (1914–1918) 57
Foucault, Michel 2, 7, 41
France 57, 85
Freud, Sigmund 90

Globalisation 23–5, 91, 110–1, 131–2
Goffman, Erving 7
Gramsci, Antonio (and Gramscian concepts) 6, 11, 24, 38–41, 44, 46, 51–2, 55–6, 63, 65–9, 76, 78, 97, 121, 123, 128–9, 147
Great Britain 57–8

Hamas 69–70, 73, 99, 124
Hamoud, Sami 76, 80
Hashemite dynasty 22
Hegemony 38–41
Hezbollah 70, 73
Hizb al-Wasat (Egypt), 26
Homo economicus 4, 8, 9, 10, 76–7, 79–81, 83, 86, 103, 113, 115–7, 118, 124, 130–5, 144–5, 146–51
Homo islamicus 4, 8, 9, 10, 72, 76, 78, 79–81, 83, 86, 93, 102, 103, 110–3, 115–7, 118, 123–4, 130–5, 144–5, 146–51

Inclusion-moderation hypothesis 22
Indonesia 130
Infitah 34, 76
Insurgent consciousness, 27
Ijtihad 32
Iran 18, 96

Index

Islah Party (Yemen) 21
Islamic economics 33–4
Islamic finance 7, 74–80
Islamic moral economy 7, 74–80
Islamic Research and Training Institute 32
Islamic social institutions 71
Islamism, definition 3, 4
Islamo-nationalist ideologies 22–3, 63
Israel 14–15, 55, 95
Italy 46

Jahiliyya 66, 88, 102, 120

Kamel, Saleh 77
Kemalism 27–8
King Hussein 56, 62
Kuwait 29, 31, 32

Lebanon 64
Liberation theology 25, 44
Lumpen intelligentsia 18–19
Lukács, György 11, 39

Malaysia 33, 93
Marx, Karl 6, 11, 119, 130–1
Marxism 6, 11, 39–41, 66, 120, 139, 147
Mawdudi, Abul Ala 49–50, 136, 138
Micro-ijtihad 20, 114, 142
Mubarak, Hosni 23, 40, 51
MÜSIAD 31, 79
Muslim Brotherhood of Egypt 40, 120, 122–3
Muslim Brotherhood of Syria 28

Nasser 4, 8, 15, 19, 59, 62–3, 74–5, 122
Nasserism 30, 33, 62

Organisation of the Islamic Conference (OIC) 75
Orientalism 11, 12
Özal, Turgut 27, 70

Palestine Liberation Organization (PLO) 56, 64, 96, 122

Pakistan 93, 97

Qutb, Sayyid 20, 65–6, 87–8, 94, 122, 137

Resource mobilization theory (RMT) 48
Riba 113–4, 126

Said, Edward 2, 12
Sadat, Anwar 29, 30, 76
Salafism 7, 21, 101, 136
Saudi Arabia 17, 75, 86, 97
Second International 39
Social constructivism 41–42, 52–53
Social movement theory 42–53
Sudan 30
Sufi Islam 27
Sykes-Picot agreements (1916) 57
Syria 5, 21, 86

Talal, King 62
Tawhid 78, 103
Thunaybat, Abdul Majid 67–8
Tunisia 5, 128
Turkey 12, 15, 24–8, 31, 70, 93, 97, 130

Ulama 18, 31
Ummah 14–15, 55, 102
United States of America 15, 43–4, 100–1, 106–9
University of Jordan 9, 83, 89, 100, 104, 125–7

Vico, Giambattista 42

Wadi Araba agreements (1994) 100, 124
Welfare Party (Turkey) 24–6
Wittgenstein, Ludwig 41
Weber, Max 6

Yemen 21, 64
Yom Kippur War 75